T0195650

Cowboy Games

Fast Draw   **Wild Bunch**

Silhouettes   **Long Range**

RICHARD M BELOIN MD

authorHOUSE®

AuthorHouse™
1663 Liberty Drive
Bloomington, IN 47403
www.authorhouse.com
Phone: 1 (800) 839-8640

Published by AuthorHouse 07/24/2018

ISBN: 978-1-5462-4922-1 (sc)
ISBN: 978-1-5462-4921-4 (e)

Library of Congress Control Number: 2018907986

Print information available on the last page.

Contents

BOOK THREE

Preface

This book is a work of fiction mixed with informational descriptions of five Cowboy Shooting Games. The locations traveled by the main characters are real places, but the clubs they visit are fictional–they are used for learning and training purposes. Specific reference to the Bar W Ranch is purely fictional, and does not refer to the many ranches in Texas and other states with the name Bar W.

The chapters follow the newlywed couple through the discovery and development of these shooting disciplines:

- Cowboy Fast Draw(CFD)–learning how to draw/ shoot wax bullets safely at an electronic target, with competitive speed.
- Wild Bunch(WB)–an extension of SASS Cowboy Action, but with more modern firearms circa 1900 to WWI.

- Cowboy Rifle Silhouettes–shooting a big bore lever rifle and pistol at varying size falling steel plates, up to 200 meters.
- Cowboy Long Range(CLR)–shooting pre 1900 single shot rifles with open sights at 300–500 yard steel gongs.

Follow the interpersonal and comical relationship as these major characters expose the extent of a commitment necessary to master these sports. These games are real activities participated by many shooting enthusiasts, and in my honest opinion(IMHO) there is no better way to enjoy your guns than to join one or more of these Cowboy Games.

Dedication

This book is dedicated to the silent group of Cowboy Shooters who keep these shooting sports alive and viable for the next generation.

BOOK ONE

CHAPTER 1

Changing Times, Again

T he wedding was the start of our continuing saga. We had two weeks before the Xmas holidays. Since we had already made our reservations for our two week honeymoon in Hawaii, we decided to spend the next 3 weeks with our families.

In our plan for the Xmas gathering, we included shopping for 5 children, their spouses, and eleven grand children that ranged from 5 years old to college students. Sue and I spent many days shopping for everyone to have one significant gift. The most difficult age group was the teenagers, and we had 7 of them. We had to give in and purchase electronic items for the teenagers–a tough group to find computer gifts.

The 5 days before Xmas were spent hosting a dinner with each family at one of our popular restaurants. During dinner, we talked more about our children and grandchildren than we did about us. This was their time and we knew that the Xmas dinner would be more centered on us. Sue went all out decorating our home for the Xmas gathering. A gorgeous decorated real Balsam fir tree from Vermont, garland and poinsettias everywhere, windows decorated with Vermont Balsam wreaths and round balls, called kissing balls, hanging in several locations, but made of Fraser fir. The house's aroma was unique and would be a surprise for all who would enter.

With the house decorated, smelling like a Vermont forest, the tree ready with all 21 wrapped gifts, we went shopping for Xmas dinner. We bought a 25 lb. turkey with all the fixings, butternut squash, garden carrots, cranberry sauce, Maine potatoes, pumpkin pies, custard pies and dinner rolls. Necessary food preparations were done the day before the party. I did the pealing–potatoes, carrots, and squash. I asked, "why so many potatoes?" "Because I am making mashed potatoes which requires more potatoes than baked potatoes." Sue did the pre cooking and everything else, including setting a long table for 23 people.

--- • ━ ● ━ • ---

The all day event started early with a photo review of our travels throughout the West. With Sue's camera SD card in our laptop, a HDMI cable to the 52 in. television provided a nice viewing screen of the many photos. We shared the narrating and managed to keep everyone's attention, including the teenagers. The most popular segment was our stay at the Bar W Ranch displaying guns and costumes(Sue had deleted the best pictures–pool side and her mini bikini).

As I was doing the last half of the narration, Sue started to prepare dinner. The turkey was cooked and Sue added the potatoes and carrots to cook in the pressure cookers. The squash was reheated in the microwave and the stove top dressing was finalized. After the photo presentation, I joined Sue in the kitchen, I started carving the turkey with an electric knife, one of the girls was deboning the red meat and one was preparing the 10 lb. spiral ham. The spiral ham was a late addition for those who don't like turkey and it was a guarantee that we would not run out of meat! Sue used the turkey juice to make giblet gravy.

With the meal ready, Sue announced, "serving will be 'line buffet style,' form a line on each side of the island, and serve yourselves. Rolls, butter, cranberry sauce and condiments are on the table." With everyone seated, I said, "the one person that has made this possible will say grace," as I asked Sue to do the honors.

The meal was a huge success and lingered with coffee and desserts. We could tell that the teenagers were getting antsy and wanted to proceed to the next event–the tree. Everyone chipped in for the clean up. The picking up, food storage, table dismantling and dishes were quickly washed. We then moved to the living room for the gifts.

Since the tree was the last event, we decided to open the gifts one at a time. Sue passed out five gifts and everyone watched to see what they got for a gift–one at a time. The process continued and one thing became very clear, we had chosen well.

Thinking we were done, one of the adults said to the teenagers, "OK boys, go get them!" A parade followed of three boys each carrying a large box. "Well Mom and Dad, getting you a gift was a nightmare until we talked with Jack and the choice was clear."

We started unwrapping the two largest boxes and the company logo hit us immediately–Dillon. We opened the boxes and saw a Dillon XL-650 with a casefeeder and the necessary accessories. My oldest daughter said, "Jack told us that you were doing too much shooting to stay with the Square Deal B reloader. He also started to let the cat out of the bag about your proposal for the coming year but he stopped short and cut us off."

"Yes, I have an idea for the year to come, but Sue has heard nothing of this and I want to discuss it with her after our honeymoon." My son asked, "can you say if it involves traveling like last year?" I said, "no, it involves staying home, and more to follow upon our return."

The week before New Years was spent preparing for the big New Year's celebration at the Country Roadhouse–our dancing hangout.

Stan Winslow, a Cowboy shooter and dancer, agreed to help us catch up on the partner dances we had missed during our traveling last summer. He showed up one day with one of the dancers from our club. Sue gasped and hugged an old dancing friend, then showed me the rock on her finger. All I could say was, "good for both of you." Miranda Blair said, "we finally found each other, and we are both very happy!"

We danced all afternoon. We learned 5 new partner dances and at least a half dozen two-step turns. We thanked them for the lesson and felt we were ready for the party. We had several days to practice these new dances and turns.

The other thing we did was to set up the Dillon XL-650 in 38 caliber on the bench. with the shotgun loader on the left. We then commandeered the other garage bench for the Square Deal B and two other sites to be reserved for the future. The carpenter and automotive tools were moved to the side shelves–out of the way. Finally, Sue was standing at the two reserved sites and gave me that look–the one I don't fare well with. Sue said, "how about a hint on what those reserved sites are for?" "You have to trust me on this one till after our honeymoon."

The New Years celebration was well organized–dinner and dance for $50 per couple with one receiving drink and champagne at midnight. Dinner was a grilled chicken with all the fixings. A 1AM breakfast was free to all present. The hall was well decorated and balloons were hanging in a bag overhead–loaded with $10 bills.

The dancing was lively and well attended in all disciplines: line dancing, partner, two-step and waltz. *I thought, the good thing about everyone dancing is that no one gets drunk. No one can perform all these moves with too much alcohol on board.* Our dance lesson with Stan and Miranda proved productive. We danced as a couple doing partner, two-step and waltz. Sue was moving away from line dancing which was more of a dance for single people.

Sue asked, "did you notice that the mean age is the 30-40's." I said, "why is that?" "Because when this club opened, the clientele was all working class single women over 21, and doing line dances only. The owner saw this as a business failure waiting to happen. He advertised free two-step and waltz lessons–plus he added no cover charge for men. In a matter of a few months, this became the social gathering center of town. You would not believe the number of married couples that met in this club!" "Wow, what a nice story, and what a nice place for us old folks to pretend we are in our forties!"

Midnight came, we locked lips in a passionate embrace, and finally hugged and kissed all our friends. We stayed for the 1 AM breakfast and finally got home by 2:30 AM for our private celebration. In the days to come we prepared for our honeymoon in Hawaii.

———————●━━●━━●———————

We wanted our honeymoon to provide us with private and quality time. Tourist sites were secondary and we planned to visit only a few memorable ones. Our two 5 hour flights, with a 2 hour stop in San Francisco, took us to Honolulu on the Big Island. Per tradition we were greeted with a lei and registered for 4 days at the Trump International Hotel on Waikiki Beach. This was a 5 star hotel with a great beachfront. The weather was 78° and the ocean water temperature was 77°.

We did choose to visit two locations. We went to Pearl Harbor and visited the USS Arizona Memorial. The other site was at the Hawaii Volcanoes National Park where we saw Kilauea, an active volcano. Most of our days were spent on the beautiful beach with its surrounding food and beverage bars.

Calypso music was everywhere. The unique island music was made by steel drums. After talking to the staff and doing an internet search, I could explain to Sue the significance of these instruments. One day I said, "these instruments are called steel pans. They are made from 50 gallon industrial drums and are a chromatically pitched percussion instrument played by musicians called 'pannists'." I saw Sue thinking and eventually she said, "what do you mean by chromatically pitched?" "A steel pan uses a musical scale of only 12 pitches. Each pitch is a half tone–one above and one below the adjacent pitch. The use of the 12 pitches produces music unique to this instrument."

After 4 days on the Big Island, we were transferred to Maui. Again greeted with a lei, we registered at the Montage Kapalua Bay resort, a luxury beachfront complex with pools and spas. This island had gardens, national parks, monuments and many beautiful beaches. Yet this island's signature amenity was the romantic and peaceful settings so appreciated by couples.

Days were spent on the beach with Calypso music and it's supporting food and beverage bars. Evenings were a daily grand production at the many local luaus. We were informed by our travel agent that luaus were a tradition on these islands and included:

1. Typical entry fee of $100 per person with a lei.
2. Continuous steel pan Calypso music.
3. An IMU ceremony. Creating an underground oven that uses a combination of hot coals, rocks, layers of leaves and topped with a mat to help steam the food. The menu often included the staple food of the island–shredded pork and island vegetables.
4. Polynesian dancing shows such as Hula dancers.

5. Ending ceremony of a Samoan Fire Knife dancer.

The days passed with us in a magical world–days we would never forget. I would never have believed that such a honeymoon could strengthen our bond, but it did. However, such times always come to an end. The last two days brought some awakening when I received an e-mail from Ranger Rooster. After a restless night and an early visit on the internet, I decided to breach the subject with Sue.

———•—◼—•—◼—•———

During lunch at a beachfront café, I said to Sue, "this wonderful honeymoon is coming to an end. Looking into the future, let's look back in the past year. Life has been a whirlwind from meeting you, going through a CAS training, our CAS matches, learning how to reload, the Bar W Ranch, the dancing at the Country Roadhouse, traveling to five western tourist bases, our finale in Nashville, falling in love, our wedding, spending the holidays with family and culminating in this wonderful honeymoon. REALLY, how do we even come close to matching that lifestyle this coming year?"

Sue chimed in, "we certainly have been burning the candle at both ends, and our lives have been on fire. For the coming year, it seems to me that we have one of two choices–either we stay the course or we relight another candle. Staying the course means a more sedentary and complacent routine from day to day–contentment. The other side of the coin, do we still have the energy and motivation to build another whirlwind lifestyle and what could that be?"

I then took over, "if you look back at the past year's events, the magic word was 'NEW'. We both have too much energy and joy of life to slow down. We need a 'NEW' challenge." She added, "great, what do you have in mind. I know you enough to know that you don't ask a question or make a statement when you don't know the answer?"

"Very good, it is now time to show you a two day old e-mail from Ranger Rooster."

Dear Wil and Sue

I just had a private meeting with Willard Stone, the real-estate mogul who owns our range, clubhouse and 50 acres. He is a life member of our club but has retired from shooting because of age and poor vision. Last summer he traveled to several Cowboy clubs and saw several Cowboy shooting disciplines: Cowboy Fast Draw(CFD), Wild Bunch(WB), Cowboy Silhouettes(CRS & CPS), and Cowboy Long Range(CLR). His current dream, he wants all five games added to our club over the next year. He wants our club to become a hub for all Cowboy Shooting

Games. To make this happen, he will finance the entire project free of charge to our club. He will pay for buildings, excavation, mounds, targets, shooting enclosures and anything else that is needed. In addition, he was at the Bar W Ranch last year. He saw you and Sue shoot, dance, riding horses, swimming(referring to Sue's bikini body) and perform the resussitation on his cousin(surprise). He claims he can spot leaders when he sees them, and you two pass the test. He feels you have the spirit of life to learn and teach these shooting sports—to make a competitive club. If you are interested, he wishes to meet with you, and you can set your price. I apparently am his second choice if you decline. Well I am still 5 years to retirement and maintaining the CAS club is all I can handle. If you decline, then this growth will likely not happen at this time. RSVP RR.

Sue looked up from the laptop and said, "so that is what has been making you pensive the last two days, heh?" I said, "YES, plus I want to do this but only if you will do it with me." "I am your wife and you know that whatever you decide, I will always support you, and you can count on me to be at your side. Yes, this is a heck of a challenge, but I know we can do it. I welcome the year ahead. Where do we start?" I looked at Sue and said, "well since you asked, this is where we start:

1. We start with CFD. There is an excellent web site with 9 free videos, a great mercantile and all the information we need.
2. Research the electronic target as the tool of the trade.
3. Watch the ultimate informational video, Hit Em Fast. I have already ordered this one and it will arrive today by overnight air.
4. Watch current videos of televised shooting matches.
5. Research the internet for other and all information available."

"Now we are on our honeymoon. We will start all this research on our 10+ hours of flight time to get home. We are flying first class which will provide Wi-Fi, but a power source is not guaranteed. So let's order a portable battery power source to support our laptops on our flights. We can have a bellhop pick it up at the nearest Best Buy. Then we place an order on the CFD website for two holsters, wax bullets and a two lane electronic target—they likely will arrive in MO before we do. Then we put all this CFD material on hold, and we go back to the beach and our routine to finish our honeymoon."

Back on the beach, we swam in the ocean followed by sunning on our lounging chairs. The conversation naturally moved onto CFD. Sue asked, "Do you have any idea of the time frame and steps needed from today to get a club up to competition level?" "Well I have been cheating, I started reading last night when your snoring woke me up. This is a rough outline to cover the next weeks:

- Research will be done on our flight home.
- Gear up with tools of the trade as ordered.
- Learn proper stance, body mechanics, draw/firing techniques.
- One week of practicing before the introductory club meeting.
- Set up a general club meeting, give a demonstration and try to convince Cowboy shooters to join this sport.
- Travel to one major state match to learn operational methods.
- Start a long training program for all new shooters. Every four new shooters will get 2 hours of personal training from both of us. A second lesson if needed.
- Hold a meeting to discuss the rules of the game.
- Hold the first practice competition and explain, at the shooter's meeting, the operational process.
- Hold the first real competition match."

"It is now February 1, if everything goes well it would be great to have our first practice competition by March 1. That will give our shooters another 2 weeks of practicing before the first real competition match. During these 6 weeks, you and I have to practice on and off throughout all this activity!"

And so, we were poised for a very dynamic year.

CHAPTER 2

CFD, Getting Started

Ranger Rooster had e-mailed us Friday evening to confirm that we would be home for the Sunday important informative meeting at the clubhouse. The next morning we boarded our plane and expected to be home by Saturday evening after an all day flight with a 2+ hour layover in San Francisco. As soon as we reached cruising speed and altitude, we had Wi-Fi and went to work. Our goal before arriving in San Francisco was to cover the CFD website in its entirety, with ample notes in preparing our CFD two related meetings–general information and shooter's meeting.

For hours we studied and went over every bit of information provided by such a great website. This included:

- Nine videos.
- Complete mercantile of all available products.

- Listings of other CFD clubs and the mileage to each club.
- Gunfighter Gazette included with a CFD membership.
- CFD Telegraph–online forum.
- CFD shooting events in the US for this year.
- Special attention to the CFD National Championship in Fallon, Nevada.
- Studied several videos of actual matches to learn the sequence of operational commands and set ups.

As the plane was starting its descent, we were both certain that we had covered the website material as much as possible, and were ready for the 2 hour DVD on our next flight–Hit Em Fast by Quick Cal. Our flight arrived in San Francisco a half hour early, and our departure was delayed a half hour. So we were looking at a 3 hour layover.

We found an upscale restaurant with a power outlet at our table. We enjoyed an extended lunch with soup, sandwich and dessert. By the time we headed to our gate, our laptops were fully charged and we finished charging our battery portable power source at the gate.

Once we boarded, we started the DVD as the other passengers took their seats. We knew that this video would be a stop, take notes and restart. The DVD was placed in my laptop, with a splitting audio adapter, we shared its presentation. Although it was a 2 hour video, it took us 3 hours to complete. We had enough notes of very important information to share with the club members at the general and shooter's meetings. We viewed the DVD for a second time–without stops.

———●—●●—●———

Arriving home, we took the time to compare our notes and we prepared our presentations–we knew we had all the information needed to get involved in this sport, After a long day at work, we showered and retired. The next morning we headed to the club for Ranger Rooster's presentation.

On the way to the club, Sue asked, "are you worried about the reception Ranger Rooster(RR) will get, especially since our order from CFD is arriving tomorrow AM?" "Not at all, RR has surveyed several club members and there was a strong support. Even if the club members declined Mr. Stone's offer, I would keep the equipment for our pleasure. I always wanted to try Cowboy Fast Draw."

The meeting convened and we had an attendance of 87 out of a potential 100 members. RR gave a presentation of Mr. Stone's offer:

- "Mr. Stone has investigated 5 new Cowboy shooting sports. CFD, WB, CRS, CPS and CLR."
- "His dream is to incorporate all five games in our club. He wants our club to become a hub for these Cowboy Games."
- "He will pay for all expenses: two new buildings (CFD enclosure and mini clubhouse for CRS, CPS and CLR), a 200 yard range for silhouettes and a 500 yard for CLR, all excavation, three new stages for WB, berms, all targets, and any extra expenses."
- "All registration income will stay in our club's account."

RR paused, Sue and I looked at the people. Everyone was literally stunned. Several had smiles and everyone was quietly talking to their neighbors. Finally RR said, "Ladies and gentlemen, this is a free upgrade to the tune of +- $100,000. All we need from you are participating shooters and your guns. We will now open the floor for a Q and A session."

1. "As a shooting hub, who are we trying to attract for competition?"
   RR answered, "We have 6 nearby CAS clubs, Cassville, Joplin, Marshfield and 3 in Walnut Shade. Many have some form of CLR, 2 have WB and none have CFD or CRS/CPS."

2. "Which sport will be first to be developed?"

I answered, "Mr. Stone suggested CFD because he is ready to start construction this week of a heated 4 season enclosure. This would allow starting the sport by March 1. The other 4 sports are outside activities and the Missouri winter temperature of 26° and snow cover is a problem."

3. "What kind of CFD enclosure are you planning?" RR answered, "35 X 60' post and beam with a steel roof, cement floor, partial wood walls, screened windows for summer use."

4. "How many shooters do you need to start one of these games?" Sue answered, "we need at least 20 members to start any of these sports, if we don't have the numbers, we will delay its development to a later date."

5. "What do we need for guns and gear to participate in CFD?" I answered, "you need one SA revolver with a 4 5/8" or 5 ½" in 45 Long Colt, one regulation holster, wax bullets and special 45 LC casings. If you have a revolver, your cost to get started to include a holster and 2000 bullets, casings and primers is +-$250." Everyone was clearly pleased with this info and I heard many, 'cheap enough.'"

6. "What are the shooting categories proposed for CFD?"

   Sue answered, "we will start with the conventional thumb draw category for both men and women—one category. Eventually we will add kids over 12 to this category. If there is a future demand, we will add a two- hand shooting category for women and children under 12 once the thumb draw category is well established."

7. "What are the clothing/costume requirements?"

   RR answered, 'Your CAS costume. Nothing new—but specifically no short sleeve shirts for men or Shady Brady hats for everyone.'"

8. "As a new club and new sport, training will be required. How do we go about getting this training?"

   I answered, "Sue and I will train everyone, free of charge. Each team of four shooters will receive a 2 hour lesson from us in our garage, using an official electronic target. When you leave, you will have fired 100 rounds, have learned the proper and safe technique of drawing and firing. If anyone needs more personal attention, you would get a second 2 hour lesson. We guarantee you that you will leave confident in your ability to do this sport."

9. "It's an amazing low cost to get into CFD. The other four games can run into big bucks. Times are hard, what do you suggest?"
"Sue and I have considered this and she has come up with a potential solution, here is Sue." "OPEN YOUR GUN SAFES, who doesn't have guns that you no longer shoot? Who doesn't have 3 hunting rifles, 3 shotguns, several 22's, auto pistols and other firearms that have not seen ammo for years? You have to choose your priorities. If you want to participate in these Cowboy Games, it is time to trade inactive guns for tools of the Cowboy shooting games. If that's really what you want, you will not miss the guns you trade or sell privately."

RR addressed the audience, "If there are no further questions, it is time to vote. How many of you wish to reject Mr. Stone's offer? Three hands went up. How many of you wish to accept Mr. Stone's offer. All we could see was a sea of hands, many with both hands up! RR asked for a non binding vote on shooters interested in each sport. The result: CFD=53, WB=41, CRS=36, CLR=31 and when asked about a pistol silhouette category, the vote was 29." Later we learned that most took one or two new sports, and a few took all four.

RR then announced, "there will be a general meeting for all who plan to join CFD, and a sign up sheet for your private lesson–check your e-mail for the announcement."

After the meeting, Sue and I met with RR who said, "well, it appears by the vote, that you have your work cut out. It's time to set up a meeting, for you and Sue, with Mr. Stone." Sue added, "and it's time for you to give the go ahead to start construction of the CFD enclosure." I also added, "it's also time to place some club orders for the following:

1. Electronic targets for two double lanes with overhead public display.
2. An audio public speaking system.
3. One Easyloader 50 press–to load 50 wax bullets at one time–for club use.
4. A reserve supply of 'Dead Eye E-Z loader' wax bullets, casings, shotgun primers, 45 caliber cleaning brushes and wax solvent.
5. Sixty booklet copies of the rules and regulations for CFD."

"We will need all of the above for the meeting in one week. Put a two day delivery on the rules booklets. If the remainder does not arrive by meeting time in one week, we will bring our gear and targets for the demonstration. Sue and I will start our training and prepare for the CFD meeting."

The next morning, after a replenishing breakfast, I called Ed's Mercantile to place an order and told him we would be there after lunch. He told me he had all the items, and since business was usually slow on Mondays, he would perform some crucial action jobs.

The next item of the day was to get on the computer and place a very important order with Dillon. I said to Sue, "in order to participate in the other Cowboy Games, we need several conversion kits and dies to accommodate the different calibers we will be shooting. So I started filling out my order:"

1. 45 ACP, 45 LC and 44 Mag–conversion kits and carbide dies
2. 30-30 conversion kit.
3. Roller handle.
4. Six toolheads.
5. Six powder dies.
6. Twelve large primer filler tubes.
7. Spare parts kit for the XL-650.
8. One powder check.
9. One low powder sensor.
10. The last three casefeed plates(LP, SR, LR).

Then UPS arrived on schedule with our order from the CFD association. As we were opening the boxes, Jack arrived. He was amazed at the amount of gear and equipment needed–to organize a new sport. Jack finally spoke, "that was a beautiful and well organized meeting you two and RR put on yesterday. I have been thinking all night and I know what direction I want to go. I don't have the reflexes and motivation to do CFD. I also don't have the vision to shoot at 200 to 500 yards with CRS and CLR. Because my love is CAS, I would like to shoot the extension of CAS, Wild Bunch, since I really enjoy shooting a pump shotgun and a 1911 auto pistol. I would also like to try pistol silhouettes to 100 yards(not 200 because of vision). I have a nice 44 magnum Ruger revolver that I would take out of moth balls. These two new sports would take me to the range to practice with my new 1911 auto pistol and my old 44 magnum revolver–going to the range is my most pleasurable hobby."

Sue immediately exclaimed, "as far as I'm concerned, choices are what this is really about. Very few shooters will do all four games, but everyone has the choice to join the ones that match their persona or interests." Jack added, "and you know, I feel very good about my choices! Today I am going to the range to take my 44 mag through the paces. Then I am going to Ed's to buy the three WB guns."

After Jack departed for the range, we unpacked the boxes. The holsters were chosen to match our different body shapes. Sue had a high riding holster with an 18° forward cant. She attached it to a 2.5" comfort belt which is worn low on the hips in women. I chose a drop loop holster with an 18° forward cant, because of my long arms and wearing my 2.5" Ranger belt higher than Sue. Both these holsters were regulation. They allowed the shooter to cock the gun while still in the holster. They also had a metal deflecting shield at the holster's open toe.

Sue kept inspecting her rig, tried a Cowboy revolver to verify that the cylinder would turn with the gun in the holster. She kept looking at the deflecting shield and finally said, "I am beginning to believe the phrase 'tools of the trade,' very interesting!"

The next box was the wax bullets, cleaning brushes, wax solvent and 45LC special casings that accept a shotgun primer. We started loading the wax bullets in the casings. It took us 20 minutes to load 50. That is when I said to Sue, "this is not going to work for us. When we start training we will each shoot 100 rounds before a rest period. RR is ordering an Easyloader–50 press for the club. It will load 50 rounds in +- 3 minutes. We need this press for us and the 50+ shooters we will be training in this garage." Sue was already on the laptop and she handed me the phone number for the press–"it will be here tomorrow night from Virginia."

Finally I said, "we are ready to shoot but we don't have any guns! Let's have an early lunch and head for Ed's Mercantile."

——————•━●●━•——————

On the road to Ed's, I brought up the subject, "are you interested in long range shooting?" Sue thought about it and finally said, "I am not comfortable shooting the heavy recoil of a 45–70 caliber with 405 gr. bullets. The guns are too heavy for me and you know that I like action. So I would rather skip this shooting sport, but that doesn't mean you should as well!" "Well Sue, you know that I love handgun shooting. I see WB, CFD and pistol silhouettes fall in this handgun category. I also like action shooting and I am not really interested in CLR. I was thinking of telling Mr. Stone during our meeting that we would get the game started and then find someone to manage it." "I agree, let's not buy guns for that sport at this point."

As we entered the Mercantile, both Ed and Eve came to greet us. Eve said, "with this kind of order, we know something is brewing at the Desperado Club. Please enlighten us. Sue started explaining the detail proposal by Mr. Stone to make our club a hub. I then added, "we are starting five new Cowboy Games–CFD, WB, CRS/CPS, and CLR. The guns we are purchasing are for the first four games. The fifth game, excluding us, will require choices of Rolling Blocks, 1885 Highwalls, 1874 Sharps, and 1895 Marlins."

I finished my words of wisdom by saying, "you know Ed that I am the organizer of all five clubs. All our club members are your customers and if you give them your usual discounts, you are going to have a thriving year."

Ed came back and said, "I have solid arrangements with Taylors, Ruger, Marlin, Mernickle leather. Starline brass and Cimarron Arms. These six companies will supply all these needs and the discounts will be passed to the customers!"

We then started going over the specifics of our order:

- Two Ruger New Vaqueros(4 5/8   Value $1200
  barrel)45LC.
  Action jobs and hammer springs changed to 14lb.

- Two Kimber 1911 auto pistols in   Value $2000
  45 ACP.
  It comes with a reduced mainspring, in case you are shooting lower velocity ammo. The pistols are for the modern class.

- Two black Mernickle holsters/   Value $600
  belts for the 1911.

- 16 extra magazines.   Value $300

- 8 double slim magazine   Value $300
  pouches(black)

- Two Marlin 1894 CB lever rifles Value $1500
  in 45 LC.
  Both have a reduced power mainspring and the Marlin jams have been repaired.

- Two 1897 Pump 12 ga. shotguns.   Value $1100

These have had a minor action job to smooth the mechanism.

- One Marlin Model 336 in 30-30   Value $500
  With a reduced power mainspring.

- One Ruger SBH-Hunter in 44   Value $800
  Mag(7.5")

- One Ruger SBH new Model in 44   Value $700
  Mag(4.62")
  Both SBH's have a 14 lb. hammer
  spring.

                    Sub Total---------------- $9000

Sue whispers, "Wil, that is $9000. We could have saved a lot by only getting one set of guns for WB instead of two." I said, "in my book my total cost for these guns is zero dollars. I pay with the generous donation from Mrs. Whitehouuse check of $5000(the resuscitation) and the theoretical dollar savings from not buying CLR guns(rolling block, 1885 highwall and 1895 lever)to the tune of $4000. As I said, that is zero per my accounting!" Now we need accessories and components:

- Lead bullets—45-230 gr. RN, 45-250 gr. RNFP, 44-240 gr. RNFP(half with GC), and 30-30 170 gr. FP-GC bullets.
- Starline brass for 45 ACP, 45 LC, and 44 Mag.

- Winchester brass for 30-30.
- Warren custom one hole pistol peep sight in 7/32" and 9/32".
- One RCBS Rock Chucker single stage press.
- One HIT Kit for the XL-650.
- One RCBS 30-30 three die set.
- One RCBS universal decapping die.
- One Lyman Universal Shell Holder pack.
- One RCBS stuck case remover kit.
- 10,000 Large Pistol primers(Federal) Two thousand LP magnum primers(Federal).
- 10,000 209 shotgun primers for wax bullets.

As Ed was finding all these accessories and adding up the final cost, Sue asks, "what is this one hole pistol sight all about?" I said, "years ago at the pistol range, I found out from pistol silhouette shooters, that the rear pistol peep sight was ideal for silhouettes. It allows you to get on target quicker, is more accurate and eliminates eye strain or the double rear sight shadow phenomenon." "Well another interesting tool of the trade!"

"Well, time to pay." Ed hands me a bag of small parts and says, "I am including these Ruger small parts–the ones that take a beating from thumb draw fast draw." Before we left, I said, "There is going to be a big demand for RNV's(4 5/8 barrel, 45 LC in the coming week. The one change that you need to do is to change the hammer spring to 14 lb. which is very important in

Fast Draw. If they have a problem setting off a shotgun primer(depending on the brand they are using) they can change to 15 lb. or as needed. We won't be moving on to WB, and the guns that go with this game, for 4 weeks. Same month span for CRS, CLR and Cowboy pistol silhouettes(CPS). This schedule gives you a chance to build your inventory."

On our way home Sue said, "I just figured out what those two unused sites are for on the secondary work bench–the Rock Chucker single press and the Easyloader–50 press." "Right on!"

When we got home, we put our purchases away. We had not seen Jack at Ed's Mercantile, and the reason was clear. We had asked him to pick up supplies for a back drop. Instead, he built our two 4 X 8' backdrops, secured them together to make an 8 X 8' wall angled some 20° downward, and on coasters. The downward angle would keep wax bullet fragments on the floor, instead of bouncing back in our faces.

I said, "now we are really done getting ready. Let's take it easy tonight. Tomorrow we start our training!"

CHAPTER 3

CFD, Our Training

DAY 1. After a replenishing breakfast, we went to the garage to start our training. Our plan on this first day was to practice "dry fire" and learn the several phases of properly performing a fast draw with the right hand. As a precaution we placed a rug on the floor in case we dropped or threw away a pistol.

The first phase was performing the Lawman's grip. I explained, "place your thumb on the hammer tip and the third and fourth finger under the grip–but you do not move the gun. A test of this Lawman's grip is to rock the gun between your thumb and your 3rd and 4th finger. If it does not rock, you are not correctly positioned. In addition, your thumb must not be behind the hammer, it needs to be at 45° to the side."

The second phase of the draw was the stance and use of body mechanics to draw the gun. Sue said, "the right leg should be a bit forward and the feet separated +- 1.5'. By using body mechanics, it helps to draw the gun. These body changes on the draw include: Right hip snapping forward, pushing your belly forward, while pulling your shoulders backwards. According to the video, let me demonstrate!"

The third phase was the actual draw–called the "thumb draw". I said, "lift the gun out of the holster, cock it as it's coming out of the holster and wrap your fingers around the grip. Keep your right arm against your body and get the gun 6 inches above and forward of the holster–and cocked."

The fourth phase was firing the gun. I continued, "with the gun out and forward of the holster, with a 'death grip,' hold the gun firmly and press the finger with a snap–don't slowly squeeze the trigger"

Sue interjects, "and we have to perform these four phases in a smooth and fluid motion–in unison?" I said, "yes. It's going to take a lot of practice, heh?"

And a lot of practice we did, all afternoon till we got smooth with some decent speed. At dinner we laughed at our escapades. I managed once to throw my gun clearly at the far end of the rug. Sue liked that, but she then shot herself in the foot–still dry firing. At one point Jack was visiting and wanted to see the value of these deflecting shields. So Sue fired a real wax bullet round directly in the holster. Jack was standing three feet away to her right. The wax bullet was deflected as expected, but impacted on Jacks left foot–protected only by a light sneaker. The single foot "turkey dance" will stay with us forever.

After dinner, we returned to the garage to practice dry firing. We added the fifth and final phase, reacting to the starter light. We set the targets to the practice mode, pressed the set mode, and got use to randomly reacting to the starter light with a thumb draw. It took some time to get familiar with the visual starting sign, and converting this sign to a physical reflex.

We were both very sluggish at first. By persisting, we seemed to become more alert and eventually we became quick as a whip. That starter light became part of an instantaneous acquired response. By the end of the day, we were both exhausted, and had not fired a real round at the target(just Jack's foot). However, we both knew how to perform this fast draw properly. "Wax bullets in the morning."

———————————◆━●━◆———————————

DAY 2. The UPS truck arrived during breakfast. "I presume that is the Easyloader–50 press." I said, "I hope so, I don't have the patience to load wax bullets manually. We need to shoot to increase our speed, and being good at manually loading wax bullets does nothing for me."

We set the target on practice mode. There was a 2–5 second random delay for the starter light to come on. We each shot 5 rounds and the average time came out to 0.85 seconds–this was our starting times after a full day of dry fire. Sue said, "can you imagine what our starting times would have been without that day of dry firing?"

After firing 35 rounds each, we cleaned the guns. We passed that special 6" firm nylon bristle brush six times in the barrel and twice in the cylinder chambers. We then passed a wax solvent soaked patch in the barrel and each chamber. A bore light confirmed the wax was out.

We were seeing a shooting pattern. Shoot 100 rounds with three wax cleaning, reload 100 rounds each and repeat. Each 100 rounds was taking 1 hour–cleaning and reloading included, followed by a rest period as needed.

We shot all day using this method. The rest period was very important. As the day progressed, the rest periods became longer. It was unbelievable how tiring it was to concentrate and react so quickly. By mid afternoon, Jack popped in. He wanted to see how CFD was done. We loaded up and fired 5 rounds each, man-to-man. Our average times came to +- 0.65 seconds from a high of 0.85 seconds this morning. Jack was stunned and impressed. He kept watching all 100 rounds and never stopped smiling. We visited with Jack during our break. He had gone to Ed's today and came back with a 45 LC Marlin lever, a 1897 pump shotgun and a Kimber 1911 in 45 ACP–ready for WB and CPS, and heading to the range in the AM.

With a solid shooting time of 0.65 seconds, we were satisfied with our first day of real shooting and looking forward to tomorrow.

Day 3. We started our day with two 100 round strings. Our times were not improving and were actually stuck on a plateau of 0.65 seconds. After some reflection, Sue said, "when you were training for CAS, I watched you and I was able to detect problems. Let's do that again. I will watch you and you watch me. We both know the proper drawing and shooting technique, we should be able to coach each other and find our mistakes."

I went first and after three shots, she said "STOP." *That word was a "deja vu" from my training days for CAS.* Sue said,: "it is very obvious, once the starter light comes on, you have a momentary hesitation before you start your draw. I bet you are losing several hundreds of a second. The solution is to react quicker, an acquired trait, that you can teach your brain. As the DVD stated, the visual reaction is a conscious function. The draw is a memory and subconscious function. One needs to control and separate these two functions."

I said, "easier said than done, but I will try. I reloaded, and worked hard on my concentration. I was teaching myself to react quicker to the start light as well as cutting my time to start the draw. It paid off, to my amazement my shooting went down to 0.58–0.60 seconds.

Sue was next. I could not detect a problem until the fifth shot. I yelled out, "STOP." Sue started laughing and said, "you finally got to blurt out that word coming in my direction, heh!" She was right, but now I forgot what I had detected. So I said, "shoot one more round so I can be sure–I was certain. "Sue, when your draw is complete, you then push your gun forward at least 1.5 feet beyond where it needs to be before firing. This converts to wasted time to extend the gun forward. Remember, the gun only needs to be 6 inches ahead of the holster, not two feet." Sue then kept on shooting and I saw her shorten her reach. By the time she was at the 6 inch mark, her shooting time had dropped to 0.56–0.60 seconds. Sue added, "Wil, this is working, let's do some more coaching."

I was next to shoot. After the second shot I heard, "STOP." Wil you can really draw smooth and fast, but you are losing time by not utilizing body mechanics to help pop the gun out of the holster. A time of 0.58 seconds is great for a person standing straight as a statue. So watch me again." Sue threw her R. hip and belly forward and her shoulders back. I then said, "women can naturally throw their hip and nearby body parts forward. Plus you have a natural 6 lb. weight on your upper body that carries your upper body backwards by natural momentum."

Sue thought and said, "well we can add a 6 lb. lead weight around your neck to see if it would help. We both broke out in laughter, and it was time to take a break.

After the break, I simulated Sue's extreme body dynamics. It did not work for me, I was missing the target. We then went to a 50% reduction of movements with positive results. In no time, my shooting time dropped to an amazing 0.53 seconds with greater than 90% hits.

Sue resumed shooting and I was watching. I saw a problem. "Sue, women tend to have a gentle hand with a gun. Grab my two fingers with the same strength you grab your gun. I said, "that is way too weak. Now put some muscle to it and give me a proper 'death grip' as the DVD keeps saying. Now try that aggressive grip with your gun." Sue resumed shooting several rounds. Suddenly, she smiled and I knew that she finally got it–her time eventually was down to 0.52–0.56 seconds.

So after two changes each, our shooting times had improved from 0.65 to 0.52 seconds. It was clear that we were correcting errors or early bad habits. We agreed that we would continue this coaching till we could no longer find things to correct. Sue added, "we had two changes each, but in actuality it is four, since we are incorporating each other's corrections."

I was next on the block. I was shooting a lot, could not hear that dreaded word and my time was not improving. Suddenly "STOP."

"I finally got you." *I wondered what she found that took so long.* "I am 100% certain that you are squeezing the trigger, and slowly I may say."

I paid better attention and started pressing the trigger in a snappy movement as the DVD suggested. It did not make a big difference, but every little bit helps. I was down to 0.50 seconds repeatedly.

For Sue's third coaching, she shot several rounds when I spotted an alarming pattern. I used the white lithium grease applied with a roller that came with the electronic target. I covered the 24 inch steel plate that surrounds the starter light with grease. Sue then fired 5 rounds, and the look on her face said it all–all 5 marks in the grease were in the lower right quadrant and actually almost on the target's edge.

I said, "Sue, this pattern, if not corrected will lead to target misses which means a lost shot." "Why is this happening?" "Something is preventing your arm from going up and to the left. Your breast is in the way of your shooting arm." Sue's eyebrows went up and I got that look–the one I don't fare well with! Since I was already in quicksand up to my armpits, I used one last effort to survive. "The bra you are wearing is allowing too much pendulousness and lateral extension of your breast."

"Let's try a sports bra or one that lifts and pushes your breasts closer together." Sue froze in place but eventually said, "I think you are right. I can feel my shooting arm hit my right breast before I press the trigger."

Sue turns around, takes her blouse off, heads for the house and comes back topless holding two bras. She asks, "which one do you suggest?" "We'll try them both, but quickly since you know Jack likes to pop in unannounced!" The sports bra result was clear. Her shot placement was now near center. The uplifting bra provided the same results. I asked, "which one is more comfortable?" "They are both comfortable. The sports bra provides a bit more compression and is less revealing.

The uplifting bra brings my breasts to a point and under my chin. Can you imagine the looks I am going to get? The sports bra is the answer." Sue shot several more 5 round strings and to our surprise her shooting times were down to 0.50 seconds. Sue smiled at me and said, "and my shooting arm was rubbing on my right chest wall as is proper, not my breast." *And I got that smile, the one I knew I would fare well with, and no later than tonight!*

After lunch I was next up. I started shooting and Sue was not stopping me–just looking. Finally, I stopped shooting and asked, "well what have you found?" Sue hesitated as if in a trance. "Wil, I have only seen a few people shoot with such a smooth performance–you are without a doubt a natural talent. You will go far in this sport. Now my only suggestion is that you tend to aggregate your shots below the starter light. Just lean your shoulders a bit more forward and your POI will be a tad higher." I tried the change, my POI was more around the starter light but my shooting time did not improve–on a firm plateau of 0.50 seconds.

Sue's performance was last of the day. She started shooting and I could not find anything wrong until I stood directly behind her. She was placing her thumb directly behind the hammer instead of 45°. When she corrected this, she found that there was less rubbing of her right forearm on her chest wall. It was more comfortable but her times did not change.

By 4 PM we were both tired and decided to break for the day. Resting with a glass of wine, Sue said, "after 3 days of intense training(dry firing, free style shooting and coaching) we are both shooting at 0.50 seconds. You are now going to go past me, you have the talent and physical ability to excel in this sport. I will predict that your shooting times will approach 0.40–0.45 seconds by competition time. I am at the limit of my ability. I am not a natural talent like you, and I don't have the physical strength in my arm to push the speed envelope much further. With a lot of practice, I may gain a few hundred seconds, but not consistently or with varying accuracy."

I added, "I have suspected this for some time and was working on a pleasant way to breach the subject, but your astuteness beat me to it. Yet I have a solution for you. You need to start playing poker with your man-on-man opponents. Start varying your slow and fast clicks, do a little of soft complaining, sound and look happy if you barely beat your opponent's shot, congratulate your opponent, show a little cleavage, miss an occasional target, then take out your fast click and blow them away. I know you can be a master at this game. Remember the DVD alluded to this several times."

Sue hummed, "so you think a little cleavage will be to my advantage?" "Oh yes, just a little, or your opponent will have a <u>premature firearm discharge</u> in his holster. Please be kind and have some sympathy!" She started laughing and said, "yes, I think you are right, and I will start working on this." "From now on, we need practice and more practice if we are to shorten our shooting times."

———————•━●━•━•————————

After a well needed shower, we changed into our western attire and headed to the Country Roadhouse for some well deserved entertainment.

After getting to our table, Stan Winslow and three other Cowboy shooters, came to visit. The talk around town was all about CFD and the meeting on Sunday. Stan said, "many shooters have already researched the subject on the CFD website. Some have even started to share the DVD–Hit Em Fast. People are enthused and looking forward to learning a new shooting discipline. We are all waiting for the meeting before we flood Ed's Mercantile–no one wants to purchase the wrong gun or gear."

One of the other guys said, "we are very appreciative of you and Sue for organizing and taking control of this new discipline!"

After they left we ordered a t-bone steak dinner. While waiting for our meal, Sue asked, "why is there so much interest in doing fast draw?"

"Many of us can still remember and relive the joy of Cowboy days with Roy, Gene, Lone Ranger, Bonanza and Gunsmoke on TV. In addition, some Cowboy shooters still believe that SASS missed the boat when they added Wild Bunch instead of CFD. Fast draw was a phenomenon of the West during Gunfighter days before 1900. WB was after 1900 during the more modern days of Butch Cassidy and the Sundance Kid."

After dinner, the DJ came to the microphone. "We have now shown you 7 partner dances, 7 new line dances and 7 new two-step and waltz turns. The general consensus is that we need to stop teaching for the summer but hopefully restart in the fall. At this point, people are satisfied with what they know. If we continue teaching, we feel that we are going to lose dancers from our ranks. We hope you approve." The applause was all the DJ and owner needed to hear!

On the table was a list of all the dances and turns we taught so far. I looked at the list and said, "how come, through all our travels, we only missed three partner dances, three two-step turns and three line dances." "They must have been more difficult dances that required several weeks to master. In any event, we are fortunate that Stan and Miranda have already given us a lesson and we have learned all these listed dances."

The dancing started and we were up dancing all the partner dances and every two-step/waltz. A slow dance was announced before the second intermission. Having Sue in my arms was a deja-vu of a year ago. I still remembered our first kiss as the slow dance finished. especially remembered Sue's exclamation, "Oh my heavens." After getting back to our table, I reminded her of that moment.

She said, "I recall it very well. We then held hands while going to our table, where you tried to separate our hands but I would not let you." "Looking back, that was the beginning of everything–we were both saying YES and accepting each other without reservations. Sue leaned over for a kiss and then said, "either we go home or we get a room!"

Day 4. The next morning, after a replenishing breakfast, we went back to practicing CFD. We followed our routine, one hour of shooting 100 rounds, shooting man-to-man and cleaning our guns every 30-35 rounds. Our rest periods were occupied with Sue reloading another 200 wax bullets and odd jobs. I was busy preparing my club meeting presentation.

We were about to start our 2nd shooting hour when Jack popped in. He was heading to the range and wanted to see how the fast draw was coming along. So we started shooting the first 5 round string. Sue was consistent at 0.50 seconds and I shot two rounds at 0.48 seconds. Jack's face was frozen in amazement. He said, "goodness, how can anyone expect to compete against you two?" Sue retorted, "we are not special talents, anyone can spend the time practicing and be competitive with us. Everyone can shoot cheaply in their garages and achieve a proficiency level respectable for competition."

As the day progressed, I found myself sharpening my moves. I was getting more responsive to the starter light, more aggressive with the thumb draw, my death grip was more sturdy, and my body mechanics were improving. I found myself snapping my right hip forward and sticking my belly out. However my pelvis was still lagging behind! I could see that Sue was varying her slow and fast clicks with great control. She was beginning to change facial expressions–a poker face.

Finally, I said, "I can't watch your face, knowing you are bluffing me, I start laughing and miss my shot every time. So I was considering a piece of plywood between us but decided against it. I need to learn how to deal with an opponent that is acting like you!"

At the end of a long productive day, Sue said, "we just emptied the fourth 1000 round bag of Dead Eye EZ Loader wax bullets. I thought a minute and said, "at the CFD meeting, should I mention that after one day of dry firing, we shot 2000 rounds each in three days time. Starting a 0.85 seconds after a full day of dry fire, you are now in the range of 0.50 seconds and I am in the range of 0.48–0.50 seconds. Isn't this info a bit discouraging. Sue immediately countered, "they all need to know that if they want to compete, they also will have to do what we did. The bottom line, it takes determination, practice and 2000 rounds downrange to train your brain and muscle memory to achieve this goal."

"My only reservation is that we used a real electronic target, what are the others going to use?" I answered, "they can use a standard CAS timer, set on a table stand at the same elevation and forward position of the gun's muzzle–the table stand placed in front of the shooter's left hand for timer activation." You draw on the buzzer and the bang from a shotgun primer will stop the timer and give a shooting time. The target should be a 2 foot square piece of corrugated sheet-metal on a wood frame that will ring out when hit." "Good to know, make sure you mention this at the CFD meeting!"

That night we were looking forward to an evening of dancing and relaxation at the Country Roadhouse. The evening started with much socialization with people becoming good friends. Sue said, "look at the way people are pairing up–just like Stan and Miranda, heh." "Yes, now let's dance, tomorrow we have a big day.

CHAPTER 4

CFD, Desperado Gunslingers

anger Rooster(RR) opened the clubhouse at 8 AM
so we could set up our two lane electronic target
with overhead display and a tarp backup. On a table we
set up the Easyloader–50 with 65 copies of an operational
manual, and displayed Dead Eye EZ Loader wax bullets,
cleaning brushes, a manual metal reloading tool, wax
solvent and Quick Cal's DVD–Hit Em Fast. Finally we
set up our laptop to the club's 52 inch TV via a HDMI
cable so we could refer to the CFD website for the videos
and mercantile.

RR filled the master coffee pot and took out 5 dozen
donuts. Club members started arriving and by 10 AM we
had a full house of 67 Cowboys in attendance. RR started
the meeting with the Pledge Allegiance to the Flag. He
then said, "we invited you all today to try to convince you
to join our new shooting sport, CFD. I will now turn the
meeting over to Wil and Sue, the organizers of this new
Cowboy Game."

"With the introduction of the 1873 Colt Peacemaker, we defined and entered the gunfighter period of 1873 to 1900. The Desperado Gunslinger Club of Missouri will try to emulate this era. IMHO, this sport is 'the most fun you can have with a gun.' It is a sport for all ages, even aging eyes since there is no aiming—this is a point and shoot game."

"Basically, this is a man-on-man competition where you speed draw a SA pistol in 45 LC, from a regulation holster, fire a wax bullet propelled by a shotgun primer at a 24 inch steel target some 21 feet away. Do it faster than your opponent and you win the shot. Win three shots out of five and you win the round. The loser gets **one X,** once you have **three X's,** in this club you are out of the competition."

"Getting down to specifics. We will now cover several subjects and items you need to know before you gear up."

A–FIREARM. "A stock RNV, Colt or clones in 45 LC caliber without external modifications except you may extend the cylinder notches. The standard barrel length is 4 5/8" but will allow up to 5 ½"."

- Action jobs are OK as well as reduced hammer springs. I use a 14 lb. and have not had trouble detonating 209 shotgun primers.
- Keep the trigger spring a stock 3 lb. A reduced trigger spring of 30 ounces as in CAS may cause a premature discharge."

B–HOLSTER. "Like the CFD website, Ed's Mercantile also carries Mernickle leather. Blocker or Tombstone leather is available on line.

- A regulation holster allows you to cock the gun while still in the holster.
- It has zero retention so use a hammer thong when not on the firing line.
- It must have a deflection shield at the open toe of the holster.
- May have up to 20° of forward cant.
- The use of a thigh/holster tie down is recommended.
- These holsters come in belt level or drop loop types(will demonstrate later)."

C–AMMO. Wax bullets. The CFDA brand is Dead Eye EZ Loader.

- 18 grain wax bullet. $30/1000.
- Push round end first, the compression at the other end snaps in and holds the bullet in the case.
- Push wax bullet in 3/8" and the 209 primer = 750 fps.
- Melting point of 190° promotes shatter on impact–less bouncing back to shooter.
- In hot weather, keep bullets in refrigerator to minimize barrel wax deposits and bullet bounce-back.

- Don't resize cases at every loading. If wax bullet is loose in the case, it is time to resize the case to prevent barrel waxing.
- Reload manually, or with a $35 manual single stage press, or use the club Easyloader–50

D–EASYLOADER–50. "This is a 2 ton hydraulic press that pushes 50 Dead Eye EZ Loader wax bullets from a shaker box into 50 cases at one time. Once the fifty slots are full of wax bullets, pull the handle 4 times. All 50 wax bullets are pushed into the case at a depth of 3/8" below the case mouth. Then take the bottom tray out and transfer/flip the loaded cases into a container. Some residual wax shavings may need to be brushed off the casings."

E–CLEANING. "Use CFDA 6" heavy duty nylon bristle brush and EZ Out wax solvent.

- Clean barrel and cylinder chambers every +- 35 rounds.
- Pass brush twice in each cylinder chamber and six times in the barrel. Follow both with one solvent soaked patch. Do the barrel first and follow with cylinder chambers. Do not follow with dry patch unless done for the day."

F–SAFETY. "Eye and ear protection for shooters. For spectators eye protection required whereas ear protection is optional.

- Leather boots and holster deflector shield are required.
- Guns can only be taken out of holster in three locations: dry fire range, cleaning site and firing line."

G–STANCE. "Feet 1–1.5 feet apart, right foot forward, knees slightly bent and shoulders forward.

- Shooting body dynamics. On the draw, shoulders move backwards, belly sticks out forward and right hip snaps forward."

H–THUMB DRAW. "This is the standard draw of the CFDA.

- Place your right thumb on the hammer at 45°, your 3rd and 4th fingers under the grip and do not move the gun. On the starter light, you lift the gun, close your fingers on the grip, and cock it as it starts to come out of the holster. Then point the gun at the target with a strong 'death grip' and fire. You want to fire when the gun muzzle is 6 inches above and forward of the holster."

I–DEMONSTRATION. I demonstrated in slow motion several times and dry fired. Then I picked up speed several times and finally I drew at full speed with a live fire. *The look on the crowd's faces was worth a million bucks.* I repeated the demo with live fire four more times.

"Sue will now demonstrate how to add body dynamics to the draw with a live fire." Sue pulls the gun, provides the draw with the real body mechanics and fires. Everyone was stunned. Sue repeated the shot with the body dynamics four more times.

Finally I said, "RR put your teeth back and close your mouth. You were suppose to look at the body mechanics!" RR said, "I was trying to but all I saw was the body portion of the mechanics." The place erupted in cackles, laughter and applause. Sue's face turned purple and I got that look–the one I don't fare well with.

After bringing order back in the room, I said, "Sue and I will now give you a real 5 shot competition with the overhead public displays of our shooting times. We started–set, starter light, double bang and repeated four more times. Our times averages–Sue was 0.59 seconds and I was 0.55 seconds. The stillness of the crowd turned into an uproar and applause. Sue added, "don't let our times scare you. Anyone can achieve the same result. Just do extensive drawing and dry firing. Then shoot 2000 round downrange and you will be in competitive range with us."

"Let's take an intermission. Sue will demonstrate how to operate the Easyloader–50 and how to load wax bullets manually, and I will demonstrate the holsters and other gear. I will also show everyone how to adjust the level of your holster to match your body type and height."

J–PRACTICE. "This is a shooting sport separate of other sports, because you can practice shooting in your cellar or garage.

- Build a target with a 2 foot square corrugated sheet metal on a wooden frame set at 50 inches high to center and 21 feet away. Use a tarp or plywood as backstop. Place your Cowboy timer on a stand to match your barrel muzzle. It will catch the shooting times from the shotgun primer blast.
- We did an entire day of dry firing before we loaded our first wax bullet. This resulted in a correct, fast and smooth draw. Rely on the DVD for proper form and technique. Use your Cowboy timer to start your draw or react to a TV scene change to draw and dry fire. Time spent on dry firing and learning a proper draw is never wasted time.
- Frequent practices are more beneficial that long ones. Stay at 100 rounds over one hour then rest and or reload wax bullets.
- Use a dedicated practice to resolve an issue.

- Wear jeans and leather boots when practicing. Even with a deflector shield, you can accidentally rake your leg or shoot yourself in the foot by prematurely firing as the gun is drawn.
- After a full day of dry fire, we then shot 2000 rounds over 3+ days to shoot at 0.55 seconds. The cost: 50 reusable casings for $40, 2000 wax bullets for $50, and 2000 primers for $70.
- Practice, practice and practice is the key to success."

K–COMPETITION. "Accuracy and consistent speed makes you a winner. You don't have to be a speed demon to win a match.

- In a match, only one person can be the 1st place winner. Yet there is the magnificent four–the top four shooters of the match. Plus there is the top 10%. Any one in this last group has the potential for top placement in the future.
- Remember, even if you lose a string and get an X, you can still win a match–even with two X's. You are always in the match until you get three X's. Some clubs allow four X's.
- It can take years for your performance game to be as good as your practice game. Game adrenaline produces anxiety and stage fright. The saving factor, all shooters suffer from the same effects of adrenaline.

- Competition day should be a pleasurable event. Socialize and watch competitors–don't be the serious type isolated away from the event. We are not competing for mega-bucks.
  When your number comes up, get serious as you enter the on deck circle."

L–CLICKS. "This unique competition of man-on-man allows you to play poker with your opponent–the goal of tricking him out of a shot.

- Vary your shooting speeds, miss an occasional shot, do some soft moaning, congratulate your opponent on missing a close shot, when your opponent least expects it, stop bluffing and blow him away with your maximum click. For more tricks of the trade, see Sue after the meeting.
- To slow your speed, the draw should remain the same. Simply delay the pressing of the trigger. Never vary your draw–it must remain a standard of competition. Associated with a late trigger pull is the softening of the death grip. That will make you shoot low–compensate by bending your shoulders forward a bit more.
- Going to your fast click requires a significant increase of intensity. Every aspect of the draw and pressing the trigger has to be maximized. Body mechanics

must be exaggerated. Expert competitors end up standing on their toes as the DVD mentioned.

- Conversely, as a competitor you must learn to read your opponent. If your opponent is playing poker with you, you can learn to anticipate his clicks. If a shooter bends his shoulders further ahead, he is going to use his slow click. Learn to recognize a change of intensity. Basically, you need to know poker bluffs, to anticipate your opponent.

"On the subject of training, Sue and I will train each of you in our garage with the use of the electronic target. Our new current plan is to train 4 of you at one time. When you leave, you will have shot 100 rounds each and feel ready to start your own practice routine. The first practice competition is 2 weeks from today, so you all have time to get up to snuff. Bring your gun, holster, wax bullets, cases, eye and ear protection and primers. We have an Easyloader–50 for your use."

"We should be able to train everyone in four days. Friday is reserved for those who need extra time or late comers. Please reserve next weekend for the working class who cannot leave work during the week. If anyone is available to fill in for a cancellation, please say so to Sue or RR. For those of you who want a training time, please see Sue or RR. Choose 8–10 AM, 10–12 AM, 1–3 PM, and 3–5 PM. We need your phone number and e-mail.

Let's go by rows, starting with row one." *As everyone in the first row got up to sign up!*

———•———•———•———

"While the signing is under way, I will discuss some subjects that may be of interest. This year the Bar W Ranch shoot will be different. The main match this year is not a CAS event. It is a split event between WB and CFD. Because of last year's demo of CFD, people showed much interest in starting a local CFD club. When a new retiree from Fallon, Nevada agreed to train the locals, a new club was formed. When a large club from Amarillo agreed to compete against the locals, the Bar W Ranch officials took the opportunity to add a match to the WB groups and make it the entire match. If this club's members choose to compete in either disciplines, we have a chance to advertize our club. FYI, we will be starting our WB club before the Bar W Ranch event. A high attendance is expected in both shooting games." *Applause.*

"The next subject is associated clubs. We will be the only CFD club in the state. Who could we attract to join us in competition? There are four existing CFD clubs within a day's drive. Oklahoma, Tulsa 180 miles and Kellyville 200 miles. Arkansas, Austin 210 miles and Pocahontas 180 miles. Hopefully, some of us will attend some of their big shoots. If we build it–they will come!." *Applause.*

"And last. How big has CFD become? The CFD website lists many state championships. These shoots have shown last year's winners to be shooting in the 0.40–0.45 seconds. Some of us will attain this level of proficiency."

"According to the CFDA website, the National Championship in Fallon, Nevada in 2017 had 249 shooters. The host club provided all the ammo to guarantee uniform velocities. The Magnificent Seven finals, to establish the fastest gun alive, was the match's signature event. The winner shot an amazing new record of 0.295 seconds!"

"Seeing that the signing is done, please take a rules and regulations booklet before leaving. We will be discussing these at a later date." RR gets up and says, "we have 60 brave Cowboys that have signed up." *Applause and many smiling faces.* I added, "see you all this week at 24 Derby Lane!"

Sue looked at me and said, "wow, we have our work cut out." "Yes, but I know we can handle it, and at the end of a week our students will be ready to perform this sport correctly!"

CHAPTER 5

CFD, Club Training

The next morning, during breakfast, we set up a training routine for all the student training sessions:

1. Show everyone how to operate the Easyloader–50.
2. Verify that the guns and gear meet the regulation standards.
3. Teach the thumb draw, body mechanics and the shooting technique.
4. Dry fire till everyone masters #3 above.
5. One team fires 5 shots, then reloads as the next team fires their 5 shots. The routine keeps repeating itself until the first barrel cleaning at +- 35 rounds. Then break for cleaning and correcting problems.
6. Resume fire for another +- 35 rounds. Break for cleaning and correcting problems.
7. Fire the last +- 30 rounds and finish with gun cleaning. Help with reloading their casings on the Easyloader–50.

8. Reschedule shooters who need a 2nd lesson or who did not break the one second mark.

———●━■●■━●———

Day 1, 8 AM–10 AM. The first team arrived with legal guns and gear. We proceeded with our established routine. The session went well. We were dealing with very attentive students, clearly eager to learn. We were pleased to end the session with three shooter's times less than one second. We then offered one slow shooter a 2nd lesson He gratefully accepted and agreed to practice this week before Friday's 2nd lesson.

While waiting for the next team, Sue said, "we have a perfect training routine. The key factor is that we each take two shooters—one does the draw as the other watches, and then we reverse the process before any bullets are fired."

Day 1, 10 AM–12 Noon. In the second group, one shooter had a non regulation holster. His comments were, "I needed to know, now I will order the proper holster." We gave him one of Sue's CAS holsters that passed regulations—one we had kept for this purpose.

Once the instructional portion of the draw was done, the shooters fired their first live round. One shooter said, "how do I know if I hit the steel target?" Sue and I looked at each other and she said, "I guess we never mentioned that feature at the meeting. If you hit the target, the public display monitor will show your time–otherwise it stays blank. Another method, if you hit the target, the starter light will start blinking, if you miss, the starter light stays with a continuous glow."

The session went well and we had one shooter that was even shooting in the 0.7 second range. The others had all achieved the goal of breaking the one second mark.

Awaiting the next team I said, "so far, everyone is arriving with 100 casings. It appears that they all remembered about shooting the 100 rounds." Sue adds, "and as they arrive, they load all 100 rounds on our press, and leave after loading their 100 rounds." "In addition, did you notice that the shooter in the 0.7 second range looked like a natural talent and of course that was Stan Winslow of the Country Roadhouse." Sue added, "and likely a top competitor against us!"

Day 1, 1 PM–3 PM. The afternoon team arrived and we immediately spotted a swagger. He boasted of practicing and drawing in 1.3 seconds.

He was a problem in that his draw and body mechanics were all wrong. Sue volunteered to take the swagger on because of the poor body mechanics and I gladly took on the other three students. These three were CAS shooters and they learned and progressed quickly. They were shooting under 1.0 second within the first 50 rounds.

The swagger was resistant to change but because of Sue's charm he eventually came around. After the training, his first 5 shots averaged 1.0 seconds and he was clearly impressed. He also left after meeting the 1.0 second goal. At the end of the session the three Cowboy shooters loaded their 100 casings, and left with many thanks. The swagger just left without saying a word or loading his casings.

While awaiting the next group, Sue felt bad and said, "we might loose that shooter." I said, "whenever you correct an arrogant person, there is the risk that you may have fractured his ego beyond repair. In this case, you corrected him as gently and as courteous as anyone could. Specifically, he will either see the light and will join our club, or we will never see him again which means that he doesn't belong in this friendly club—and it's not a loss."

Day 1, 3 PM–5PM. The last team arrived and went as smooth as possible. Three shooters were easy to teach and broke the one second mark just before their last rounds. I had one elderly gent who was slow and his shooting time was way high at 1.5 seconds. His problem was very obvious. Once his draw was completed, he hesitated to pull the trigger. He admitted, "I have shot pistols all my life and had aimed at my target. This point and shoot discipline is a tough trick to learn for an old dog. Yet, I am enjoying this game and I will practice to pick up my speed." Sue interjected, "we see your motivation and we would like to offer you a second lesson on Friday." *The gent's look said it all—and I thought he was going to kiss Sue.*

As we were relaxing before dinner. Sue summarized the day, "I think we had a very successful day. We have 2 shooters that got a second lesson, 13 students that are satisfied and well trained, and one shooter that we may lose." I added, "and one natural talent–in a pleasant man who will become a top competitor." Sue looked at me and added, "if you don't want Stan Winslow to walk all over us, maybe we should practice for an hour before dinner, heh!" One hundred rounds later we put our gear away till tomorrow.

After dinner, Sue brings up the very important subject, Rules and Regulations of the CFD game. We quickly decided that we needed a special meeting with the new club members–to be held Sunday AM after the club training week.

I started going over the booklet(the same booklet that we passed out at the last meeting) and started to prepare my presentation of the most important features–as well as a handout for the meeting. Sue took the list of shooter info gathered at the signing and prepared a CFD e-mail list in her address book.

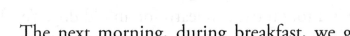

The next morning, during breakfast, we got a call from a student scheduled for the first class. He sounded terrible and admitted that he woke up with a terrible cold. We immediately gave him a spot for Friday. Sue got on the phone and easily called in a replacement.

Day 2, 8 AM–10 AM. The group with an on call substitute arrived to start the day. The instruction and dry fire portion went well. When the time came for live fire, one man seemed more anxious than need be. As the starter light came on, both shooters hit the target. The nervous nellie surprised everyone. He fired the gun as expected but the gun came out of his hand, and landed some 6 feet away on the padded rug. The result was a spontaneous eruption of laughter, including the student. Sue commented, "well at least you didn't throw your gun at our expensive target." The shooter was obviously embarrassed so I immediately chimed in, "looks like you have too much adrenaline on board. Just put this behind you and let's try again. I could not help it, I started laughing again, as did everyone else. The shooter was such a good sport that he was also laughing. Despite the event, all four students were well trained, including the gun hurler, and left having broken the one second mark.

Day 2, 10 AM–12 PM. The team arrived, one woman and three men. The lady appeared a bit anxious. She admitted that this was her idea to learn this sport along with her husband–yet afraid that she could not perform. Sue took the lady and I took the three men. The men were aggressive shooters and had probably been practicing.

They all were hitting 0.8–0.9 seconds and would make top competitors in the sport.

With Sue's slow, gentle and reassuring technique, the lady quickly relaxed. Her training went well and confidence set in a bit later than usual. She finished the session shooting 1.4 seconds. When offered a second shoot on Friday, the lady started crying and mumbled, "thank you so much. I will never forget what you did for me today, and I will practice before Friday."

Day 2, 1 PM–3 PM. During the team's gun and gear check, one shooter presented a problem. He had a revolver with a welded side thumb extension on the hammer, a 3 inch barrel and a holster without leather covering the gun's cylinder. We had to inform him that he could not train here with that gun and holster nor compete in the club's events. We offered him one of our guns and the spare holster. He refused saying, "well to hell with you and this sport!" and left in a huff. Sue immediately got on the phone and called in a substitute who lived in our condo complex–he was here in minutes.

The training was otherwise uneventful and every shooter left satisfied, and with 100 loaded casings–like everyone else. They all shot and broke the one second mark.

Before the next group arrived, I said to Sue, "what is the disgruntled man's name?' "His name is Daryl Scollins and here is his address." "Remind me to e-mail

RR tonight and give him this information. This is a dude with revenge in his eyes."

Day 2, 3 PM–5 PM. The last team of the day had a unique problem. One shooter had a very old fast draw holster without a deflector shield but legal in every other aspect. We decided to train him since he had jeans and steel toe work boots.

The session went well and everyone was breaking the one second time. Before departing, I gave the shooter missing a deflector shield a gift. I had made a deflector shield out of 0.08" thick steel. It was 4.5" long, 1 3/4" wide and the 1" tip bent at 45°. I showed him how to attach it to the holster's curtain. I said, "I am giving you this because there is no reason for you to buy a $130 holster when the holster you have is regulation, but without a deflector shield." The guy was very thankful.

Before the team left, they all loaded their casings. One shooter said, "I am selling some unused expensive guns and will order this Easyloader–50 press. Several of my friends and neighbors will be able to enjoy it as well." We gave him the phone number to place an order.

We then practiced our own shooting for an hour and shot the usual 100 rounds. After dinner, I did some more work on my Rules and Regulations handout and Sue was still building her e-mail addresses.

Day 3, 8 AM–10 AM. The next morning three of the trainees were having way too much trouble with the training, dry fire and shooting. The fourth shooter quickly picked up this game and within 50 rounds was almost in the 0.75 range. He realized that the other three needed more help than he did so he was first to leave.

We worked hard with these three and finally got them to come close to the 1.0 mark. When they were reloading their cases, Sue said, "are these three shooters that inept or are they a group that doesn't know if they want to be in this sport?" I answered, "I think we have one bad apple in the bunch that is hindering the other two. Let's offer all three a second lesson and see what happens!" After the offer was made, two students were very happy to attend on Friday. The third one declined. He said, "this is not for me, but thank you for the training. This is what I needed to make up my mind. I will be seeing you in Rifle Silhouettes and Long Range." "Glad to have you in those games."

After they left, Sue said, "are you aware who the shooter is who easily shot in the 0.7 second range." "No." "He is Stan Winslow's friend from the Country Roadhouse, George Blakely."

Day 3, 10 AM–12PM. The next group were police officers with no CAS experience. Two men and two women, all four were carrying and shooting Glocks(auto pistols without hammers). When asked to place their hand in the Lawman's grip, all four wrapped their entire hand and thumb around the grip. Sue said, "now you need to forget everything you learned in the 21st century. We will take you back to the 19th century to learn this sport."

These four officers were very eager and motivated. They picked up the moves very easily. By the time they were done shooting their 100 rounds, they were hitting at 0.8 seconds smoothly and accurately. As they were leaving, two were leaving their service belts/glocks on the bench. I said, "you are going to look funny getting out of your cruiser with a fast draw holster and cowboy pistol. Better make a change.!"

Day 3, 1 PM–3 PM. The trainees arrived, and another surprise. Four ladies and all good friends. We spotted the problem immediately. Two ladies had an average body, one had an over endowed bustline and one was flat chested. The problem of the over endowed was quickly resolved with a sports bra.

We started our training, as the shooting started, the flat chested lady was shooting low as expected. Sue explained, "you don't have the natural momentum to throw your upper body backwards. Bend your head and upper body more than usual." The result was clearly beneficial. Sue got genuine praise and thanks from these ladies. They all met the 1.0 second goal.

Day 3, 3 PM–5 PM. The last team of the day provided some unique issues. One student had developed his own draw–not illegal, just clumsy and slow. Sue's diplomacy went to work. "Draw 5 times and let's see what your time is. Then you draw 5 times according to the standard thumb draw." The shooter quickly saw a shaving of 0.3 seconds off his time–nothing more was said.

Another student did a perfect draw, then brought the pistol to his face and aimed at the target. I said, "what the hell is that?" The student said, "I have been a target shooter for the past 40 years, and have aimed at my target. I have trouble with point and shoot." I said, "well when you leave here you will be comfortable with point and shoot."

We worked hard with these two shooters. Whereas, the other shooters easily picked up this draw and shooting technique, and were also quickly shooting in the 0.8 range. I asked, "you guys have been practicing, heh. Do you know Stan Winslow?" One answered, "yes, Stan has started a practice group in his garage. Six of us meet every evening after work, and practice." Sue added, "and you two are Jim McGinnis and Paul Smart, heh" One gent said, "yes, and see you Saturday night. Thank you for the training session."

The two problem shooters were offered a second lesson and graciously accepted. As they departed, we did 1 hour of shooting our 100 rounds. Sue was holding strong at

0.50 seconds, and I was progressing in the 0.45–0.48 range.

After dinner, we again worked on our projects. Sue finished her e-mail addresses and then started photocopying the handout on CFD Rules and Regulations, as I finished my presentation. Before bedtime, I said, "according to my math, we should have an easy day tomorrow with only 12 students left." "Well no, I had a call from one of two couples who heard about us training people for CFD. They seemed like pleasant people who would gladly buy a club membership if CFD was for them. I booked them as the last team of the day." I answered, "well the word is getting around and we haven't even had our first match!"

———————•—◦•◦—•———————

Day 4, 8 AM–10 AM. The team arrived with regulation guns and holsters. One shooter was not using the standard Dead Eye EZ Loaders, he had another brand of wax bullets. I looked and recognized the brand. I said to Sue, "these wax bullets don't shatter on impact, so get ready to duck, they will bounce back at us."

As soon as live fire began, Sue managed to catch all five shots on her body–one on her upper left arm, one on her left breast, one on her high abdomen, one on her very, very, very low abdomen and one on her very, very, high right thigh.

I said, "women have fragile blood vessels and bruise easily. Better check the results." Sue went in the house and came back to the garage giving me that look–the one I don't fare well with. She then grabbed a large metal garbage can, stood behind it and held the cover as a chest and head shield. On the next 5 shots, we heard, bing, bing, bing, bing and bing. Despite the laughter, we got through the lesson with good results. The other three loaded their cases with the Easyloader-50 press. The variant wax bullets did not fit in the press and the shooter agreed not to bring these bullets to any practice or competition at the club.

Day 4, 10 AM–12 PM. This was the first team to not have a single issue, learned quickly and even left 15 minutes early. They were well prepared for competition.

Day 4, 1 PM–3 PM. This team provided an interesting dilemma. All four shooters had a disability. Sue had scheduled them together as a chosen group–intentionally. I said to all four students, "the shooting sports in this country allow modifications to compensate for the specific disability, as long as we maintain a level playing field for all contestants. Let's work with each of you individually:"

1. This shooter had only half a right thumb for a right hand thumb draw.

A gunsmith had welded a hammer extension that compensated for the absent half digit and even allowed a 45° application to the hammer. 'We watched his draw and it was as normal as could be–APPROVED.

2. This shooter was missing his right ring finger. He demonstrated a proper grip using his middle and 5th finger. The gun lifted out of the holster properly, safely and with a good death grip. APPROVED.

3. This man's disability involved an old stroke affecting his left leg. He had difficulty standing and balancing. He performed his draw while wearing a clasped crutch on his left forearm. He could not use body mechanics for fear of losing his balance. So he did his thumb draw and fired while standing straight. He was clearly safe. APPROVED.

4. The last student had a "familial tremor." The tremor was so severe that his thumb would shake and fall off the hammer. He told us that he had been referred by the CFDA to a certified gunsmith capable of performing the internal modifications and install a fanning hammer. Although fanning was not recommended for CFD because of the damage to a stock gun, this gun had been modified for this purpose. We watched him do a safe draw, firm hand grip, and proper fanning. APPROVED.

We trained all four as easily as any other trainee. They all left with shooting times breaking the 1.0 second mark. All were pleased to be included in the club team.

Day 4, 3 PM–5 PM. The last team was the married couples without a club membership. They had done their research and had been at Ed's Mercantile. They arrived with new Ruger Vaqueros and regulation holsters. They did not have casings or wax bullets since Ed was out. We gave them our loaded ammo and started the training. We trained the men and the women watched attentively–and vice versa. They were quick learners and smiled through the entire two hours. It became clear that they wanted to stay with the sport. I gave them a synopsis of the CFD meeting they missed, and invited them to Sunday's meeting on "Rules of the Game." They were informed to see RR on Sunday for memberships. Before they left we showed them how to use the Easyloader–50 press.

With everyone gone, Sue said, "it has been a smooth 4 days. We have 50 men, 12 women and lost two–a man out of his comfort zone and one angry disgruntled man with the illegal gun and holster." "I have given his name and address to RR." "We also gained four new club members which will please RR. For tomorrow, I have scheduled all the repeat lessons at 8 AM and we should be done easily by noon. At 1 PM we have a luncheon meeting with Willard Stone."

We then did our 1 hour of shooting, had dinner and had a relaxing evening at home without projects.

———●●●———

Day 5, 7AM. After breakfast, we went to change for the lesson. Unexpectedly, Sue comes out of the bathroom, standing nude with hands akimbo. She gives me that look–the one I don't fare well with. I immediately saw the problem. She had five perfect bullet bruises–left upper arm, left breast, high abdomen, very very low abdomen and very very high right thigh. After I stopped laughing, I hugged her and said, "beautiful battle scars for the cause." She answers back, "I can accept three for the cause but not the two very very personal ones. Thank you."

Day 5, 8AM A lively bunch arrived. Each one claimed they had a good week of practicing fast draw. We watched their shooting technique and let them shoot freely. They all broke the 1.0 second mark and a few were between 0.9–1.0 seconds. They all exhibited a comfortable stage presence and were all having a good time. We let them shoot till noon and most shot 200 rounds each. As they left, I said, "they will all blend in well with the remainder of the team. It was worth the extra time."

———●●●———

We arrived on time at the Stone Hotel. Mr. Stone's assistant escorted us to his office-suite lounging area. Mr. Stone came out of his office to greet us. It was immediately clear that this 81 year old man still displayed power and leadership. We sat on settees facing each other and the house lady brought coffee. He asked her to delay lunch for one hour.

She agreed and he thanked her–*I acknowledged Sue's glance, that thank you was a plus for us.*

Mr. Stone went right to the subject on his mind. "I have no heirs and I am in the process of organizing my assets and my will. I have only one relative, a cousin and otherwise the remainder of my assets will go to charity and one special cause–the Desperado CAS club."

He explained how he has enjoyed shooting CAS at our club, and how he hopes to change the club into a hub of Cowboy Games–for Missouri and surrounding states. He explained that his dream was to develop five new shooting disciplines at the club.

"I am setting funds aside for the building of four new buildings, an enclosure for fast draw, a mini clubhouse for Silhouettes and Long Range, roofed facades for WB, and roofed stations for CFD practice. The funds include excavation for new ranges in WB, Silhouettes and Long Rangel. A large monetary reserve for purchasing the many steel targets from our own local steel target manufacturer. Basically, I have given RR a blank check to purchase anything he needs to make this happen, and I have set up a trust fund that will continue when I'm gone."

"Now my lawyers tell me I need an alternative person or persons to take over the club and the works–including control of the check book. This is a precaution in case we lose RR. I also need organizers who are willing to set up and develop these five shooting venues–and I hope you two will fill those two positions. Enough from me, how say you?"

I started, "we are grateful for your generosity and we would be honored to be your alternative replacements for RR. We would also be glad to develop these five disciplines. As of today, we have spent 50 hours training and preparing ourselves for the CFD game. We just finished training 64 new members, over a week's time, on how to perform safely per standards of the game."

Sue took over, "we are having a meeting soon to discuss the Rules and Regulations of the game. As soon as the enclosure is built, we will have our first practice competition. We are fortunate to have 64 Cowboys eager to proceed."

Mr. Stone interrupted and said, "the construction materials have arrived and construction started yesterday. I am told that the enclosure will be 100% completed in 7 days and ready for use at that time."

Sue continued, "after the practice match in two weeks, and the first real competition match in three weeks, we will start organizing the WB with the other three games to serially follow."

I then added, "we will organize and manage all four games, CFD, WB, CRS and CPS for one year. We will also organize Long Range but choose not to participate or manage this sport. We are action shooters and Long Range is not our game. We will need to find a manager for this game."

Mr. Stone chimed in, "what extra do you need from me?" "We need nothing, but RR will need some help. He needs physical help with maintenance and match workers. There is a limit to volunteering when too many activities are needed." Mr. Stone put up his hands, "say no more, I forgot all about this need. I will notify my lawyer today to set up an employment trust fund. I will authorize RR and you two to pay anyone as club helpers at a rate equal to double the state's minimum wage rate, and I am sorry for not recognizing this need."

There was a pause and Mr. Stone took over. "I will now pat myself on the back. I chose you two and I was right. You are clearly organized, dedicated and true leaders. This club will prosper under your direction. So now how do I repay you financially for your work and plans?"

Sue jumped in, "we are doing this because we enjoy the Cowboy Games and we need the challenge." I added, "besides, we are financially secure and we don't need money–your generosity towards the club is way beyond, and more than enough."

"So, RR will continue to manage the club without pay and you don't want pay either. I guess my only cousin was right about you two and RR. You all didn't know, Constance Emma Whitehouse is my cousin–ha ha ha! I also heard how she gave you your entrance fee back to the tune of $5,000– ha ha ha. And yes, I saw the resuscitation!"

Mr. Stone added, "Wil and Sue, you need not wonder, you and RR will be taken cared for, in due time. Thank you for making my dream a reality. I will be at your first practice competition–incognito, and will give a $500 cash prize to anyone who can pick me out of the crowd. Oh and let me say, in my entire life, I have never seen so many full grown men drop to their hands and knees and vomit in unison, that 6 inch cardiac needle certainly did do the trick! Ha ha ha."

On our way home Sue said, "I am pleased how the meeting went. I am especially pleased to see a trust fund for future employment needs. That was a nice touch you came up with and I am certain that RR will appreciate it." I thought and said, "I just can't wait to tell RR who Mr. Stone's cousin is, ha ha ha!"

After we got home, we practiced our usual 1 hour/100 rounds and then had dinner. We were too tired to go to the Country Roadhouse so we decided to skip it until tomorrow night.

CHAPTER 6

CFD, Interim Activities

After a replenishing breakfast, we were about to plan our day when Sue got a phone call from Miranda Blair. She would come over at 1 PM with Stan to review the partner dances and two-step turns they taught us a few weeks ago. Apparently they had missed one partner dance.

With the major portion of the afternoon already committed, we decided to do some intensive practicing of our fast draw. We managed to shoot 300 rounds each and be done by lunch time. Our shooting times did not really change. Sue was holding at +- 0.48 and I was at +- 0.44 seconds–a plateau we were having trouble escaping.

At 1PM, Miranda and Stan arrived. Sue immediately said to Miranda, in private, "every time I see you lately, you seem happier every day." "Miranda said, "not only are we engaged, but we have moved in together. This is not our first rodeo, and life is good for two 50 year old lonely people. " "When is the wedding?" "Time will tell, all in due time."

We then talked to Stan, "So we hear that you have started a practicing session after work." "Yes, I have and three of my friends are doing quite well." "What are your shooting times?" "We are all approaching the 0.6 second mark and improving every day." "Great, and if you continue, you may catch up to us."

For the next two hours we were taught the new dance, as well as reviewing the ones we learned a few weeks ago, We were done by 3PM and visited with them—they were quickly becoming good friends.

After they left, we took an hour to do our 100 round shooting routine. Then we did a quick review of the new dances before we headed out to the Country Roadhouse. As soon as we got to our table, Stan showed up with his three friends: George Blakely, Jim Mcginnis, and Paul Smart. George thanked us for the recent training session, Jim added the fact that it had improved their times dramatically. Paul then says, "our goal is to be on your coattails by the practice match and to equal your speeds by the time the first real competition match is held."

Stan added, "by the way, you have had some very well organized meetings on CFD, and we are all looking forward to tomorrow's meeting—even if the subject matter can be dry." Sue adds, "but it all depends on the presentation, and Wil is quite good at keeping people's attention, heh?"

We danced all evening. We realized, again, that since we knew so many partner dances plus danced all the two-steps and waltzes, that Sue was moving away from line dancing. She explained, "when I was single, line dancing was a blessing. Now I have a dance partner, and leaving you at the table to do a line dance is not so cool any more." "I understand, but still dance some of your favorites. You have too much energy for me to keep up and an occasional fast line dance is relaxing for me!" *I thought, the relaxing part is to watch Sue shake her body parts!*

Before we went home after the last slow dance of the evening, Sue said, "did you see Stan and Miranda dancing?" "Yes, and it looks to me like a wedding at the Country Roadhouse is in the making."

———◆━◆●◆━◆———

The 2nd CFD meeting was scheduled at 10AM–for the purpose of electing a president/vice president, naming the club, and reviewing the Rules and Regulations of this sport. We were at the clubhouse at 8AM and there were already 5 cars waiting. People were coming early to load their 45 casings on the club press. Sue comes up to me and says, "people are arriving with the usual 100 casings to load, but some have as many as 300 to load." Just as I was about to ask someone why they had so many casings, I saw someone place a sign on the vendor table that read, "I will drill your 45 Long Colt casings for 209 primers. Cost $10 per fifty cases. $5 extra for primer pocked cleaning–chamfering and deburring.

I stepped up to the man and asked for more information. He said, "I worked 40 years in a machine shop and when I saw the 45 casings at $40 plus shipping for 50 cases, I knew that I could do the job as well with my quality drills on my drill press. I fabricated a vice to hold 45 LC cases without damaging them and went to work. Here is a sample of my work." I examined the samples, was pleased, and I told him that I would get RR to mention him at the meeting. "This is a great benefit for our shooters. Thank You"

RR announced the meeting at 10AM sharp. He added that he would stay after the meeting till everyone had loaded their casings. He volunteered to mention the man who would modify casings at a fair price. After the Pledge Allegiance to the Flag, RR started the meeting with an election for president/vice president. That took one minute and I was elected president and Sue was elected vice president. RR then handed us the meeting.

Sue started by announcing, "we had a productive training week. We started with 62 students, lost 2 and gained 4 for a total of 64. Yes we had two new couples that are now club members. Please say hello to: Claude and Gail Rockford and Cyrus and Jane Moorehouse–as they stood up. *Applause.*

I then took over the meeting. The first order of business, RR just told me that because of the heavy demand for the press use, he will pay a retiree to open the clubhouse between 9–11AM and 6–8PM, until we hold the first real competition match–courtesy of Mr. Stone. He will need work applicants after the meeting." *Applause.*

Rules and Regulations of the game.

GUNS. "Four additional tips:

- The cylinder notches can be deepened if you have a cylinder that jumps the notch.
- Grips can be thickened or thinned to match you hand.
- Hammer knurling can be smoothed or enhanced.
- Birdhead grips are not allowed."

HOLSTERS. "Three omitted items:

- Modern contemporary holsters used in World Fast Draw are not allowed.
- Your belt can be notched 1/4" to keep holders in place.
- If you have an older fast draw holster without a deflector shield, I have a sample of a homemade shield to show you and how to install it."

OPERATIONAL METHODS. "At competition matches:

- Your man-on-man competitor will be chosen randomly. At registration, you will pick a number.

Numbers will be chosen for serial competitors as you get on deck.

- Because of a high number of expected shooters, this club will eliminate shooters with three X's.
- Spin your cylinders after loading your gun–to prevent high primers which will cause a lost shot. Also, after spinning, learn how to move the empty chamber under the hammer–unique for different guns.
- On the firing line, load your guns only after the "load and make ready" command. Then keep your hands off the gun.
- With a "down range" command, all hands off guns.
- After the "line is ready" command, you may apply the Lawman grip carefully without moving the gun. Thereafter, you will hear the "set" command. This will be followed with a 2–5 second random pause until the starter light comes on.
- After the 5 shot string, you will hear the "unload and show clear" command as well as the "dry fire" command.
- It is not yet determined who will give the commands. Either the Range Master or the announcer!"

HAND JUDGE. "Every shooter will be a hand judge officer:

- Once you get out of the on deck circle, you sit down next to the current shooter on the firing line.

Your job is to assist the shooter. You will hand him his 5 live rounds after the "load and make ready" command.

- When the shooter has correctly loaded his gun with an empty round under the hammer, you sit down to signify that your shooter is ready. If there is a problem, stay standing till the Range Master comes to investigate.

- Once sitting down, watch your shooter. If he performs any illegal move, for example, drawing his gun before the starter light, it is your responsibility to make the claim. Stand up and the Range Master will come over. There is an extensive list of issues the hand judge must watch for. Check your handout or Rules booklet.

- Be kind and fair. You are next to the firing line and you will get the next shooter as your hand judge."

VIOLATIONS–TECHNICAL. "First violation=a warning. Second violation=loss of shot. Third violation=loss of round. See your handout for a more complete list, but here are the common ones:

- Trigger finger in the trigger guard before the draw.
- Premature lifting of the gun before starter light comes on.

- Feet ahead of the firing line.
- Discharging your gun with the muzzle behind the front of the holster pouch."

VIOLATIONS–PROCEDURAL "All=loss of shot.

- Apply the Lawman's grip carefully. It is a touch grip. If you move the gun, it is a procedural. Check the book for others."

VIOLATIONS–MINOR SAFETY. "1st violation= loss of round. 2nd violation=match D/Q.

- Touching your gun after a "down range" command.
- Breaking the 170° rule.
- Unsafe gun handling.
- Discharging gun in holster.
- Dropped gun on the firing line.
- Leaving the firing line without unloading and showing clear."

VILOATIONS–MAJOR SAFETY. "All=Match D/Q.

- Loading gun other than on the firing line.
- Having live ammo on your belt when in the contest area.
- Use of alcohol or drugs during match."

In closing, "read your handout and your Rule's handbook. You will all be hand judges and you need to know the rules and violations. One of us will also be a floating "side judge" to assist all of you till you get comfortable with the task."

RR took over the last portion of the meeting–naming our CFD club. RR pointed out that he would like the name to include the word Desperado. This will indicate to other clubs that it is a subdivision of the parent club. RR added, "would anyone like to propose a name?" Hands went up and names were given: Shootists, Vaqueros, Pistoleros, Cowboys and Cowpokes. I interjected, "RR, what do you think?"

RR got up and said, "all those suggestions are good, but I have a different idea. Since we are the first CAS club to host this new Cowboy Game in MO, I believe that we have first choice. As Wil said at the beginning of these meetings, *'we are trying to emulate the gunfighter era between 1873 and 1900,'* I suggest that we call ourselves, the Desperado Gunslingers."

The place went dead quiet, Sue broke the silence with, "I like it" and I followed with, "so do I." Someone in the crowd got up and said, "that is a wonderful name and I make a motion we adopt it." The motion was quickly "Seconded." "All in favor, raise your hands."

RR then revisited the employment issue. "We will have five new ranges to take care of, plus all the administrative duties that involves. Mr. Stone recognizes this need and is willing to provide a good wage for some easy work. I am willing to offer all of you a part time job, but I am going to ask you all to reserve this benefit for those who need the extra income–the retirees or workers who are having a tough time making ends meet. So come see me to sign up."

Otherwise, the meeting is done. The practice match is in two weeks and the real first match is three weeks from today. So practice, practice and practice–a reminder, the clubhouse will be open for the next three weeks from 9–11AM as well as 6–8PM, so come with your coffee, use the loading press, and visit a while.

Sue and I waited for RR to be done with job applicants. When done, we sat down with a cup of coffee, discussed how the meeting went, and what RR found out about the job applicants. He said, "I had 15 applicants, 11 men and 4 women. I gave the women administrative jobs and the men mostly range and physical jobs. These people really needed the extra income. No one could believe the pay they were offered." I interjected, "I think Mr. Stone recognized the financial need and wanted to help them, don't you agree?"

The next morning, during breakfast, I said, "we have two weeks before our first practice match. How should we organize our days?"

Sue came back with, "what we need the most is a lot of practice, but 8 hours a day for two weeks is overkill." I answered, "I have an idea. Let me make a few phone calls while you pick up some groceries. "OK, but I expect to be enlightened when I return."

An hour later, Sue returned, quickly pulled in the garage, and had a strange look about her. I asked, "what is wrong?" "When I got to the store, I noticed someone getting out of his car and just stood by his car. I actually walked to the store with my hand on my revolver. When I had my groceries, I asked security to escort me to my car. That man was still standing by his car. On my way home, I think he followed me." I said, "thanks to your awareness to your surroundings, we may just have had a warning of some impending danger. I think I am going to call Detective O'Brien and mention it to him."

After the call, Sue asked what he had said. "He recorded the info and his only recommendation was to wait, try to get a tag number and not to leave the house without us being together. I did mention the trainee who left here in a huff and appeared angry. We'll see."

"Anyways, I had a productive day. How would you like to travel 700 miles over 4 days, visit four actual functioning CFD clubs, and spend three nights in a motel?" "Oh wow, you know I like to travel, especially if it involves guns and shooting. Tell me more!"

"Well, we have researched the sport, have trained ourselves, trained 64 club members, and watched every video possible. Yet, we need to see, in real life, an actual CFD club match. So I propose this trip, leaving Friday, to Oklahoma and Arkansas where we will visit their clubs on Saturday and Sunday and be back home by Monday."

"I am ready and eager. Why motels when we have a camper?" "Because this is a quick business trip where all our energy will be spent doing some quick moving to cover 4 clubs over two days–not spending time setting up and closing the camper."

"So today is basically done, and we are not leaving till Friday morning. So we have three full days. How do you want to spend all this free time?' "Well, while you were gone for groceries, I got a call from an old patient. He has a small rough lumber mill with five employees. Apparently, the owner and employees got a whiff of what we were doing with CFD and they started investigating the web site and watched the DVD Hit Em Fast."

At this point, they have reserved at Ed's. six RNV's and six drop loop holsters. If we agree to train them, they will pick up their gear for the training." "So what did you tell him?" "I said that I had to check with my new wife, the boss------ bla-bla-bla." "Wil Summer, what a bunch of bull ticky. When do we train them?" "Well they are closing shop tomorrow at noon to go get their guns and gear at Ed's and will all be here at 8AM Wednesday. In addition, to compete with us, they will gladly pay the club's membership fee."

"This sounds like a good bunch of people." "Yes, the owner has done very well with these 5 dedicated workers. He is paying them full wages while traveling to Ed's and training here. What the workers don't yet know, the owner is paying for their guns and holsters as a long over due bonus." "Wow."

Tuesday was our day to practice all day. We each shot 500 rounds by 4PM. Sue was irritated at staying on that plateau again. I was aware of one improvement, we rarely missed the target. By the end of the day, my gun broke. Guess I am rougher than Sue on the thumb draw. I had to replace the hammer plunger, spring and pin–from my vigorous hammer cocking.

That evening we worked together to prepare a package for these six new shooters to include: CFD Rules, web site, name of DVD, general club meeting handouts, as well as CFD multiple meeting handouts. The next morning we were up early and were ready by 8AM.

The team arrived in two vehicles. After introductions, we gave them a presentation of the essentials discussed in the old meetings. We then went over our training routine. We spent a lot of time with the thumb draw, death grip, body mechanics, and dry fire for 30 minutes.

They had arrived without casings or Dead Eye EZ Loaders because Ed was out. We gave them our loaded ammo and showed them how to reload them on the Easyloader–50 press.

Before their first live fire. Sue and I gave a demonstration of a 5 shot string at the targets. Sue shot .50 seconds and I matched her. Eyeballs were popping out. When we explained how we had shot some 3000 rounds each, they relaxed. I then shot several rounds at +- 1.0 seconds, and explained that no one would leave today without achieving that goal. Their improvement beyond today was their responsibility.

The training session went well, Four hours later they were all ready to go home and continue their training. We showed them how to load wax bullets manually as well as on the Easyloader–50. As they were leaving we included:

- An application form for the club membership, signed by us as their sponsors.
- Sent them to the clubhouse tonight at 6PM where they can purchase, at cost, some cleaning brushes, solvent, casings and wax bullets–and load them on the club's press.
- Informed them of the clubs open hours for the next 3 weeks.
- Gave them the dates for the practice and first match.
- Gave them advice on proper attire–long sleeve shirts, jeans, Cowboy hat and boots.
- Encouraged them to stick to the 100 round rule to avoid fatigue and burn out.
- We showed them how to set up a target in their garage and how to use a Cowboy timer to start them and record times.

We exchanged phone numbers and e-mails. Each one was encouraged to call us if they had any questions, not to wait till the practice match in 2 weeks.

After lunch, Jack showed up wanting a demo on how we were coming along. Sue and I went man-to-man for a 5 round string. Sue averaged 0.49 seconds, and I hit 0.44 seconds. Jack just about collapsed to the floor. He said, "I cannot believe my eyes. You two have turned into dynamos or you are natural talents. You have trained yourselves to this level of proficiency as well as training Cowboys all last week."

Sue chimed in, "we are not natural talents or dynamos. We are just pig headed and determined to master this sport." "It has actually become a well received challenge and we are really enjoying ourselves." Speaking of CFD, we are leaving Friday till Monday for a tour of other CFD clubs, for our education. Would you pick up the mail and watch the place.? Keep in mind, we had one unpleasant experience with a trainee last week. If you see any strangers snooping around, try to take their tag number."

That afternoon we practiced again. By dinner time, Sue says, "I feel like we should put our guns away until we come back from our trip, I need a break!" I immediately agreed and said, "I have a great idea for tomorrow. Let's go get the materials to construct two standard targets to serve as temporary practicing lanes at the clubhouse. This is the ideal time to have practicing lanes since the clubhouse is opened 6 hours per day when the loading press is available on the premises. All they need is their timer and we will include an elevated stand to hold their timer at muzzle level." "That is an excellent idea, but lets go get the materials after dinner. That way we can start building in the morning, heh!"

"Tonight we will send a group e-mail telling everyone of our additions to the clubhouse–inviting all to not only load their casings but practice at the same time, and reload their casings again before leaving."

The next morning we started with a solid 4 point base of 2X4's with a 1.5" threaded pipe holder. We attached a 48 inch pipe with a drilled hole to attach a bolt that would hold the 24" steel target some 50" high. By 10AM we were headed to the range with two high wire stands for the timer and ammo, as well as two targets.

When we arrived with the targets and stands, RR was there with a dozen fast draw shooters. We quickly set up the targets in their own bay. The steel targets were angled to keep any bounce back to the wooded areas. RR explained that there is so much demand, that he is changing the club's open hours to 9 hours per day. First shift 8–11AM, second shift 11–2PM and third shift 6–9PM. All three shifts manned by three different employees. In addition, he will authorize the construction of two more targets and stands with a roof over the shooters, as mentioned by Mr. Stone.

Sue says, "why not, this clubhouse is a great place to hangout when you are retired and or training for CFD" We then told RR of our traveling plans on behalf of the club. RR surprised us by saying, "I want you to bring me the bills for food, motels, mileage and any incurred expenses. There is no way you are going to pay for this–I insist!"

Since this was a day of rest for us, we stuck around the clubhouse till 2PM. We talked and socialized with several of the club shooters who were sticking around after practicing and loading casings. Sue and I quickly saw that this gathering location was going to be very popular.

We then went home to pack for our investigative trip.

———●━●●━●———

CHAPTER 7

CFD, Traveling

We traveled southwest into Oklahoma some +- 200 miles. This was an easy route on a major highway. We arrived early and scouted around to find a motel. We found a four star motel with a full breakfast, and only a few miles to the CFD range. As prearranged during my call with the Range Master, we had agreed to meet Friday evening at the range. That way, the Range Master(RM) could walk us through the range and answer all our questions–since he would not have the time tomorrow morning before the match.

We arrived at the range at 7PM. The Range Master(RM) was waiting for us at the clubhouse and there were several Cowboys practicing fast draw. After introductions, the RM said, "I am very glad to see a club developing within our access. We need the competition and comradery. So what do you need from me?" Sue answered, "we would like to see your shooting facility" I

95

added, "and see how you operate and organize a shooting order and shooting match."

"Fine, let's begin, our clubhouse holds 75 shooters for lunch, it is heated with two propane stoves since we use this clubhouse year round—its construction is board and batten. We have an outside attached cook shack and a string of porta potties. Our CFD enclosure has a concrete floor, full plywood backstop, steel roof and partial sides for 20' each side with screened windows for summer ventilation. The enclosure is 35 X 60'. The first 20' is fully enclosed with sliding doors at the rear and the last 40' is fully open. In the winter we have a propane stove in the 20 X 35' section. In the summer, the sliding doors are fully open and all the windows are open. This makes our shooting enclosure a four season building."

"The 20 X 35' section is locked up. The audio system, folding spectator chairs, electronic targets, and control consoles are left in place. This is an important feature to minimize our work load."

"Next to the enclosure is the practice range. We have four steel targets set at 21'. The shooters stand under the roofed enclosure with an elevated table for their Cowboy timer. It is a rain or shine practice range. We have 45 club members, everyone has a key to the clubhouse for the use of the Easyloader—50 press and a winter warm up spot."

Sue interjected, "is this club just for fast draw?' "No, like most locations, CFD has evolved from another sport. Let's walk around the bend in the road." Suddenly, it became clear, there were 10 permanent facades for CAS. The RM added, "we are all CAS enthusiasts and enjoy these permanent stages. We can use these ranges for practice and or pleasure. We also have a plinking range on the 11th stage. We have 75 regular CAS participants, and yes they all have a key to the clubhouse."

On our way back to the CFD enclosure, Sue says, "I am glad RR added two more steel targets and a cemented floor/steel roof for inclement weather at our practice range?" "Yes, that was a great idea,"

The RM finally says, "now lets talk about the method that we use to process CFD shooters. Please realize that every club has specific variations that fit their needs. You will also develop your own, but this is how we do it."

"When you register, you take a random badge with a number and you wear it all day. We don't use real or alias names. At the beginning, the announcer calls 4 badge numbers, for example, 31, 44, 12, 50 to the firing line, then calls 5, 13, 17 46 to the hand judge seat, and calls four numbers to the on deck circle, 22, 27, 41, 42. Now we are ready to start the competition. In this club, I give all the commands; load and make ready, line is ready, set, shooting begins, commands repeated four more times till finally, unload and show clear command, followed by the shooters move up command. The runner or announcer then refills the on deck circle and the process repeats itself until all the shooters have gone to the firing line."

After the first groups have all had their turn on the firing line, we restart the 2nd group the same way and thereafter for several more groups–all groups have randomly chosen numbers so each shooter has a new competitor for each string. In this club, you need 4 X's to be eliminated. The club is growing and we will eventually have to go to 3 X's for elimination." I said, "we are already there with +- 70 shooters."

The RM adds, "if you ever get over 70 participants, you will have to go to two day shoots or eliminate at 2 X's in order to have a one day shoot."

I asked, "have you ever considered speeding up the process with a 10 shot group?" "Never, how would you like to end up with a speed demon and have to walk off the firing line with 2 X's–really?"

Sue asked, "how many workers do you need to run a match. "We are still using volunteers, but the idea is quickly growing for hiring actual workers. This is what you need:

- Runner–to fill up the on deck circle and run shooter's scorecard to the scorekeeper. Assist anyone else in need.
- Scorekeeper.
- Announcer/operator. To assist the RM and activate the starter light after the set command.
- Side judge to assist the hand judges and the RM.

- Range Master.
- A back up for the RM and Side judge."

"So if you two are the Range Master and the Side judge, you need 3 workers and a back up to replace you when it's your turn to shoot or you need a break."

We thanked the RM and as we were leaving, we shared names, alias, e-mail and phone numbers. The RM's alias was Ramrod Ellis. He surprised us by saying that several club members were going to the Bar W Ranch Shootout, and hoped to see us there. We told him that we would be back in the morning as spectators.

The next morning, after a replenishing full breakfast at the motel, we headed to the range. We got there at the beginning of the shooter's meeting. Ramrod Ellis started the meeting with the Pledge Allegiance to the Flag. The meeting was short since the participants were all club shooters. The one announcement, "we have two guests today, Doc Derby and Ladyslipper from Springfield MO. They are starting a CFD club in MO. If they ask you any questions, feel free to answer. I would like us to help them as much as possible."

The action started and went along as smoothly as possible. We watched for a half hour without a spoken word. The participants were enjoying the event, they were socializing with spectators, and some were watching their friends shooting.

Sue finally spoke to one shooter coming off the firing line. She said, "you are shooting at 0.45 seconds and you just beat a speed demon shooting 0.35 seconds." "Yes, but he was shooting beyond his capabilities, he missed the target three times and that is what got him an X. Some people never learn, you can't win if you don't hit the target."

I asked another shooter, "is there much use to the side practice range on the steel plates. An eager shooter answered, "this range is a gathering site for retired Cowboys during the day and for workers at night–for everyone on weekends. Even if we can practice in our garage, it is much more pleasant to come here and compete against our friends, and enjoy the club house with our bagged lunches and a thermos coffee. This club and range is alive with activity every day of the week–because of the CAS stages and the practice CFD range."

Sue asked another shooter. "What is the average times for the match winners?" One lady said, "usually the winner is shooting in the vicinity of 0.40 seconds. Occasionally we have a speed demon as winner in the 0.35–0.38 second range. Remember we have been doing this for three years and going strong."

As we were leaving, we stopped at the lunch wagon to pick up a kaiser roll sandwich, coffee, a pastry, and headed to the next CFD range for the after lunch shooting event.

We arrived at the next club after their lunch break. Since they only had 45 shooters, they expected a short afternoon until the signature event of the match–the Magnificent Six. As we watched the last of the main event, it was clear that there were speed demons vying for the last six positions. One of the spectators was heard saying, "these guys are pushing the envelope beyond their abilities."

The established elimination method for the Magnificent Six was a 2 X system, or loose two strings and you are eliminated. The contestants were tense and working hard. With 4 eliminations, we were down to two contestants. Sue said, "watch the guy dressed in black, he is a speed demon from the Magnificent Six elimination."

The guy dressed in a tan outfit won the round. Sue said, "the guy in black was bluffing and gave away the string and got an X. He shot too fast, whereas the guy in a tan outfit shot a solid 0.43 seconds. The guy in black was playing poker, he groaned loudly with a verbal expletive when he missed the target. Now wait and see what he does on the next string, when he knows the guy in tan has a fast click of 0.43 seconds."

The second string was as expected, the guy in black shot a consistent 0.41 seconds and beat the guy in tan. So now they each have an X. Whoever gets an X next will be in second place. The guy in tan was working very hard, beyond his ability, and was obviously very tense. The guy in black easily won at 0.39 seconds.

At the end of the match, we learned an important tactic. All the Magnificent Six got a medal around their necks. Position 3–6 each got a bronze, second place got silver, and first place got gold. A shooter said, "that way we are honoring the best 6 shooters of the match." We left at 4PM and headed several hundred miles east to Arkansas. We got there late, found a motel with its own restaurant. Had dinner and went to bed.

* * *

In the morning, we skipped the continental breakfast and headed to the range. At the range, we got a full breakfast at the food wagon, and had our meal in their clubhouse. During breakfast we noticed the many vendors set up on the perimeter wall.

After breakfast, we walked the grounds. They had a nice enclosure for CFD also a 35 X 60', but without a side practice range. They had a CAS range of 10 stages with permanent facades. Sue said, "this is the third enclosure we see. They are all the same size and same set up. I guess Mr. Stone had done his research when he chose this same enclosure for our club."

Since we were early, few of the expected 55 shooters had arrived. We went back to the clubhouse to visit the vendors. One table had an elderly gent with an obvious weak right arm. We struck up a pleasant conversation with him. As we thought, because of an old stroke, he was selling his fast draw gear and a Ruger New Vaquero. He also had 3000 Dead Eye EZ Loaders, 200 casings, 3000 shotgun primers, brushes and wax solvent.

The gentlemen brought up an interesting point. He said, "the two of you need a spare gun. Thumb drawing is hard on the internal mechanism of a revolver. That is why I carry these extra parts: hammer plunger, spring and pin as well as a pawl. You all need a spare gun." "OK, make me an offer for everything on the table–a complete set up without a holster."

"Wow, I did not expect that. Instead, why don't YOU make me an offer." "No, I am not a good haggler." Sue whispers, "retail new is worth +- $1000. The gentleman said, "how about $500 cash for the lot." I said nothing, pulled out my wallet and handed him six $100 bills. He said, "wait, you gave me too much." "No, I gave you a fair amount for a more than fair request. Thank You."

We brought all our purchases to the car and Sue said, "you had all that cash on you, really?" "Not a problem, we are both carrying a concealed weapon, heh."

At the shooter's meeting, after the Pledge Allegiance to the Flag, the Range Master (Marshall Samson) started with a strange announcement. "This has been a difficult year for the CAS and CFD clubs. We lost some good friends to health and then the furniture factory closed. We have had to rebuild the fast draw club. Although we use to be 70 members, we are now 50. The problem is that 20 are beginners.

Consequently, all violations will be explained but not counted against anyone. Also, we have guests from Missouri who are planning to start their own club. Wil and Sue Summer–please answer all their questions freely."

I said, "this is a good training technique that we will use at the practice match. Let's see what the common errors and violations are. I suspect the experienced hand judge will be standing often and the side judge will be helping the inexperienced hand judge."

- The first violation was the gun's premature lifting before the starter light came on. The hand judge was standing and the RM came over. "You would have lost the shot, even if you had beat your opponent. Do it a second time and you would be D/Q."
- The next one was a bit funny. The shooter discharged his gun while still in the holster. The deflector shield sent the wax bullet toward the hand judge who jumped off his seat and fell to the ground. The RM came over and said, "you just lost the string and got your first X."
- Another shooter, while loading his gun, started to speak to his hand judge and accidentally pointed his gun at the judge. Breaking the 170 ° rule. The RM came over with the bad news.
- The next one was more serious. The shooter was using his 45 colt as his concealed weapon. He

shows up on the firing line having forgotten he had a loaded gun–match D/Q.

- This one was unique to CAS. Cowboys often carry their match ammo on their gun belts. In this case, a shooter showed up in the contest area with live ammo–match D/Q.
- The inexperienced hand judge missed the next one. The side judge saw the violation. The shooter fired his gun before the muzzle cleared the holster pouch. The RM corrected both.

We decided by 11AM to move on to our last club an hour's drive away. En route, Sue asks, "do you think that one practice match is enough to cover all of the potential violations?" "No, but we will be using either us or RR as side judges to watch for mistakes. At some point, the only way to teach all beginners is to 'sink or swim.' An applied violation will be an event that will fixate in your memory bank."

• • •

We arrived at our last club by noon. We were greeted by a Cowboy who said that he noticed our MO plates. "I assume you are Wil and Sue. I am Roger West and I am the one you spoke to recently. I sprained my thumb yesterday and so I am not shooting today. I would like to be your guide. Have you had lunch yet?" "No." "Well

105

let our club treat you to our hot beans and salt pork–
Arkansas style."

During lunch, Roger used the non-pressured time to
cover some very important issues. "We are not affiliated
with CAS. This is purely a CFD club and we use real
people's names. We have the standard enclosure and a
free side range with steel plates. Every club member has
keys to the clubhouse and this is a great gathering and
socializing center for all the members."

I commented, "this is the second club we see with this
arrangement and we certainly agree that it is a great way
to keep a club alive–which we just implemented."

Roger then said, "here are some quick tips:"

- "We live in a small town but have 100 club members.
  Most shoots have 70 contestants, although we
  prefer 60 for a match to get done by 3:30PM
- During a match, offer caffeine and decaf drinks.
  Every shooter has different needs to compete.
  When it gets hot, offer free water to everyone.
- Don't accept thin flimsy sunglasses as eye protection
  for shooters and spectators. Offer durable plastic
  glasses/side shield with a clear or tinted glass. Also
  remind spectators that wax bullets can bounce
  back, so don't stand sideways if you don't have
  side shields on your glasses.
- Shooters provide their own ammo at our closed
  club matches. When we have open shoots we still

load our own ammo but if there is a question of velocity, we chronograph the round. Eventually, we may have to provide club ammo to guarantee uniform velocity.

• Start you club with two double lanes. Not three doubles like you will see today. Once you can handle two double lanes or you have to process 75 shooters with a 3 X elimination the same day, you can add another double lane.

Since Roger was so talkative and a great source of information, Sue asked, "what do you hear of the CFD match at the Bar W Ranch?" "Well I hear that the group, started locally by the man from Nevada, is well trained and may be a difficult group to beat. The proposed match is now limited to 100 and will do an elimination at 2 X's. Plus they are only accepting trained and experienced shooters from legitimate clubs. It's going to be a real hot match to watch and participate. The first day will be the general elimination down to the Magnificent 10. The second day will be the signature event, a 3 X elimination of this top 10 %."

Sue looked at me and said, "remind me today, to call Eleanor Beecher at the Bar W and reserve a spot for us on the CFD and WB team–and possibly add some spots for some of our club members."

My question was, "what are your plans for expansion in the future?" "It's clear to my club that if we don't include kids and women, our club will eventually deteriorate and loose its popularity. The fact that the club is a daily gathering site will help delay this downhill course. However, this year we are adding two hand shooting for women and kids under 12. Any 12 year old who can demonstrate proper thumb drawing can move up to adult status."

"Have you entertained starting a Shootist category with 7 ½" barrels?" This was brought up but was voted down. We decided to add Cowboy Silhouettes instead. We have the 200+ yard location to make a range and we feel this is a non CAS discipline that people are interested in. We would have both rifle and pistol silhouettes. We don't want to add CAS to compete against the many clubs in the area. We feel the silhouettes will attract new people and with the targets left as stationary ones, people can practice any day and use the clubhouse as a meeting place—a win-win situation for us. Plus we might attract your club for both CFD and Silhouette competition, heh."

We watched the competition and suddenly some shooters produced a large amount of white smoke, and some did not. Roger did not wait for our question, "some shooters use this smoke screen as an irritation and a distraction for their opponent. It is not fair and don't let it start in your club. This is the last match that this is allowed. Either everyone uses 3.5 grains of Triple Seven or everyone just uses a 209 primer. The original intent in using a black powder substitute was for show—now it is used to throw off your opponent's concentration."

The competition was moving along nicely until a sudden ruckus was developing on the firing line. A shooter and hand judge were in a loud and violent verbal exchange. The RM came over and was observing and listening to the loud banter. A side judge whispered in the RM's ear and the RM yelled, STOP.

To the shooter, the RM says, "you had no right to confront your hand judge in this manner—all you had to do was lift your hand and I would have come over to settle the dispute." To the hand judge he says, "you also had no right to confront the shooter in this manner—all you had to do was stand up and I would have come over. Both of you need to settle personal differences somewhere else. I am now charging both of you with a Spirit of the Game violation. You are both D/Q. In addition I am throwing you both out of the range for today and banning each of you for one week. IF YOU EVER DO THIS AGAIN, YOU WILL BE BANNED FROM THIS RANGE FOR ONE YEAR, OR FOR LIFE IF THE BOARD VOTES YOU OUT PERMANENTLY."

Roger looked stunned. He said, "I am sorry you had to witness that event. We have been in operation for 4 years and we have never had any confrontation. We are all friends!" I said, "things happen, it was a real learning event for us, and I especially liked how the RM handled the situation."

Sue then asked, "do you have any idea what the side judge whispered to the RM?" "Yes, he probably said that the shooter's wife was the hand judge's mistress!" "Oh my, that would do it." I added, "what were the odds that a random pick of shooter and hand judge would put them together?" "Probably 100–1, heh!"

Before we left, Roger wanted to show us his Silhouette targets that had just arrived from our Missouri manufacturer. In a shed we saw the standard Chickens, Hogs, Turkeys and Rams. Full size for rifle and half size for pistol. Roger explained, "The club members want to use the standard knockdown silhouettes that reset from the firing line. We have plates on a railing, individual knockdowns, upright poppers, and new types on order. During non competing days, these targets will be stored away. We will leave fixed targets, of the same size and yardage, for practicing. All these targets reset by pulling a cable at the firing line. We don't want people going down range to reset targets. The faster we reset the targets, the more we keep the spectator's attention." I added, "Very interesting, according to our club president, we will be getting the reactive targets that reset automatically by power, We also wish to avoid a slow moving competition, which will push spectators to leave and never return."

We thanked Roger for his assistance and hoped to see him again at the Bar W Ranch. We left by 4:30PM and were on our way back to our motel when we got a call from Willard Stone. "Just to let you know that my good friend, Roger West, just called. He had a nice visit with you guys. He is the one who convinced me to add CFD and Silhouettes. So RR spilled the beans about the resetting of the silhouette targets with power, heh! Anyways, I hope you had a productive tour." "Yes, it's been a very rewarding visit and we'll add many tips to our own club."

At the motel, I asked the desk clerk where we could have dinner and do some country dancing. His eyebrows lifted and he said, "go to McCutcheons Bar and Grill. I am a regular and let me call to get you a reservation for tonight. This is a great Cowboy hangout with a top of the line band for country dancing" He gave us directions to the club. We had just enough time to shower, and change into dancing apparel.

McCutcheons was a huge place, at least twice the size of our Country Roadhouse, and on a Sunday night a full 6 piece band was setting up, We ordered their specialty, Barbecue Strip Steak with steak fries and coleslaw. While waiting for our meal, Sue says, "if this band is any good we might be back in the future when we come to compete for CFD and Silhouettes. It would be nice to have a second dancing venue."

To our surprise, Roger West came to say hello. "So you do country dancing as well. Now I know you will be back to compete with us because you will love this band. You will also appreciate the sophistication of our dancers and our instructors." The band started promptly at 8PM. They sounded great. A good beat and tempo. They could easily duplicate the quality of a CD. The vocals were perfect.

They started their repertoire with three line dances which Sue performed. Then we had a medium to fast two-step. It became obvious to me, "wow these dancers know many more turns than we do. We might learn something tonight!"

The next selection was their first partner dance. It was a Sidekick to a song by L. Parnel–Knock Yourself Out. Later in the evening we recognized many partner dances: Shadow, Shottische, Sweetheart Cha Cha, I only see you, Besr ofFriends, and too many to mention. We were glad to sit out a partner dance, that we did not know. There was a simple and quick one called a Quickstep that we picked up and were able to follow the crowd.

Sue said to me, "these dancers are like professionals. They know so many partner dances and they all do the two-step and waltz. What a fantastic place and an incredible group of dancers. Even if we don't come back to town for shooting, we should come just for dancing, and make it a 3 day event since they have a band Friday through Sunday."

The band's breaks lasted only 15 minutes but were more frequent than long breaks. Enough time to rest but not time to gear down and stop dancing, which can happen with long breaks. After the last break, they announced the dance lesson for the evening. The instructors started, "tonight we are teaching you a routine. This is not a new dance, it is actually a combination of 10 moves from two-step and partner dances. Each move is an old standard that flows into the next move. All you need to remember is the sequence."

It was interesting and actually easy to remember. It became clear that this would be a nice addition to two-steps and waltzes, as it continued to travel along the counterclockwise line of dance—the standard perimeter floor etiquette.

The routine was called Walker #1, named after the instructors. The Walkers also announced that they would teach two more routines over the next two weeks. That would end the teaching season until next September. As soon as we sat down we wrote the names of each move and turn: shuffles, vines, rock steps, pivots, cha cha's, swings, promenades, around the world, hammer lock and turning vines. It was then brought to our attention that someone was going from table to table selling a DVD—the Walker's three routines for the people who have trouble remembering. As the sales person reached our table, I paid the $20 and I saw Sue tear up her written list of Walker #1.

We danced till midnight and then returned to our motel. The next morning, after a replenishing breakfast, we headed back to Springfield.

———————————

On arriving home, Jack came to greet us. Jack was obviously interested in the Cowboy pistol silhouettes in the Arkansas CFD club. This would be a location he could access in one day and provide competition beyond the home club. He admitted that he had started practicing 50 and 75 yards using 1 gallon jugs. I said, "better add 10 round speed shooting at 40 yards using ½ gallon jugs– which includes a 5 round manual reload."

Jack then told us of an incident that happened Friday evening. "As I was outside changing an entrance lightbulb, I heard the horn toot of a car door locking. I looked up and saw a man walking to your front door. Instead of ringing the door bell, he started looking into the front picture window, then into your garage door window. I came up with my cattle cane and told him the owner was gone. When asked why he was looking in the windows, he said, "just wanted to make sure no one was home." I said, "ringing the doorbell would have been a more acceptable approach. Get out of here, and if I see you here again, I will call the cops!"

"He then gave me a huff and left. I took the auto tag # of his red Rogue SUV. I then called the police station to make a report of the event. They called me right back and said that the vehicle was registered to a Daryl Scollins. Since you had already made a report of possible retribution, the police said they would pay him an official visit today."

We thanked Jack and I immediately called the police station and asked for Detective O'Brien. His secretary said that he was at our Desperado range on a vandalism investigation." I called RR and found out that some time during the night someone had shot up the backstop with a shotgun and had blasted away at the steel roof. RR then told me that he had given the name of Daryl Scollins as a person of interest. I then spoke to Detective O'Brien and told him of Jack's encounter with the same man. Detective O'Brien then said that he was placing an all points bulletin on the man. The CIS team had found a strange cigarette butt whose filter type did not match the workers brands. They sent if for DNA analysis.

Meanwhile, Mr. Stone came over to inspect the damage. The workers were about to start making repairs. Mr. Stone was obviously upset at this senseless act. He immediately called his office and authorized the construction of a steel chainlink fence around the range. He also placed an armed guard from 4PM to Midnight and a second shift from Midnight to 8AM until the fence was secured.

According to RR, "Mr. Stone is not preventing any club member from entry. He wants all club members to have a set of keys to the clubhouses and the entrance gate. It would be the responsibility of the last person leaving the range at anytime of day or night, to lock the clubhouses and the gate. Keys for all club members would be distributed at all events till everyone was issued a set of keys."

After ending our call with RR, we had dinner and then spent the evening with phone conversations with our families. By bedtime, we realized we had a full week of activities in preparation for the first practice match next Sunday.

CHAPTER 8

CFD, The Practice Match

That morning, we talked about our week's preparation for the practice match on Sunday. Sue pointed out. "the most important thing is to practice to try to cut down on our shooting times. Six days is excessive, we have to find something else to fill our time between shooting exercises!" "I agree, lets shoot 100 rounds and then go to the club to see how the enclosure is coming along. Besides, we have to unpack the club's CFDA order, and verify that the electronic target is functional."

Upon our arrival, Mr. Stone came to greet us. I said, "it's likely that the vandalism culprit is the man that refused our training because of his illegal holster and gun. We are sorry for this extra expense." "Not to worry, RR explained everything to me. You did what was necessary. As you can see, a fence company is already at work, and the backdrop and roof repairs are almost done."

"Actually, I am glad you are here, the cement forms are about to be built. What size floor plans do you want?"

"After our trip, every enclosure we saw was 35 X 60'. The platforms for the practice range were 6 X 25'–this gives each shooter a 6' square for a table and standing room—with a steel roof over the four lanes."

"Great, how about the shooting enclosure." "From my travels, I noted a partial full walled portion and a large open area." "How do you want the divisions?" "Again, everyone we saw had 20 feet of sidewalls with screened windows, and a front wall of sliding doors. This allowed a heated winter enclosure and a security section for leaving the shooting targets and accessories." "What heat source do you want?" "A propane stove just like the clubhouse. In summertime, we open the windows and the sliding doors for a completely open arena." "Perfect, I like it!"

"And by the way, you will have a set of keys for the clubhouse and fence gate by Sunday–to distribute to all your CFD members. RR will distribute the keys for the CAS members at the next shoot. We will add more keys for the CRS, CPS and CLR mini clubhouse in the future. I never want to see a club member locked out!"

We then went to the clubhouse and started opening the boxes from the CFDA. We displayed the wax bullets, casings, brushes and wax solvent with our cost prices. We then set up the Easyloader–50 and checked its operation. Next, we set up the electronic targets and fired some rounds to verify proper function. We even set up the audio equipment to make sure all was working properly. Finally, we locked up the targets, consoles and audio system.

With our bagged lunches, we got to visit with some of the CFD shooters who were practicing. Several had questions that required us to do a demo. After lunch, we went to the practice range and helped some of our students. As we were watching them practice, Sue said, "I think we just found the activity we needed to use up our spare time this week."

"Yes, you are right. We need to spend some time here, but we don't need to both be here at the same time. I propose that you shoot in the morning and I assist the shooters as needed. At lunch we both meet at the clubhouse for a snack. I will then go home to practice while you become the afternoon instructor. We meet at home for dinner and we both come here again for the evening shooters." "Perfect plan, I suspect the word will quickly get out and we are going to be busy, heh?"

As we were leaving for the day, the construction foreman stopped us. "I am building four tables with a bench for each of the shooters in the practice range. How high should the table be to hold the timer?" Sue drew her pistol and held it out at her shooting position. The foreman measured the height of the muzzle and smiled. He then added, "we will be pouring the concrete at 4PM. It has a hardener and drying agent and will be ready for use by tomorrow morning. During the day, we will be adding the tables, but we will not interfere with people who wish to shoot. The roof will be added in the early

119

mornings, before 8AM daily, until it is completed–thus it will not interfere with daytime shooters."

That afternoon we had an intense practice. My times were slowly improving. I was shooting at 0.42 seconds but Sue was holding at 0.48 seconds. I again brought up the subject of strength and speed. I said, "I think you are right about men having more strength in their arm than women. However, you will be competing against all competitors since we don't have a women's division. I think it is time for both of us to start lifting weights. I would also benefit from building muscle strength–I have been wielding a stethoscope for years, not a hammer!"

"On second thought, lets not start weight lifting until after the first real competition." "Why." "Because there is bound to be some initial muscle soreness at the onset of these exercises. This would likely hinder our draw initially, until our strength starts improving." "OK, we will start an exercise program once we start preparing for the WB game." "I am certain you will do well, with some poker, at 0.48 seconds."

The next morning, I was off with a thermos of coffee and a cheese sandwich. It was nice to be only five miles to the club. I got there at 8AM, opening time, and had breakfast with several shooters. I explained to them what I was proposing. I gave them a choice of either me watching them or wait at the club for shooters to seek me.

The consensus was to initially watch till all errors were corrected, then disappear for an hour. Then return and repeat the correction of errors if necessary, and disappear again. This recurring system would allow shooters to shoot freely but still be corrected if necessary.

I liked this approach and the morning just zipped by. At 11AM, Sue showed up with a cold lunch and coffee. I explained the routine we had established that seemed to be a perfect win-win for everyone. Sue also brought a small tool box. "What is that for?" She opened the box and said, "I brought a pistol vise, an armorer's tool kit and all the small parts to repair a RNV." "Great, I will also bring it with me." "Plus I left one full set of internal parts at home in case we break a gun while one of us is here at the club, with the tool box."

I went home to practice. Sue showed up at 4PM. We prepared dinner and Sue told me how her shift had gone. "Well I was right, the word got around already. I had a full house of shooters. I watched a dozen shooters, made some changes and did not get to the clubhouse till 1PM. Thinking I could take it easy, I spent the rest of the afternoon answering quick questions. At 2PM I encouraged everyone to leave. The foreman and his workers were waiting to build the concrete forms. I am late, because I watched them. By 3PM the forms were done and the concrete truck arrived. I left at 3:30PM as the workers were polishing the surface with their trowels."

At 6PM we arrived for the evening event. Twenty shooters were waiting, and they weren't only day workers. The word was really getting around. We followed the same routine and were not free until 7:30PM. During our intermission, we were surprised to see Ed and Eve arrive. We greeted them and had a nice chat.

They wanted to see how things were progressing and an evening drive had been planned all day. We showed them around the clubhouse and then brought them to the CFD enclosure and practice range. They were full of questions and certainly enjoyed their tour.

Eve then said, "the real reason we came was to make a contribution to your club. There is no doubt that we are experiencing a financial windfall, and the orders are already in for the WB guns. Everyone wants a 1911 Kimber, actually people are placing their order for WB, CRS, CPS and CLR. Their orders are all the same, 'order me whatever Wil and Sue got from you.'"

We were escorted to their pickup. Ed lifted the rear door's cap and the truck bed was full of boxes. Eve said, "40,000 Dead Eye EZ Loaders–for your CFD members. Many thanks for your business." We unloaded the truck and placed the boxes in the clubhouse, and thanked them for their donation. As they were preparing to leave, RR shows up asking where the boxes were. Ed said, "I had asked permission from RR to make this donation. I wanted everything aboveboard."

———•————•—•—————•———

By Wednesday, very few shooters needed assistance. Many were shooting in the 0.55 second range. At lunch, we started passing out the free wax bullets from Ed's Mercantile. I had reserved 15,000 bullets for the employees who were having financial issues. Everyone else got 500 free bullets–no repeats per the honor system.

As I was sitting in the clubhouse, with no one needing my help, I saw Willard Stone arrive with his assistant/driver. I went up to him and said, "what brings you here today?" "I am just ahead of an excavator and a bulldozer. We are excavating the range for WB. The site is a hill that will be excavated out to build the berms for three WB lanes and backstops for each lane. After one day of excavation, the workers will start building the three facades. What kind of facades do you want.?"

"According to the many videos I have watched, we would like a roofed bank facade with three open shooting windows. The middle range would be a field range with three separate roofed tables down range. The third would be a jail design, with a roof, three barred windows, and one open window."

"Great, and according to my measurements last summer, each lane should be 50' between berms and 75' deep. Do you agree?" "Yes, that sounds great." "One last thing, here are 100 sets of keys for the gate and clubhouse. Start passing them out at registration this Sunday."

Sue arrived at lunch for the change of shift. I said, "I think this may be our last day coaching shooters. Most of them are shooting independently and don't need our help." "Ok, I will finish the afternoon and we will both come tonight as our last official visit."

Sue got home by 3PM. We shot one more round and had an early dinner. We were at the range by 6PM as workers were arriving. We handed out their free wax bullets and watched them shoot. They were also shooting independently. We spent the entire evening visiting with RR who had come to see the WB range excavation. I asked, "how can you keep up with all the changes that are occurring here?" "e-mail, anytime Mr. Stone does something regarding the club, his assistant e-mails me. Whenever a worker spends a shift here, they e-mail me. Some of these mails are as short as, 'no problems.' Even the construction foreman gives me an update daily."

'By the way, have you seen the final designs of the WB stages and facades?" "NO." He hands us the architect's designs. Sue says, "wow, what a nice job–paint included, heh!"

As we were leaving, we reminded RR that Saturday was training day for the runner, scorekeeper, side judge, announcer and RM. Since RR had to learn all these jobs, we would start with him at 8AM. RR said, I will be ready, and will know the rules of the game by then."

———◆━━●━●━━◆———

Thursday and Friday ended up as free days for us. Although, the majority of our time would be spent practicing fast draw. We decided that some play was in order. We loaded our truck with all the new WB guns and headed to the club. We needed to get familiar with our new guns–especially the pump shotgun and the 1911 auto pistol.

We set up on the CAS range and started off with the 1897 pump. We had the habit of taking the butt stock off our shoulder for cycling. We eventually learned to keep the shotgun up on our shoulder and cycle it while keeping our eyes on the sight/target. The second problem was learning how to load two rounds while on the firing line. With the action open, one round goes over the bolt and the other round goes in the magazine. After closing the action–bang, recycling the pump–bang. We continued shooting until we both got comfortable with the weapon.

The 1911 Kimber auto pistol was a joy for me but a new thing for Sue. I had plenty of experience with auto pistols prior to my joining CAS. I spent a lot of time with Sue. She did not have the strength to rack the slide by "pulling" it with her left thumb and first finger. So I taught the method where she held the slide with her left thumb and fingers, as she pushed the gun into the slide with her right hand."

The next maneuver was releasing a magazine. "Release it with the magazine falling straight up and down, not sideways. A sideways release is a good way to break the 170° rule. To reload a magazine you can turn the guns on its side, but keep the muzzle down range."

She shot the gun for a long time before she finally got a jam. I yelled, STOP. "Kimbers are known for not jamming, finally you got one. Let me show you how to clear a jam. Release the magazine which you may need to pull out, if it doesn't drop, then rack the slide to remove the jammed case, and insert a new magazine. It's that simple. The next jam is yours to clear–if you get another one today."

We also shot the rifles to verify they were functioning properly. Both rifles were shooting low at 25 yards and we had to elevate the rear sight by two notches.

After a coffee break at the clubhouse, we went back to shoot all three guns for pleasure and familiarity. We got home by lunch time.

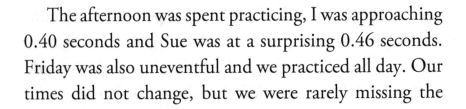

The afternoon was spent practicing, I was approaching 0.40 seconds and Sue was at a surprising 0.46 seconds. Friday was also uneventful and we practiced all day. Our times did not change, but we were rarely missing the target. One thing we finally noticed, we shot quicker with regular coffee on board–throughout the day.

Friday evening we went dancing at the Country Roadhouse. Stan and his triple appendages–George, Jim and Paul came over to tell us they were ready for Sunday. Their shooting time would remain a secret till the competition. Stan asked, "do you have a bit of final advice?" Sue said, "get a good night's sleep and control your caffeine intake. Some caffeine is good, but too much will ruin your game."

The dancing started and the evening was going smoothly. Suddenly, Sue says, "lets do the #1 Walker routine." We performed it without errors. We danced some more and repeated the routine two more times. As the dance finished, we were swamped with, "what was that?" "Where did you learn that, what is it called, would you teach us this routine?" The club owner was listening and then moved over to the DJ.

The DJ announced that Sue and I would teach this routine. We explained where we learned it, and the fact that it was a conglomeration of well-known turns and moves. It only required the recall of the sequence of turns. The "teach" was quick and simple. The DJ started another two-step and the dancers were able to perform #1 Walker with ease. Later, I said, "maybe we can learn #2 Walker by watching the DVD, if we ever have time, heh."

Saturday, training day arrived. We were at the club by 8AM. RR was already waiting with coffee and donuts. RR made it clear that he knew the rules of the game, cover to cover, and was ready to learn the operational commands and shooter's progressions.

We spent three hours with him. He was a quick learner. He learned every job possible, knew all the commands and was obviously the resident expert on the rules of the game. We quizzed him on different violations and he never assigned the wrong penalty. It was clear that he knew the rules better than Sue and I–and that was reassuring.

By 11 AM we started training the remainder of the helpers. The side judge, Sandra, had taken the training but decided that this sport was not for her. She preferred learning the rules and would function as a side judge, or whatever job needed a replacement. We trained the runner, Dixie, and scorekeeper, Jean, together. The side judge was also learning their jobs. The final job was the announcer. This job was done by Lynn, a shooter's wife, and she was already informed on the commands. Her husband Lyle would park the cars, then would shoot.

Sue and I decided that at the practice match, we would mostly stand aside and allow the helpers to work as much as possible, especially RR to function as RM. This was also a learning day for the workers.

The training was done by 3PM. Workers arrived to move some 75 folding chairs to the new enclosure. They also moved the target system and audio equipment to center stage. The three of us set all the equipment up and tested it with our guns. The new helpers got to see the shooting in action and the side judge/announcer got to use the controls to activate the starter light. The score keeper got to see the scores and added them to individual scorecards. Bottom line, everyone was ready for our first CFD practice match.

———————●—————●—————●—————→

The day had finally arrived. Registration was smooth. Everyone took a random numbered badge, was given 500 free wax bullets, if not already taken, and given a set of keys for the gate/clubhouse. I took badge #36 and Sue took badge #49. We then set up the audio system, the electronic target, and were ready for the event.

At the shooter's meeting, after the Pledge Allegiance to the Flag, RR announced that the club and gate would now be open all day. The first club member to arrive will unlock the gate and clubhouse, and the last person to leave had the responsibility to lock both up.

I then took over. "Welcome, we have 64 shooters. I have several announcements:"

1. "Today is a practice and an opportunity to learn. If you get a violation, it will be explained to you, the penalty assigned but not registered against you. This is a freebie day.

2. "Every three lost shots, you get an X and you will be eliminated once you accumulate three X's."
3. "If your hand judge stands up, you did something wrong. I or RR will come over to explain."
4. "When the runner or side judge calls your number, be prepared to step up. If you don't show up, you loose the round and get an X."
5. "The most important safety command is STOP or DOWN RANGE. That means, freeze and all hands off your guns."
6. "Be kind, all hand judges will become the next shooters."
7. "The helpers are: side judge–Sandra, runner–Dixie, scorekeeper–Jean, and announcer–Lynn. The cooking crew is Charlie and Ben. Maintenance is Curt. Parking is Lyle. Clean up, closing and storage of equipment is Milt. Registration is Diane.

"If there are no questions, lets go do some fast draw." RR took over, before we knew it, the firing line, hand judges and on deck circle were full and ready to go. The commands were given and the shooting started. People were getting the process. The first three firing lines of 12 shooters were free of violations.

Then the violations started: discharging gun before the muzzle cleared the front of the holster, premature movement of gun before the starter light, discharging gun in holster, dropping a gun on firing line etc.

Calling the violation was not only enlightening for the shooter, it was a great lesson for all.

Sue and I each had our turns. We each won our first four rounds. I was shooting 0.45 seconds and Sue was shooting 0.50 seconds. We had both made it to the Magnificent 8 by a late lunch time. Lunch for Sue and I was a pastry and coffee(sugar and caffeine). Stan and his three appendages had also made it to the Magnificent 8 and they were also having very light lunches–regular coke and cookies.

———•——•——•———

Going in the Magnificent 8 elimination, the pressure was on to maintain your best practice speed. We needed to get our fast clicks out if we wanted to win. The competition was fast and furious–best three shots out of five wins and the competitor is eliminated. The last four shooters were Sue, me, Stan and one of his appendages, Jim.

Sue won the draw and took Jim on as competitor. He won the first string with a speed of 0.48 seconds to Sue's 0.50 seconds. I then saw Sue pull out her poker face. She missed the next target–now down two shots. Her third string was a fast click of 0.46 seconds and found Jim snoozing at 0.50 seconds. Jim could not hold on to his lead, Sue won the last two strings with times of 0.46 and 0.47 seconds.

I then had to compete against Stan. I knew his times all centered around 0.45 seconds as eliminations brought us to this point. I decided to simply give him a straight five fast clicks–the best I could produce. I missed the first target, trying too hard–and Stan was smiling. I then settled down and produced three fast clicks, 0.42, 0.41 and 0.40. Stan was no longer smiling but shook my hand. I said, "your 0.45 seconds is nothing to laugh at, congratulations on a job well done."

So here we were, husband and wife vying for 1ˢᵗ and 2ⁿᵈ place. What to do? All spectators were way too quiet. RR gave the commands and the shooting began.

> I won the first shot by speed.
> Sue wins the second shot–I missed the target.
> I won the third shot by speed, plus Sue missed the target.
> The fourth shot was a draw at 0.46 seconds.
> The fifth shot–*what do I do, she is my wife, do I throw the shot and go to another shot to break the tie, or do I go for it, now.* I did what was right to me, I went for it and shot my second 0.40 second of the day. A clear winner.

RR took over the awards ceremony he invited Jim to the firing line and placed a yellow medal around his neck, Stan got bronze, Sue got silver and I got Gold. After much applause and congratulations, people started leaving. Everyone was clearly pleased with the process. RR reminded everyone to practice before next Sunday for our real competition match.

Then RR stopped all the shooters from leaving. He said, "go in the clubhouse. There are 10 spectators lined up with a number 1–10 on their chests. Vote for one and add your name. Whomever chooses the number of Willard Stone wins $500–the more winners the merrier"

We all went in, looked at each spectator and voted. When everyone was gone, RR started going through the ballots. He says, "we have one winner. Sue, how did you know. She answers, "a little old lady does not have breasts that high, especially when one points up and the other points down." To everyone's surprise, Mr. Stone starts pulling off his latex mask and makeshift bra.

With everyone gone, we sat down with Mr. Stone and RR. RR said, "you two did one hell of a job setting up this CFD club and did some great training. Don't you agree Willard?" Willard looked at us and said, "all in due time!"

As we got in the car I said, "I am mentally and physically spent"

Suddenly, Sue scoots over the console and plants a very passionate kiss on me. I finally get free and say, "my goodness you are beginning to kiss like, like, like, like well I like it, but what was that for?" Sue says, "for not letting me win today. You are an honest person and for that I respect you more and more each day. Now take me home so I can thank you properly!"

———◆—●—◆———

CHAPTER 9

CFD, The Competition Match

The next morning, we got up late and we were totally exhausted. After a replenishing breakfast, we sat in our recliners with coffee and quietly watched the news. It was clear that after several weeks of planning, training and directing the club into a successful practice session, we were mentally and physically spent, Sue said, "I don't want to do a darn thing today."

We were so tired that we took a 2 hour nap. Upon awakening I added, "maybe we could at least get up and change out of our pajamas." "OK, as long as you don't try extracurricular activities, "Not a chance," as I strained to get out of my lounger.

We spent hours in personal thought and contemplation. By 3PM I said to Sue, "I need a break away from CFD. We have all week before the first real competition on Sunday. We need to move away from the rigors of intensive training. I know we need to continue practicing our fast draw because Stan, his three friends and newcomers by the names of Lyle(Gerry Rigger) and Charlie(Butcher Blok) are fast coming up on our heels. All six of them are getting harder to beat."

Sue looks at me with a blank stare and says, "I have been sitting here for hours and just cannot come up with a plan for the week, I also know that when you bring up a subject, you already have a solution, so out with it!" "Yes, let's start doing research on Wild Bunch Shooting, and start reloading for the 45 ACP and 45 Long Colt cartridges that we will need in this sport. In addition, we will add some practice time periodically to maintain our skills and possibly improve." "For the rest of the day and evening, let's make contact with our children and invite them to the match on Sunday. I am certain that some will be happy to attend the event to see what we have been up to."

Tuesday morning we tried something new. Without breakfast or coffee we tried our fast draw. After 35 rounds, with horrible results, we put our guns down and had breakfast with several cups of coffee. I explained, "without the caffeine, we don't seem to have enough energy to activate the musculature to respond, or to visually react to the starter light. This is such a dynamic sport. It requires a visual astuteness and fast muscle reaction that are sensitive and responsive to caffeine, I plan to mention this at the shooter's meeting on Sunday."

After our one hour practice we started the WB research. Sue started with the many internet videos of actual shoots.

I started with the official SASS Rules handbook. As I went through the handbook, it was clear that this sport was an extension of CAS. Yet there were specific rules and situations that applied specifically to WB. I went through half of the book and took notes to prepare a handout of special issues–to be discussed at the first WB meeting.

Before dinner we practiced our 100 rounds. That evening, Jack showed up. He said, "I have been following your footsteps. I did research on videos, articles and the rule's handbook. With all the gear I picked up at Ed's Mercantile, I have been practicing. The WB range is up and ready for targets. So I have two questions, when do we get steel targets and why did I buy a black holster/belt rig per Ed's suggestion?"

"Men are not clean shooters and when you shoot sooty cartridges like 45 ACP and 45 LC, in short order your tan holster will be filthy and not cleanable–black never looks dirty. As far as the WB targets, RR is arranging a list of volunteers for Saturday morning. We need to put out 140+ steel targets. Some are falling targets or railings with several knock down plates, and some are non falling permanent plates for practice. These are heavy items. If you can help, notify RR by e-mail."

Wednesday was uneventful. We did our 100 round practice and then I finished the WB handbook and my meeting handout. Sue made 75 copies of the handout and I e-mailed RR to request an order of 75 WB Rule's handbook from SASS mercantile.

Wednesday afternoon, we put together the Dillon XL–650 and started loading 45 ACP for the 1911 Auto pistol and 45 LC for the rifle. We loaded both with Clays powder at 900 fps. Sue asked, "why 900 fps." "Because, RR told me that the targets would all be set to fall if hit with a 230-250 grain bullet at 750 fps and that included a low hit on the plate. We have a reduced power mainspring if the 1911stock spring is too strong for 900 fps, and Ed included this extra reduced power mainspring for plinking with light loads in the < than 750 fps range. I am certain that an edge or low shot, will drop the targets with 900 fps.

We divided the reloading process into two separate jobs. I started to operate the press and that is all I did. I added a lead bullet, pulled the main handle, and a finished round fell in the hopper–at a rate of 600 rounds per hour. Sue was the helper. She added powder to the powder measure and Hot Shot lubed cases to the casefeeder. Loaded primers to pickup tubes and when she had the time, loaded field grade 12 gauge ammo on our single press(not light loads as was used in CAS). These loads were standard box-store loads that would guarantee the knocking down of shotgun targets. Every hour we changed positions to prevent muscle fatigue. We reloaded till 4PM and then shot our 100 rounds before dinner.

Thursday was a discovery day for Sue. We shot our 100 rounds after morning coffee and a light breakfast. At the end of the practice session, Sue said, "I just got an idea of what I can add to my poker game since I am not budging off the 0.45 second plateau. While I perform this idea to perfection, you should check the many videos of actual WB shooting events to pick up some important shooting sequences."

An hour later, I had seen enough videos. I started watching Sue and discovered what she was doing. She had developed the ability of placing edge shots–and I mean shots right at the edge of the targets. This would give the competitor a false sense of security that Sue's next shot would be a miss. That is when I said, "wow, you are going to drive your opponents mad with those edge shots. Now mix edge shots with your slow and fast clicks, a little cleavage, and facial expressions–and I pity your opponent! It will become known as man-on-man nightmare."

For lunch, we went to the local diner. Several of the workers were there for their daily visit. Stan, Lyle and Charlie came up to our table. They made it clear that everyone was practicing. The practice range at the club was like a mass production of shooters. Everyone wanted to improve and many were on our tails. Stan said, "watch these two guys, Lyle and Charlie, I bet they will be in the Magnificent 8 on Sunday. Just so you know, our goal is to unseat you and Sue."

Sue cracked up and added, "you guys may beat me but you are going to have to get up real early to beat this guy. He is showing signs of a natural talent and is improving every day. Lyle added, "and Stan is also improving faster than anyone else and is likely a natural talent as well." Sue countered, "yes, we know this and we encourage you, Stan, to move ahead of us." I added, "Stan, with the interests and talent you are exhibiting, would you consider being our second in command while we move on to start WB, CRS, CPS and CLR. RR would always be available to assist you?" "Well, let me think about this and I will let you know Saturday night at the Country Roadhouse!"

We got back from lunch at 2PM. The discussion with Stan and friends motivated or psyched us up and we decided to practice shooting 200 rounds to see if this would change our shooting speed. Fortunately, both our guns broke by the end of the 200 rounds. My gun's pawl was worn off and would not rotate the cylinder to the next groove. Sue's gun just froze and the hammer could not be cocked. We watched the dismantling video again and quickly took the guns apart. The repair was simple, I changed my pawl and changed the hammer plunger, spring and pin on Sue's gun. A 15 minute repair job was done with plenty of parts left over. It was so obvious why that spare gun, we had purchased during our trip to CFD clubs, would be so important for us.

Sue brought up an interesting subject. "What will be the protocol for handling a broken gun during competition?" I answered, "I and RR have been working on this for some time. This is our plan: to finish the string, the shooter will accept any gun from friends or our spare gun. When the string is done, the broken firearm can be brought to the clubhouse where Ed's Mercantile gunsmith will repair the pistol at part's cost plus a labor charge of $20–assuming a simple fix of interchanging parts. Anything more complicated and the gun goes to the shop. The alternative is to continue sharing guns and repair your own gun later."

Sue added, "one of these days, I will ask a question that you won't know the answer–with a smile!"

By Friday morning, we needed a break. We went shopping for groceries and other items. Getting back home, I backed the SUV to the garage. Sue had her hands full so I unlocked the garage door. My key did not fit in the lock without some unusual grinding noise which I dismissed. As I opened the door to let Sue in, I saw, in the hinge space, a sight that no one ever wants to see–someone was standing behind the door with his back to the wall. I followed on Sue's heals and slammed the door with all my strength against the wall. I heard a loud scream, Sue dropped her groceries and pulled out her concealed weapon when she heard the scream. I pulled the door back and saw a 6 foot man with a crowbar over his head ready to hit me in the face. I reflexly responded with a self defense move and shot him in the foot/ankle area. The man dropped to the floor, like a pole-axed beef at a slaughter house, and the crowbar went flying in the garage.

The man was groaning in pain as I leaned down and said, "if you try to get up I will shoot you in the knee, and likely you will never walk without assistive devices, if at all. If that doesn't stop you, I will shoot you in the groin– and I guarantee you that will knock you out." Meanwhile, Sue was calling 911 to report a house invasion with a lethal weapon. The dispatch reminded us to hide our guns as the police arrive, to avoid confusion–never greet a policeman with a gun in hand.

Shortly thereafter the police arrived. After quick questions, they handcuffed the perp. As they rolled him to cuff him, he screamed out in pain from the movement. The officers were not apologetic. As the ambulance arrived, Detective O'Brien was right behind them. As he entered the garage, he shook our hands and then looked at the perp on the floor. "I see you shot him in the ankle." "Yes, he was going to brain me with that crowbar." "And why is his nose crooked?" "Because he accidently walked into a door! Then we gave the detective the fine details of the event. Detective O'Brien then looked at the perp, "well Daryl Scollins, we have been looking for you all week since the DNA came back on that cigarette butt from the Desperado Club."

"You see Doc, Daryl here is a two-timer in the drug trade. This will add B & E charges, aggravated assault, home invasion and vandalism at the club CFD enclosure." As the EMT's and police were loading him and heading to the ER because of the gunshot wound, Sue asked, "if he's in the drug trade, are we to expect revenge form the drug bosses?" "No, they will look at Daryl's behavior as stupid non business related activities. They don't want any additional public exposure and will quickly forget about this idiot. Can you come to the station by 4PM today to sign your statements and file charges.?" "We'll be there."

Sue was still upset, she added, "I never realized that setting up a shooting game could provide a risk for our security." "It's simply the risks of leadership. Sometimes you have to say no to someone, and not everyone will accept the word no. We must not let this one event ruin our goal of establishing four more shooting games. OK?" "I agree."

"Now, we are both upset enough to throw off our shooting game. Let's put the guns aside and dance. Let's learn Walker #2 routine and we can teach it tomorrow night at the Country Roadhouse." We watched the video, stopped it every three moves, and practiced the moves till we learned them. Then we restarted the video and added three more moves. We kept doing this until we learned all twelve moves. One thing was clear, these were more complicated moves than the #1 routine and two moves were actually very complex double moves. After practicing it over and over again, we finally became smooth and proficient. We decided to break the routine into four separate sections. We would teach the first two sections and allow dancers to practice them while dancing, and would teach the last two sections half way through the evening.

After dinner, we shot our 100 rounds. I was finally sneaking below the 0.40 seconds. Sue commented that I was shooting at 0.37 seconds about 60% of the time. This would be useful on Sunday.

———•—◀—●—▶—•———

Saturday morning was dedicated to the WB range. RR had 6 volunteers who were bringing the steel targets by pickup and trailer at the new WB range. Sue was assigned the pistol plates, poppers and shooting trees and I was assigned the rifle counterparts of all three targets. RR took on the close and far shotgun knockdowns. We had a blueprint that RR had prepared in triplicate for each of the three ranges.

Every target was pre-drilled at the factory, but there were hundreds of nuts and bolts to be tightened. Everyone was carrying a ratchet & socket set in 7/16, 1/2 and 5/8". It took four hours for the nine workers to set out 140+ pre-painted knockdown and permanent targets.

As we were leaving for the diner, RR said that he had made an arrangement at a local hardware store to purchase several cases of Rustoleum flat black spray paint at cost. We would paint every target before each match, and people practicing could paint their own.

After lunch, we did our last practice shoot of 100 rounds, I was now consistent at 0.37 seconds and felt confident that I could maintain this speed–at least for tomorrow. Sue was still consistent at 0.45 seconds but very good at edge shots. We then practiced the #2 Walker routine again, and knew we were ready to teach it. We changed and headed to the Country Roadhouse for dinner and dancing.

We asked Stan and Miranda to sit at our table and they gladly accepted. We had a great visit. Stan proposed a friendly bet. To the winner of the match, 2000 wax bullets for the winner. Sue refused to take the bet, but I did.

Eventually, Stan said, "I have thought a lot about your offer of taking the CFD 'second in command' while you are both developing the other Cowboy games. I would be honored to do so." Miranda jumps in and says, "he is proud that you asked him to step up and I know he will do a fine job." I added, "and I am certain you are capable and will be successful. I think you may want to review my club and rule's handouts tonight. We never know what tomorrow will bring with spectators. If you want my handouts, use the club photocopier to make copies."

Before the evening of dancing started, the DJ came to ask if we would teach the #2 Walker routine. We said yes, but would like to break it up in two sections, one early in the evening and one in mid evening.

The music started, and early on we saw people were adding the #1 Walker routine to their two-step and waltzes. It was clear that people liked this new variation to two-step and waltzes.

When the time came, we had everyone in the house up to learn this new routine. We taught half and asked the dancers to incorporate these 8 moves into a routine and we would teach the other half later in the evening. It worked out well. The second half was taught, and then the dancers incorporated each half into a fine and pleasant routine. The owner came to thank us on a fine job. He said, "I am willing to offer you compensation for each lesson you teach." Sue stopped him and said, "our pleasure. This is our home base and we would never consider charging you." The evening continued and we had a great time dancing and visiting with our new friends.

Match day had finally arrived. We were at the clubhouse at 6AM with RR. Over coffee we discussed the day and felt certain that we had dotted all the I's and crossed all the T's. We opened the enclosure and activated all the electronic targets and audio equipment. The employees started arriving by 7AM and were setting up for registration. One was assigned to getting a release of liability from registrants, and assign a random shooter number. Two to get the shooter's name, phone number, e-mail updates. The cost for the day's participation was $15.

As the contestants were arriving, Sue saw a cavalcade of three cars from different MO counties. She greeted them and then came to see me. She said, "we have some very interested spectators, some have a personal interest and some are interested in starting their own club." "OK, would you give them an introductory guidance of what they will see today, and invite them all to stay after the match for a more formal discussion of what they need in equipment etc.–I'll try to get Stan to do that presentation." "Good idea."

Once registration was complete, the bell was sounded for the Shooter's meeting. After the Pledge Allegiance to the Flag, I started the meeting:

- "The first WB meeting will be held next Sunday at 10AM.
- Many of you are complaining of sore thumbs from loading wax bullets. For those of you who cannot come to use the club's Easyloader-50, This hand

reloading tool called the Silver Press is the answer. To demonstrate–place a case in the bottom, and a wax bullet on top, push wax bullet down in the case with this palm pusher, then pull the case out as you twist it out of the press to remove excess wax shavings. And presto, you save your thumb for only $40. Available at CFD.

- Today your penalties are real, so be careful.
- Please answer spectator's questions freely.
- Please get to know the employees since they are permanent workers for all new Cowboy Games
  Runner–Dixie   Scorekeeper–Jean
  Side judge–Sandra   Announcer–Lynn

- If your gun breaks you will be offered my spare RNV to finish the string(with 5 free shots to get accustomed to a new gun). After the string, Ed's Mercantile gunsmith is at the clubhouse and will replace internal parts at cost plus a $20 labor charge. Or you can finish the match using a friend's shared gun and fix your own gun later.
- Control your caffeine intake to match your needs.
- Visit the vendors in the clubhouse, Many shooters are emptying their gun safes to purchase some more Cowboy guns for the new games–there are some good deals to be had.
- The last item, do not confront a shooter, if there is an issue that cannot be resolved by the hand judge,

then the RM will be the only one to resolve this issue. The RM today will alternate between RR, me and Sue.

Are there any questions. One gent raises his hand, "I see a full house of shooters and many spectators. Is there any room for this club to expand the CFD division or are we at our max?" "Today we have 65 shooters. The answer depends on the demand. We can start shooting a half hour early and can handle up to 75 shooters in a one day match with a 3X elimination. If we go above 75 shooters we have a choice of two day shoots or do a 2X elimination. Depending on the demand we have a choice of putting the matter to a general vote of CFD members or establish a five member advisory board. Time will tell."

"If there are no further questions, lets go do some gun-slinging."

The match progressed smoothly. The workers were very good at their jobs, the shooters were respectful and Sue and I had very little to do. RR was in charge and was obviously having a good time. There were few violations and the violators understood their errors. By lunch time we realized that in order to process all 65 shooters by 3PM, we needed to continue shooting through lunch.

I frantically worked with Sue and Sandra, and devised a system that would keep the next 30 shooters in the enclosure and send the other 35 to the lunch wagon. We randomly picked 30 badges and wrote the order on the on-deck chart, called out the 30 numbers and sent all the others to lunch. When the first batch was done lunch, we reversed the process–giving us an extra hour of shooting time.

By 3PM we were down to the Magnificent 8. Sue, myself, Stan, his three friends George, Jim and Paul and two expected shooters, Lyle and Charlie. RR announced that this would be a 2X elimination until the last two shooters were left and then we would change back to a 3X elimination.

George, Jim, Paul and Lyle were the first four eliminated. That left me against Charlie and Stan against Sue. Stan and Sue went first. Sue did her best poker and edge shot, but Stan would have none of it. He threw a 0.43 and 0.44 seconds against Sue's 0.45 and 0.46 seconds.

I then went against Charlie, I gave him two moderately fast clicks at 0.43 seconds and eliminated Charlie's 0.46 seconds. Then came the final round, Stan against me. *I thought, he just beat Sue with a best time of 0.43 seconds. I suspect he is able to hit a .40 second draw–possibly an occasional 0.39 second. So to beat him, I need to put out my best practice time of 0.37 seconds.*

The final match was ready to go and RR reminded us that this was a 3X elimination. The first round went off and I missed the target to the left. Stan's time was 0.40 seconds, but he did not know my time since when you miss the target, there is no time on the public display. I then adjusted windage by rotating my body to the right.

The next two rounds was mine. I shot a 0.39 seconds to Stan's 0.40 seconds. Spectators were aghast at the time's proximity. I was now ready for the last round.

Retrospectively, I recall being in the zone of extreme concentration and I actually saw the starter light's early flickering in slow motion, and the gun just came out of the holster by pure muscle memory. Stan was smiling at the scores. He shot 0.38 seconds and I shot 0.36 seconds. *I thought, I had no control in performing the draw. It was done by pure instinct, autonomic reflexes and muscle memory. I had heard these physiological mechanisms mentioned many times, but this was the first time I really experienced them in real time.*

The applause was thunderous. Stan shook my hand and I saw Miranda hold up two bags of those orange wax bullets. RR came up to congratulate us and invited all members of the Magnificent 8 to the center stage. He placed a yellow medal around the neck of the bottom 5 shooters, bronze to Sue, silver to Stan and gold to me. As the applause ceased, RR announced a meeting at the clubhouse for all spectators who are interested in getting involved with the sport.

There were some 26 spectators who came to the meeting. I started the meeting and said, "There are three reasons to learn CFD–to start your own club, to join an existing club or to shoot for personal satisfaction. If you want to learn we will train each of you for 2 hours in teams of 4 students–free of charge. We will guarantee that you will shoot 100 rounds and be able to hit the target in one second. You need to show up at your class with a gun, holster, eye and ear protection. You can gear up with the other items at a later date."

"Now I would like to introduce the shooter who will be your instructor–second place winner Stan Winslow." Stan went ahead and discussed the type of gun needed and it's modifications. He then went through the different holsters with deflector shields. He pointed out the great deals to be had at Ed's Mercantile. He also directed everyone to the CFD web site and especially to Quick Cal's DVD, and much more!

Stan said, "depending on the number of people signing up, I will hold classes in my garage during evenings and weekends." Stan then went through a question and answer session. Registration was started and it became obvious that no one of the 26 attendees left without registering their info and choosing a lesson time.

As Sue and I were heading to the car, W. Stone intercepted us and simply said, "Thank you for building such a great team."

At the car was a mob of our own family. My college grandson said, "grandpa, I never thought you could draw so fast. I thought this was going to be a boring day, but what a 'high' this day has been." My son added, "there is no doubt, you killed Matt Dillon. Nice going."

Sue's daughter added, "mom, you looked sharp out there and I was so proud of you!" "A very quiet one of Sue's granddaughters said, "grandma, I want to learn how to do this, and I want to start now." Her mother looked at Sue and said, "this child never asks for anything and finds too many things boring. At age 12, I firmly believe that her wish is bonafide. When can you start training her?"

"I see her eyes are determined, arrange for the bus to drop her at our home after school and we will give her a week's training. Pick her up after your work and we will see what a week brings. This kind of thing is why we had an Annie Oakley or now have Holy Terror in CAS.

We then explained to our family that the remainder of our summer would be spent at training a team of shooters for WB, CRS/CPS, and CLR. My son asked, "does this mean traveling to compete." "Other than the Bar W Ranch we will be staying close to home this year."

We then headed home to prepare for game 2–the Wild Bunch.

BOOK TWO

BOOK TWO

CHAPTER 10

WB, Training and Club Meeting

Being done with CFD for the next few weeks, we picked up an egg/bacon sandwich, several thermoses of coffee, and headed to the clubhouse. As we were enjoying our breakfast, one of the shooters on the WB stages came to talk with us. He said, "Doc, there is much confusion as to who should reset the targets." Sue adds, "we have set up a simple fair system, and we'll be over shortly to explain and get implemented."

Arriving at the WB range, I said, "as a shooter is loaded and ready for the firing line, he has to decide how he wishes to shoot his forty rounds. If he plans to shoot at only fixed targets he can proceed from the firing line, shoot his 40 rounds, step to the unloading table and let the other shooter step up. However, if that shooter wanted to shoot at only targets that were reactive or falling targets, it is that shooter's responsibility to pull the cables, that reset 5 to 10 targets at a time. After shooting the 40 reactive targets, he also steps off the range to the unloading table–and the cycle repeats itself for the next shooter. We are providing a worker to pick up brass to speed up the process."

The shooting started and we joined the mix at the stage with the shortest waiting line. We followed this same pattern at all three stages, and we did the full cycle three times before 2PM. We then headed home to prepare for our special student, Sue's granddaughter, Bailey.

We prepared a 5 day course of training theory and practical techniques. Actual practice was included each day. The one thing I impressed on Sue, "treat her and train her as an adult, it would be a waste of everyone's time to treat her as a child. Plus, as you teach her, I will sit on the sideline. I can demonstrate technique initially, and maybe later provide some suggestions, but that is all I should be doing. You need to impress on her that you are the teacher and that I am your helper. OK?" "I agree."

The bus arrived at 3:20PM and Sue was ready, The first words out of Bailey's mouth were, "Mom said that I was 12 years old, but actually I am going to be 13 in two weeks, I wrestle with boys and I am strong, and I really want to learn this sport." "Say no more, that is why you are here and I will happy to train you, so let's get started."

After adjusting the belt and holster, Sue instructed her in the hand and thumb position. I then demonstrated the thumb draw in slow motion and Bailey followed my lead. I picked up speed and she again followed without difficulty. Sue then showed her the proper position of the unholstered gun followed by the death grip of the pistol, with her right arm against her chest wall. Bailey was a quick learner without the usual preset ideas of how it should be done. She followed the directions without doubt or questions. She did a perfect trigger push without asking what was meant by an unrelated trigger squeeze.

As she started to draw and dry fire, I said, "it's different teaching someone who has no preconceived notions like the men and women we taught during the club training, heh!" Bailey dry fired for a half hour and Sue even added some body mechanics before live fire.

Bailey's first live fire was a visual awakening for her. We both encouraged her to increase her speed in a slow progression. Within 50 live rounds, to our surprise, she was hitting the target within 1.0 second. The look on her face was worth a thousand words.

Without knowing that Bailey's dad, Sam, had arrived and quietly snuck in the garage, Bailey drew and hit the target 5 times with her best time at 0.8 seconds. Sam exclaimed, "wow, you're making my daughter a gunfighting enthusiast." Sue added, "better still, we are training a natural talent." I also added, "Dad, this young lady has a future in this sport." We could tell that Sam was very pleased with our comments.

I then took the time to explain to Sam how to build her a steel target for home practice. Told him about the CFD web site where, in the future, he can purchase wax bullets, cleaning brushes, wax solvent and 45 LC casings.

Plus, we told him to stop at Ed's Mercantile and pickup a RNV in 45 LC, to purchase some 209 shotgun primers and to get her this model specific belt/holster rig in black.

I then added, "since her birthday is in two weeks, we are making Bailey an early birthday gift, we are paying for all her gear. I will call Ed and have him send me the bill as well as tell him to supply the gear for 5,000 rounds. Sam and Bailey were both pleasantly surprised. Sue added, "clean your gun and that is it for today, see you tomorrow." Tonight, after your homework, we want you to watch this DVD–Hit Em Fast. Sam added softly, "do you really think she will have homework tonight, heh!"

———•—◦—•———

For the remainder of the week, we found ourselves in a very comfortable rut. Every morning, we had coffee at home and then headed to the club with two egg Mcmuffins and two thermoses of coffee. We visited with a bunch of WB shooters, and then joined the lines to practice till noon. Shooting at reactive targets was such a joy, it was clear that a miss was unquestionable–"when it don't go down, it's a miss." We found that most of our misses were with the 1911 pistol. This was secondary to unfamiliarity and lack of experience–but every day we got better. We had no problems with the rifle or shotgun.

At noon we headed home for a light lunch and reloading until Bailey arrived. The two of us shooting ate up a large amount of ammo and we had to reload each day to keep our supply up. In addition, we kept up orders on the internet for shooting components–bullets, powder, shot and wads–for all three guns.

Bailey arrived with her dad early, and with a box of supplies. Bailey said, "Dad took me out of school early(I only missed physical education and study hall) and we went to Mr. Ed's Mercantile. Wow what a place," as she opened her box with a full gear for fast draw.

Wil and Sam sat and watched the entire lesson. After a short dry fire session, Bailey started shooting live rounds. Sue did some coaching as she had done with me when we were training. Periodically, I would watch Bailey to do more coaching. Bailey picked up the new changes without hesitation. The most drastic change today was Sue's training of more body mechanics. Bailey followed directions and within a short time, her right hip snap just about threw the gun out of the holster. Sue looked at me and said with a chuckle, "remember how much trouble you had with body mechanics?" I didn't give her a chance to say more, "yes, but remember, you are not showing an old dog a new trick!"

As we were behaving like spectators, Sam said, "I actually took a personal day off today. In the morning, I built her a target and back stop per your specifications. When we get home, I suspect her home work will not take long before we find her in the garage. I also made an elevated stand for the Cowboy timer you gave her. That way she can shoot independently."

I relieved Sue watching for errors, which were few. Unlike adults, a corrected error was never seen again–an advantage of a young shooter.

At the end of the lesson, Bailey was shooting an occasional 0.7 second and was happy with her progress.

At their departure, Sue said, not knowing of the newly built home target, "till your dad makes you a target, practice your dry fire. Once you have a target, stay with the routine of cleaning your gun every 35 rounds and rest after 100 rounds–like you do here. See you tomorrow and remember to leave your gear home, you will use mine when you are here. We don't want gun stuff in school or on the bus, heh!"

The remainder of the work week continued with the same routine. Morning breakfast at the club house, practice WB till noon and reloading in the afternoon till Bailey arrived. Every day, we saw an amazing improvement of Bailey's skills. By Friday, we had nothing to add to her training and she finished the day with a 0.6 second time.

Sue said to her, "you are completely trained and you are on your own. We would like you to come here once a week so we can watch your technique and see your accuracy on the electronic targets. Shortly thereafter,

Stacey arrived and gave Sue a big hug and said, "Mom, you have made your granddaughter a very happy and motivated little girl. Stacy got all emotional and Bailey said, "Mom! it's a personal accomplishment, not an emotional upheaval."

Saturday was not a day to go practicing at the WB range, with all the shooters expected. So we decided to reload all day and go dancing that night. The day was going well and we finally generated a surplus of ammo for the next practice week. At 2PM the phone rang. I said, it's Bailey and I answered. Bailey was crying and unable to speak. Finally, she started speaking and said, "grandpa, I broke my gun." "Oh is that all it is, come over and we we'll fix it, OK" "You think, it is really badly broken and I can't pull the hammer back." "Not a problem, come over."

Sam, Stacey and a despondent teenager arrived. We showed everyone the video on dismantling the RNV. We then dismantled it with Bailey's nose almost touching the gun. The hammer plunger was bent. We changed it and its spring and rebuilt the gun. We also pointed out the pawl which can wear down and the cylinder would not turn to the next cylinder stop. We gave Bailey a new pawl, hammer plunger and spring with a spare cross pin. "The next time you will repair it yourself with mom or dad's help, as long as it's a locked hammer or incomplete cylinder movement—otherwise you bring it to us." Before they left, we showed Bailey how to operate the manual

Silver Press to help her load her casings, and gave her the press we had recently ordered. Bailey gave us both a big hug and a warm thank you, and left with a smile.

After they left, I asked Sue why all the tears?" "It's about the fear a little girl has of losing the only hobby she has ever had. I can understand how catastrophic it meant to her. It also means that she is really serious about this sport, and I am real proud of her."

We had three hours before going to the Country Roadhouse. We practiced the Walker routines #1 and 2. We also learned the #3 routine in case there was a demand from the dancers. Upon arrival, we were greeted by Stan and Miranda. We took a table for four and visited.

Stan had been busy training the group of spectators. Of the group of +- 25 students, we were going to inherit at least 10 more club members and likely a dozen visiting shooters. When asked if this meant a two day shoot, I said, "Sue and RR and myself prefer to go to a one day 2X elimination for monthly shoots. The yearly championship shoot in late fall will be a two day extravaganza with a 3X elimination, vendors, and a dinner/dance event." "Stan adds, "I hope dinner will be a pig roast with the fixings!" "Yes those are our plans."

Sue was watching Miranda throughout the discussion. Finally Sue asked Miranda, "so what is new with you?" Miranda acted like a cornered rat and eventually said, "so you did not hear?" "No." "Well, Stan is training me to shoot a rifle so I can participate in Cowboy Rifle

Silhouettes–and I'm enjoying it." Sue and I both exploded in laughter and praise. Stan said, "now honey, I know that is not what you really wanted to say, so say it." "We have agreed to a fall wedding and are in the process of arranging a wedding in this club, just like the wedding you had here last fall. Please keep this quiet like you did. It was great getting the announcement and invitation all at once. The surprise is still talked about today." Double congratulations were extended and our pleasure was felt by both Stan and Miranda. Stan added, "your support is very important to us, so thank you."

Our dinners arrived and we had plenty of time for coffee before the dance started. Once we were rolling in two-steps and waltzes, it was clear that everyone were performing the #1 and #2 routines. After the first intermission, the DJ asked if the crowd wanted the #3 routine taught tonight or wait till next fall. A show of hands was clear, tonight was the night to teach it before the summer schedule.

Sue and I got on the floor and started with the first four moves and continued till the entire routine was presented. I was amazed how the moves were so different from the other two routines, but were still moves present in some of our partner dances. The dance then restarted with a two-step, and dancers were incorporating #3 Walker routine in their dancing. The remainder of the evening was uneventful and we danced to our hearts content. We went home by midnight, to prepare for the first WB meeting tomorrow.

———————•━━•◦•━━•———————

"Welcome to the Desperado Club Wild Bunch division. We have +- 70 shooters in attendance and we hope to convince all of you to join this Cowboy Game. Were you to join, the thing I want you to bring away from this meeting, is knowing which gun to purchase and which shooting category you plan to participate. First, some household chores. Pick up your key for the gate and clubhouse, and remember the rule, the last person to leave locks up the clubhouse and gate."

"We have a brand new WB range with two facades and one field range. Use it at will. Remember the usage rule, the person on the firing line chooses whether he will shoot 40 rounds at fixed targets vs. reactive targets. If he chooses reactive targets, he must reset his own targets. The club workers will paint all 120 match reactive targets the day before a match, and that day the WB range will be closed."

"As many of you know, WB is simply an extension of CAS. All SASS rules apply plus some rules specific to this sport, which I will eventually discuss. It involves more modern guns of the period between 1900 and WWI. It's a fast shooting, more movement, and more rounds per stage that still demand accuracy. Each stage has 40 targets that move or fall–with a proper hit. Moving on to the tools of the trade."

A–FIREARMS.

The lever rifle is a big bore caliber of either 44 Mag or 45 Long Colt. It can have regular open sights or tang mounted peep sights of the era. Receiver sights are not acceptable. The levers can be standard loops or large John Wayne loops. The big issue is the travel distance of the lever. Maximum distance is 4 1/8". This means that some short stroke CAS kits will not work in this sport. Other allowed features are: colored sights, ivory bead sights, lever wraps, 16" barrels, front sight hoods, and slip-on/ lace recoil pads. Ed's Mercantile has in inventory the Marlin 94 Cowboy for +- $750. The reason I recommend the Marlin over an 1873 is the money you save, which is better placed on a higher quality 1911."

"The shotgun is usually a replica or original 1897 model with an external hammer and a magazine tube that holds five 12 gauge rounds. Ed has the Cimarron model for +-$500. The old Winchester Model 12 is also allowed in this sport but expensive to buy. You can use your double barrel shotgun, but you are at a disadvantage with two shots to the five shots in the 1897 pump."

"The 1897 is often called a 'Trench Gun," because it was used in the trenches of WWI with devastating effect. Other acceptable accessories are: ivory front bead, 18" barrel, internal choke tubes that do not extend beyond the muzzle, and lace or slip-on recoil pads. Before I forget, slam firing on close knockback or knockdown shotgun targets is allowed." There was a pause, then many statements of approval were offered. I eventually added, "slam firing can be an enjoyable part of this game. Those who have never seen it will be surprised and will easily pick it up."

"Now the handgun, the 1911 auto pistol in 45 ACP. 'Which 1911 do I get?' This is probably the most debated subject on the matter. Well, it comes down to, 'you get what you pay for!' " "With this in mind, Ed has broken down the choices into three categories, which he carries in the store. Action jobs are $75 extra."

"The first is the economy grade. Springfield Armory has the GI Series. This is a decent entry level in stainless steel for +- $650."

"The second is the mid level grade. Ed suggests two brands. The Springfield Armory has an upgrade loaded series. For the money, it is a quality stainless steel firearm for +- $800. The other brand is the Colt Combat Commander, Series 70 or XSE, also in stainless steel."

"The third is the top quality grade. Ed recommends the Kimber Custom II–CDP, also in stainless steel. This is the well known 'low jam gun' for +- $1,000. This gun is a precision instrument. Note: the Kimber Gold Match model is not allowed in WB."

"Yes, Ed likes stainless steel auto pistol for ease of function, lower jams, easier action jobs and easier to clean. Ask Ed and the positive list will be extended. Ed has three other favorites: Remington R-1, Ruger SP 1911 and Cimarron 1911. When Ed was asked how and why he had his list of favorites, he said that it was what other clubs requested, or he had less returns of malfunctioning/ broken guns. According to Ed, no one needs to spend several thousand dollars for a Custom 1911 to participate in this sport! The production runs mentioned above are more than adequate precision firearms for this game."

POWER FACTOR.

"Power factor is determined by: bullet grains X velocity/ 1000. For example, a 230 grain bullet–multiply by the velocity of 750 fps and divided by 1000 equals a power factor of 172.5.

In math equation: 230 X 750/1000 = 172.5 PF."

"WB requires a minimum PF of 150. So if you reload, be certain you are reloading at a velocity of 750 fps or use a chronograph to verify your velocity. At a match in this club, we are not going to chrono your load, but another club might chrono your load. In this club, the targets are set to fall with a power factor of 150. Sue and I want a bit of a buffer. So we reload at 900 fps for both pistol and rifle–and the targets fall without hesitation. Incidentally, WB max velocity allowed for pistol is 1000 fps and for rifle it is 1400 fps. Also WB minimal bullet weight is 180 grain. Only lead bullets or lead polymer coated bullets are used, to protect our targets. Jacketed bullets are not allowed."

For reloading 12 gauge shotgun shells, use #6 shot which hit harder than smaller shot. Also, load field grade shells per manual. If you have an old vintage 1897 shotgun that only holds 4 rounds of standard 2 3/4" shells, you can shoot 2 5/8" shells from B+P and get 5 rounds in the magazine.

OPERATIONAL METHODS.

"Although I will have more on this subject at the shooter's meeting, I want you to start thinking about safety at the loading table, and when you are shooting this week, start putting this info into practice."

"When you arrive at the loading table, all three guns must be unloaded, the actions open and no magazine in the 1911 pistol. Cycle each gun and show the loading officer that the guns are unloaded. Then drop the hammer of all three guns, in a slow controlled manner, onto an empty chamber. You may then load, 10 rounds in the rifle magazine, 5 rounds in the shotgun magazine, a 5 round loaded mag in the pistol, and holster it. Please note that all pistol magazines are loaded with 5 rounds max–to match the pistol arrays of 5 targets before you need to reload."

CATEGORIES.

"WB has basically four shooting categories. Men's Traditional or Modern category and women's Traditional or Modern category. Yes, men and women have their own categories just like CAS. So what separates the Traditional and Modern categories? It is the 1911 pistol different specifications as follows:

TRADITIONAL

- "Basic four. 5 inch barrel with standard barrel bushing, and maximum of 8 rounds per magazine. Action jobs and stainless steel guns are allowed.
- Unloaded pistol weight of 40 ounces with one empty mag.
- Non adjustable military style rear sights with front blade. Fiberoptic and red dot sights not allowed.
- Other standard specs: mag release, thumb safety, slide release, recoil spring, solid trigger and spur hammer."

MODERN

- "Basic four above are the same.
- Barrels up to 6 inch are acceptable.
- Max weight of 42 ounces with one empty mag.
- Adjustable rear sight with plain front blade is the standard, but fixed military rear sight can be used.

- Painted sights, colored sights or colored inserts are OK.
- Extra slide serrations are OK.
- Extended mag release, thumb safety, and slide release are OK
- Beavertail grip safety is OK.
- Match triggers and light weight hammers are Ok."

"It is true that the handgun specs separate the two categories. Now if you already have a pistol that fits the Traditional category, you have the choice to shoot in either the Traditional or Modern category–but not vice versa. What you may not know is that the Traditional category requires ONE HAND SHOOTING"–followed by boo's and Oh No's!

I added, "if you shoot single handed duelist or gunfighter in CAS, then Traditional category is your game, or for others it can be a new game."

"I may also add that there is another category that some clubs have adopted–Traditional and Modern Senior categories. This is based on clubs that have become too large and or have an excess of shooters over 65. Only time will tell if we ever need to add this category."

Someone asked, "what is the actual ratio of Traditional vs. Modern category participation?" "I researched this and the best answer comes from the 2018 Winter Range Championship. There were 98 WB shooters. 49

participated in the Senior division and 49 participated in the standard division. The actual results are:

Traditional Senior--------22
Modern Senior-----------27

Standard Traditional-----14
Standard Modern---------35

As you can see, the Seniors are evenly distributed, but the Standard division is 2:1 in favor of the Modern category. The statistics don't matter, it is up to the individual shooter. Sue and I did not have a 1911 and had to purchase them. We did not want to shoot single handed and so we decided to go with a SS Kimber in Modern category.

HOLSTERS AND POUCHES.

"This sport requires a specific holster for your 1911 handgun. Ed's Mercantile carries the Mernickle holster. Ed's standard is the black belt and holster combo for $300. This holster provides wrist relief with a forward cant. This allows you to grab your gun without bending the wrist. If you have a black belt, the holster is $140. This holster has a retaining strap for gun security, which is unsnapped for competition. The holster must cover the gun's barrel from the muzzle to the ejection port."

"Several magazine pouches are needed. It is strongly suggested that you have a minimum of four double pouches and magazines to match. The Mernickle pouches are newly redesigned to be slimmer, narrower and molded to the magazine to avoid pouch collapse. This change allows more pouches on the belt. Magazine pouches must be worn vertically and on the opposite side of the body than the handgun.

Double pouches sell for +-$38."

"Extra rifle rounds and shotgun shells are worn on belt slides as is used in CAS. Some shooters like to wear a Bandolier, but they are very heavy. This sport is engineered for very few necessary extra rounds."

OTHER INFORMATION.

"To simplify the shooter's meeting, I would like to point out some other tips that may apply before you decide to join our club.

- Before you shoot your 1911, decide how you will rack the slide backwards. There are two standard methods. The first is to grab the rear slide serrations with your left thumb and first finger and pull back. The other is to place your left hand over the slide and hold it while you push the gun forward with your right hand. It is a personal choice. I perform the first method and Sue uses the second one.

- SASS rules apply, a miss is 5 seconds, a procedural and minor safety violation is 10 seconds, and a failure to engage a target is a 30 second violation. A missed target or a target that does not fall cannot be reengaged.
- In this game, unlike CAS, a dropped round or magazine on the ground can be picked up and used.
- At the end of a shooting string, the RO must certify that your pistol is unloaded before you holster the pistol and go to the unloading table to check your rifle and shotgun.
- A broken gun stays on the shooting table. The rifle and shotgun should have their actions open and the pistol have its slide locked back—all if possible. Do not hand a broken gun to the RO.
- The dress code is the same as CAS plus the era to WWI.
- Our club name will be, The Desperado Wild Bunch, as an extension of the Desperado CAS club."

NEIGHBORING CLUBS.

"What do we have for neighboring clubs? It was simple with CFD since we were the first one in the state, With

WB, it is a different matter. Within 70 miles, we have five CAS clubs that also host WB matches. Some of these WB clubs have been in existence for several years."

"These 5 WB clubs are: One at Marshfield–26 miles. Two in Walnut Shade–39 miles. One at Cassville–59 miles and one in Joplin–70 miles. In addition, Marshfield will host the WB State Championship this summer. These are all accessible within one day's drive. It is very likely, we will share shooters and eventually will start hosting club competitions once our club is more experienced."

"Sue and I will be visiting some of these clubs next weekend. We hope to learn from these clubs and bring their knowledge to our club. Since we will be gone next weekend, we are planning a double weekend in two weeks. RR has scheduled a special WB weekend. Our practice match will be Saturday and Sunday will be our first real competition match. This means you have two full weeks to practice for WB shooting."

For those of you who wish to join our club, there is no membership fee this first year. We need your name, address, phone number and e-mail address. See you in two weeks or on the range starting tomorrow. PS–as you are leaving, pick up your copy of the SASS rules handbook and my handout for today. Start reading the rules, especially the violations–it will make it easier for all of us. Thank you for coming."

After the meeting, we had an impromptu get together with RR and Willard Stone. Sue reported that 68 of the 70 shooters in attendance signed up and plan to be back in two weeks for the entire WB weekend.

Mr. Stone added that with this type of enthusiasm, he wanted to provide something special for Saturday evening that WB weekend. He offered to provide a caterer and a free dinner for all participants and their spouses. He asked RR to e-mail all the new WB registrants and ask them to reserve Saturday evening for the dinner and a Country Dance. Mr. Stone wants the club members to start looking at their shooting club as a social venue as well. RR looked at us and smiled. That is when Mr. Stone added, "yes, I know that Wil and Sue are Country Dancers and very capable of teaching two-step and waltz. I am not trying to be deceitful, I happen to know that dancing two-step and waltz would take hold like a grass fire in this community. I am hoping that the free dance may become an igniter of future activities, heh!"

The last subject was our expenses for our CFD trip and the trip planned for next weekend. "Your CFD expense account was paid by RR out of club funds. That is not acceptable. Whenever RR purchases something on his club credit card, I pay for it—that's the way it should be." Mr. Stone hands Sue and me our own credit card named Desperado Club with our personal names. "In the future, whenever you purchase anything for the club or spend on the club's behalf, use your card and my accountant will take care of it. This includes your upcoming WB trip and any trip in the future–including the Bar W Ranch event in 3 weeks."

On our ride home I said, "it was a good meeting and we are lucky to have a generous benefactor. So let's get ready for our trip and more."

———•—•—•———

CHAPTER 11

WB, Planning and Traveling

After getting home Sunday evening, Sue did the phone rounds with the family. I took the opportunity to call the nearby WB club's contact person since Sunday evening was a good time to find them at home.

These representatives were very happy to have us come down and see their clubs in action. All four clubs had either a practice or actual competition next weekend. The RM would meet with us before shooting started and a guide would follow us through out the matches. It came down to a Friday night event, two on Saturday and a big all day competition on Sunday.

During our morning breakfast, we set up a week's schedule to culminate by Friday noon. Monday was dedicated to setting up the new shotgun knock-back, also called dumping targets. These targets were to be set up at the same distance as the close pistol targets and were made for slam firing.

Arriving at the range, there were some 30 shooters waiting for us. RR had sent a group e-mail notifying WB shooters that Sue and I would demonstrate and explain slam firing on the new dumping targets. After setting up the targets on the ground, Sue explained, "the 1897 shotgun does not have a disconnect so it will continue to fire as long as the trigger is depressed, allowing slam firing on the forward motion of the forearm." Sue demonstrated with an unloaded shotgun. With the trigger depressed, every time she pushed the slide action completely forward it would automatically fire.

I then added, "the bolt is released when the shot is fired. During recoil, you bring the fore-end rearward while keeping the gun on the shoulder. Then you push the forearm forward which brings in the next shell. This forward motion pushes the supporting hand toward the target and the eyes/body follow to allow a point & shoot at the ground dumping target." I then loaded 5 rounds in the magazine and slam fired at 5 dumping targets. I hit all five and each one went from a set 45 degrees to a flattened plate on the ground. "Like all knockdown targets, the shooter is responsible for pulling the cable to reset the dumping targets at practices."

Someone asked, "so you don't aim?" "You can but most shooters develop the point & shoot technique for speed. Slam firing is an acquired method that can be as fast as an automatic weapon. Let me add, a dumping target at close range does not require a hot load to knock it flat.

This is a shotgun target that is very responsive with your light Cowboy loads, and does not require the field grade shells you are using on the other knockdown targets."

Having set up 5 dumping targets on two stages, shooter's were taking their turns slam firing. By noon everyone was getting somewhat comfortable. That is when I noticed that Willard Stone was watching the group doing the slam firing. I approached him and said, "what brings you here today?"

"When I got that e-mail from RR, I had to come and see what this slam firing was all about. May I say, I really like it. It is a great addition to this game. What gave you the idea?" "Discovered it during our research on the sport. I may add, that is why Sue and I are leaving this Friday to visit 4 WB clubs. I know we will come back with new ideas."

As we were still talking, a lunch wagon arrived. The owner/cook put out a sign advertizing a $3 lunch of two choices. Burger with chips and a drink, or bowl of chili with rolls and a drink. I asked, "who authorized this?" "I did, for the next two weeks until the first matches, there will be a noon lunch wagon—to encourage the WB shooters to come and practice. There will only be a limited menu of two items which will change each day." "The price is too low for a hot lunch." "You may have guessed that this lunch wagon is my property and the cook is well paid. The prices are just to cover food costs and to appeal to the shooters."

During lunch, the subject of the long range and silhouette range came up. The range is now excavated and RR will take the added responsibility of setting up the permanent steel targets from 25 to 500 yards. I wanted to talk to you about the mini clubhouse for the new range. What are your ideas on the needs of this game.?"

"After discussing it with RR, it is clear that the long range and silhouette range will be used year round. The building does not need to be more than 40% of the main clubhouse square footage. It should be a warm up shack with a propane stove or furnace. It should also have a wind protected shooting railing for summer or winter use." "I agree, and construction will begin in the next 48 hours."

We spent the remainder of the day slam firing our shotgun. As close as the targets were, we initially had misses. It took a while to stop aiming and follow the point & shoot techniques. We finally headed home at 4PM knowing that we would revisit slam firing again.

Tuesday was dedicated to practicing the 1911 pistol. Arriving at the range, the WB range was mobbed. All three ranges were being used. A quick look showed us that the shooting was very well organized. We took our pistols and headed to the CAS range. We would shoot at the 5 close pistol targets, and run to the next stage to shoot the next 5 pistol targets and occasionally the 5 rifle targets. The pistol targets were at +-6 yards but the rifle targets were at least 20–25 yards.

It quickly became clear. The close pistol targets were easy to hit. The rifle targets were a problem. Running between stages, even if only 25 feet, was generating adrenaline and motion difficult to control. This is what we practiced all morning. After a hot lunch of beans and hot dogs, we went back to practicing the 1911 pistol.

The afternoon program was operational technique. At the first stage, you draw, rack the slide and shoot 5 targets. Drop the spent magazine on the shooting table(not the ground) before you start your run to the next stage. On the run, keep the pistol pointing down range, with the slide locked back, as you pull out a new magazine with your left hand. Once at the next shooting table, insert the magazine, release the slide and shoot. If the next stage requires shooting another gun first, place the pistol on the table with the slide locked back. The pulled magazine can also be left on the table. We practiced this method repeatedly as well as shooting at the more distant rifle targets.

The other thing we practiced was clearing a jam. Sue asks, "would you describe the common jams and how to clear them." "Ok, there are many different ones, but the three common jams are:

- Failure to chamber a round. This occurs when you push a magazine in the grip but you don't get it deep enough to engage the mechanism. When you rack the slide, pulling the trigger gives a click. The cure, tap the bottom of the magazine and rack the slide–you are good to go.

- A double feed. With a double feed the slide will not move forward. Look in the ejection port and you will see a round behind the one in the chamber. The cure, pull the magazine and rack the slide twice, insert a NEW magazine, rack the slide and you are good to go.

- A stove pipe. This means that a round did not fully eject from the port and prevents the slide from going forward. The cure, pull out the magazine and rack the slide several times to clear the gun of any rounds. Then insert a NEW magazine, rack the slide and you are good to go. This method is also used to clear the many other rare events. This means, clear the gun of rounds and magazine and restart loading again".

"Note that clearing a jam usually ends up wasting a magazine since it's usually short of five rounds which is needed in WB shooting. That is why you have 8 magazines in you belt pouches, plus one loaded magazine in your hand as you arrive at the loading table."

Sue had another question, "why not insert a magazine into the gun while running, so when you get to the next shooting table you are ready to release the slide and start shooting?" "Because of brain training and muscle memory. You train yourself to respond with one move with another automatic movement. Let it be that when you insert a magazine, it is time to release the slide and start shooting. If you load a magazine on the run, you may automatically release the slide while running. Now you are running with a loaded gun and that is a stage D/Q. RO's are accustomed to seeing a gun with the slide locked back when on the move. That is why we practice moving between stages with the slide locked back."

By the end of the day, Sue had a strange event. If you have 5 rounds in a magazine, once you shoot 5 rounds, the slide will lock back. Sue had a failure to lock back. She looked at me with a "what happened?" I said, "pull the slide and a sixth round will eject. The only sure way to load magazines with 5 rounds is to place 5 rounds standing up on a table. Load the magazine and repeat. If you count 5 rounds from a bucket of reloads, you will get distracted and end up loading four, five or six rounds. Not good in competition! Another method is to place your ammo in 50 round plastic boxes. Each row is five rounds for each magazine." At the end of the day, since we had been running all afternoon, we were glad to go home for rest and recovery–and possibly do some reloading after dinner.

Wednesday and Thursday were both uneventful days. We got up late, had breakfast and headed to the WB range for practice. We shot the three complete courses with all guns. We found ourselves spending as much time in the clubhouse socializing with shooters taking a break. It was clear to us that we were comfortable, with the guns and the WB targets, and requiring less training time.

The one subject that got our attention was the information on how Ed's Mercantile was dealing with the supply and demand. According to several shooters, the prices were at least 15% lower than most retail gun shops. Ed was getting daily deliveries of guns and other supplies. He had hired two more employees to serve the public and had added a local gunsmith to do the action jobs so popular with shooters. We never heard a negative word from any shooter doing business with Ed.

We headed home early Thursday afternoon. Bailey was expected after school with Sam or Stacey. Bailey's first words were, "I cannot move away from 0.6–0.65 seconds, I am stuck there." I said, "so you are on a plateau and cannot get off it, heh?" Sue added, "let's watch you and see if there is a problem." We watch for some fifteen rounds. Wil said to Sue and Sam, "Her body mechanics are perfect, and her hip snap is literally popping the gun out of the holster. Her thumb draw is ideal. Her accuracy is excellent. Her visual response has significantly improved since she has been doing the TV screen changes, with a fast draw and dry fire. I see a lot of good points that don't need changes. I only see one thing that needs improvement."

Sue finished my statement by saying, "Bailey, once the gun is out of the holster, you are slow to get the gun into firing position. Or, your gun transition is too slow." Wil added, "you need to increase the strength in your right arm. You need to do exercises to increase the strength of your biceps/triceps muscles." "Continue shooting and I will keep watching while grandpa prepares an exercise schedule for the next 6 weeks." "All you will need are barbells of 2, 5, and 10 pounds plus a solid pipe across a door for body pull-ups. Stay on this schedule and you will not experience exercise muscle soreness which could slow you down temporarily. We will check on your progress next week."

Friday morning was a slow day since we were leaving at 1PM for Marshfield where we would meet with the RM and guide at 2PM. Sue asked what our itinerary was and I said, "after our visit in Marshfield, we would travel to Walnut Shade, in the evening, and take a motel. Saturday would be spent watching a full competition. In the evening we would travel to Joplin and find a motel. Sunday would be spent at an all day competition." Sue asked. "What happened to Cassville?" "They sent me an e-mail last night to cancel because the practice was changed to next week."

After breakfast, Sue said, "Let's go shoot 100 rounds of fast draw to maintain our skills. We have plenty of time to pack before lunch." I agreed. We started shooting and found our skills had deteriorated. It took 300 rounds each to regain a respectable speed. We both agreed, that in the future, we would try to shoot 100 rounds each day–we had worked too hard in training ourselves to loose our skills.

We arrived in Marshfield by 1:30PM. We were early so we could visit the WB range before meeting with the RM. We walked to the WB range and were pleased to see the same set up as we had built. The right facade was a bank, the center stage was a walk through field course and the left facade was a jail. The targets were a mixture of racks of falling plates, rails of sequential falling plates, individual knockdowns, ground poppers or knock-back shotgun targets, and upright poppers. They did not have any fixed targets.

The RM arrived and after introductions, we walked to the range for a target layout explanation. The RM started, "let's start with the bank's three windows. Window 1 has a five shot shotgun at ground dumping targets as well as 10 pistol targets at individual knockdowns. This is to signify a bank robbery where the tellers are fighting the robbers, while in the bank–with a short range pistol and shotgun gunfight."

"Window 2 signifies the robbers trying to escape to their horses, and the fight continues with pistol and shotgun. The targets are now farther down range as the robbers are escaping. The shooter has to reload 5 more shotgun rounds and shoot at flip up shotgun targets(hit a red plate and a flag pops up). The pistol targets are smaller and farther down range, and require some precise aiming."

"Window 3 represents the robbers running away from the bank empty handed. The tellers are still shooting at the robbers but are now using their rifles. The sheriff also arrives on the boardwalk and fires his pistol at the robbers. That is why the rifle is shot at the window but the pistol is shot by stepping on the deck to the right of the window."

"Now moving to the jail, the sheriff sees an outlaw gang coming to free their jailed gang member. This time he uses his rifle to shoot at the approaching gang, for ten rounds at 25 yard targets. He then moves to the center window for the closer shots with 5 shotgun and 10 pistols. His last shots are 20 pistol rounds at close encounter from the third window. All 20 shots are at alternating large and small close targets."

"Finally the field course. This represents a bold bounty hunter going to the gang's hangout to collect the bounty on the outlaw's heads. He encounters lookouts at two different locations. He uses his 10 rifle rounds at the first lookout, his 5 shotgun at the second lookout and has a major gunfight at the outlaw's camp. This gunfight uses 25 pistol rounds to bring an end to the confrontation."

Sue adds, "wow, what well written fantasy scenarios. Wil, we need to write similar scenarios before our match. Since WB is an extension of CAS, we need to follow tradition." "Yes, I agree. I also noticed that the targets for the jail location have been changed around to not match the bank stage." "Yes, we like to vary the targets to avoid repetition. We have also been known to change all three stage layouts after a couple of matches."

"What is the size of your club?" "We have an average of 50 shooters that are mostly an extension of CAS. Our membership is made up of all ages which keeps a nice balance. We shoot in the four standard categories–men and women traditional or modern categories. We don't have a senior division at this time because of membership resistance."

"What about paid workers vs. volunteers?" "We don't have fixed targets that require 3 spotters. We have two paid positions per stage, loading and unloading table officers. The remaining positions are volunteers–RO1, RO1 assistant, scorekeeper, and two brass pickers. The RO1 assistant resets the cables once the main RO and scorekeeper document the misses, procedurals, and other penalties."

"What is your major cause of procedurals?" "We have some 40+ targets per stage, so it is common for a shooter to shoot at the wrong array." "Why is this sport so popular since it's very similar to CAS?" "It's popularity is based on two reasons. There is a lot of shooting, especially with the auto pistol, and there is an immediate visual gratification to seeing targets fall from your shooting ability."

We finished the evening by watching the shooting for two hours. The shooting was well matched to the target layouts. The shooters were very capable gun handlers, accurate and especially smooth in pistol loading and changing magazines. We were witnessing a well oiled machine. Before we left, we thanked the RM and invited him and his shooters to visit our range some time this summer. We then drove to Walnut Shade, had dinner at a family restaurant, and chose a motel close to the range for easy morning access.

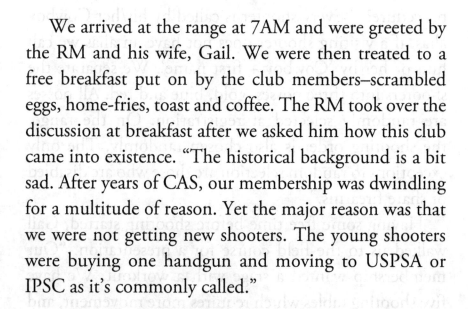

We arrived at the range at 7AM and were greeted by the RM and his wife, Gail. We were then treated to a free breakfast put on by the club members–scrambled eggs, home-fries, toast and coffee. The RM took over the discussion at breakfast after we asked him how this club came into existence. "The historical background is a bit sad. After years of CAS, our membership was dwindling for a multitude of reason. Yet the major reason was that we were not getting new shooters. The young shooters were buying one handgun and moving to USPSA or IPSC as it's commonly called."

"In an attempt to capture a younger crowd, WB was born. In short order we attracted a large crowd of 40 year old shooters. This group, along with some older but progressive CAS shooters, formed a solid foundation and the club membership grew to 70 members within one year." Gail added, "we are also close to Branson and we are getting shooters from that area, both as club members and visiting shooters. These two reasons keeps our match attendance at 75 shooters."

The RM then informed us that Gail was a WB shooter and would be our guide today. We certainly acknowledged that a RM had his hands full with registering 75 shooters, running a shooter's meeting, supervising three shooting stages, and trying to get so many shooters to shoot all three stages by 4PM–then followed by an awards ceremony.

Gail took over. Sue asked, "what is your registration procedure?" "Every shooter is called by his/her Cowboy alias, if a visiting shooter does not have an alias we call him or her by 'Cowboy + first name'. We separate the shooters into three posses–gold, blue and red. All posses are randomly selected at registration. On the range, the shooting order is also chosen randomly. The only exceptions to random selection are those who are disabled or share firearms."

Having some free time before shooting started, Gail walked us to the field course for a presentation. "Our membership wanted a stage with a workout. We have five shooting tables which requires more movement, and maneuvering with two guns in hand. In actuality, the shooter moves downrange, stops at 5 tables and shoots at the targets set 45 degrees to his movement path. For example, you shoot 5 shotgun and 5 pistol rounds at table 1. Then move both shotgun and pistol, in a safe manner, to table 2 where you repeat the sequence of 5 rounds each. Then you move to table 3 with the pistol. At table 3 you shoot 5 rifle and 5 pistol rounds, then move to table 4 with both the rifle and pistol in a safe manner, and shoot 5 rounds of each again. The last move brings the pistol to table 5 where you have 10 difficult small targets awaiting you."

After the Pledge Allegiance to the Flag, a shooter's meeting ensued. We then followed the shooters to the range and started watching the match progression at all three stages. That is when we started with questions for Gail.

1. "Everyone is running between shooting tables."
   "Yes, distance between tables converts to seconds. A short moving time can make you a winner."
2. "Is the auto pistol the major gun in this game?"
   "Yes, the rifle is always 10 rounds and the shotgun 5 or 10 rounds. The pistol is never less than 20 rounds per stage. Everyone likes the auto pistol. We even have one yearly match with 40 rounds per stage of only pistol shooting. This is usually our most attended match."

3. "How do you handle dropped rounds and magazines?" "This club's house rule is that you can pickup a magazine or single round off the ground or shooting table. It may not be allowed at other clubs, and it's up to visiting shooters to clarify the house rules."

4. "What is your rule on moving with a pistol?" In this club, any movement with a pistol is done with the slide locked back. So you drop your empty magazine on the shooting table before moving to the next."

5. "Do you split your posses into half workers and half shooters?" "Yes, Each 25 member posse is split into A & B. That way the shooters can enjoy their time shooting and socializing when not working."

6. "What is your most common violation?" "Because we frequently move two guns at a time, we have a high incidence of breaking the 170 degree rule. If done with an unloaded gun, it is a Stage D/Q. If it is done with a loaded gun, it is a Match D/Q. PS. Our house rules for moving a rifle with 5 rounds remaining, require the shooter to open the lever before moving to the next stage."

As we watched the remainder of the competition after lunch, it became clear that this was a serious bunch of shooters, having a good time, and no one appeared stressed out. Sue started paying attention to the shooter's times. The facade stages of +- 40 rounds, and little movement between windows, showed times of 45–65 seconds. The shots sounded like automatic fire between guns and windows. It was obvious that an aggressive 40 year old can move and shoot fast.

We stayed after the match to see how the awards ceremony was organized. They had 12 plaques on the table and one trophy. Each of the four categories had a first, second and third place. The names were called for the plaques, with enthusiastic applause. The last award was a trophy for the match winner. It went to a young 30 year old man.

Sue made a list of the twelve winners, entering their name with their 3 stage total shooting time. In addition, she was at the photo shoot for winners, and took photos of each winner, then placed a name and time to each shooter. Sue smiled as she said, "I think I could beat all these six lady winners, but time will tell." I looked at the men's times and realized that I would have trouble beating the third place winner."

We then thanked Gail and the RM for their support and hoped we would see them again this summer.

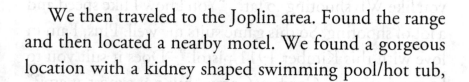

We then traveled to the Joplin area. Found the range and then located a nearby motel. We found a gorgeous location with a kidney shaped swimming pool/hot tub, an upgrade restaurant on the premises, and a dance hall/bar with a country band on Saturday nights. We lucked out for all three amenities. We registered, reserved a table in the bar and the restaurant. Got in our swimsuits and headed to the pool. I kept staring at Sue in her mini bikini and realized she still wore it well.

We dove in the deep end, swam and floated on noodles. Then the pool got busy and waiters were taking drink orders pool-side. We both ordered a Grey Goose Vodka Martini with olives. Sue asked, "don't you feel bad making Mr. Stone pay for our trip?" "I did at first, but after a second Martini, I have no guilt in my being. We really worked hard to get to this point and we are only half way." "Yes, it has been a lot of work, but we have enjoyed every step of the way, heh." "Yes, Mam."

After sobering up in the shallow end, we went to our room for a shower and dressing for dinner. Sue wore a nice low cut black dress with a somewhat short skirt. I had a casual shirt with a sports coat and dress pants. The restaurant was over the top elegance for a motel. We ordered the Chateaubriand for two with the assorted vegetables and red wine. We had plenty of time before the country band started at 9PM.

The dinner conversation was spontaneous. "How do you like WB shooting so far?" "You know I like speed and a lot of shooting. So this game suits me well. Plus, I am in love with this Kimber 1911 pistol." "Does it suit you to be good at many Cowboy Games, but not expert at any?"

"Yes, I am very comfortable being a strong competitor, and I am happy to be shooting different games. That allows me to do a lot of shooting at all the practices, and shooting a lot is what I really enjoy."

I added, "I can follow your logic, and I also enjoy a strong showing at all the games. But I want to excel in fast draw. I have the urge to push the envelope to my maximum ability, and shooting freely in my garage allows me to reach this goal. You may find me spending more time in the garage than at the range. It is OK if you go to the range without me, or I hope I can spend extra evening time in the garage for that purpose." "Not an issue, I understand where you stand. Being a natural talent gives you the edge to become an expert in CFD."

After a fine dinner, we stopped at the bar. We asked the receptionist what the dress code was. She said, "Cowboy boots and hat, jeans and a western shirt." Sue said, "we are going to change out of our dining clothes and be right back." "At the room, I said, "you are a beautiful person, and I don't mean because you are in your underwear." Sue jumped into my arms and planted a passionate kiss. She added, "let's go dancing and later we can put this room to good use, heh."

At the bar, the receptionist showed us to our table and took our drink order–beer and wine. The band was nearly set up and we saw a sizeable dance floor. Their first two dances were line dances and Sue did not get up. Instead she held my hand as we watched the floor full of women. The men were all sitting down and watching. Sue said, "isn't it classic? Men won't line dance here as in the Country Roadhouse." When a nice two-step was played, everyone was up. They were a sophisticated group of dancers.

After several two-steps and waltzes, the bar manager came to talk with us. "I see you can hold a candle to my local dancers. Where are you from and where do you dance?" After explanations were given, we asked, "tell us how you have come to have such a sophisticated group of dancers." "I employ an instructor year round. With her husband, she started teaching partner dances three months ago, and you will be seeing these dances performed tonight." "Great, we know several partner dances and we hope to join your dancers."

The partner dances we performed included: Best of Friends, Cowboy Cha Cha, San Francisco, Mambo Rock, Shottische, Rings, Hello Heart, The Sidekick, Texas Waltz, The Florida Stroll, McGraw Stroll, and of course the Blue Rose, There were a few we did not know and we decided to sit and watch. Sue made a list of the three new ones that we might learn by watching them on YouTube.

After an entire evening of dancing, we retired to our room for private time. In the AM we were spending the day at a range close to Joplin.

We arrived at the range at 7AM for their match day breakfast. We had our replenishing breakfast of French Toast, Canadian Bacon, and Vermont maple syrup from a small family orchard in Jay, Vt. During our meal, the RM and an assistant came to join us. The RM said, "glad to see you and welcome to our match. This is Randy who will be your guide today. Randy is a WB shooter who recently broke his arm and will not be shooting today. The RM barely finished his meal when he was called to the registration desk because of a problem.

Randy quickly took over. "First of all, I am glad to see a new WB club close to us. Our shooters like to travel to other clubs and one more club is ideal for us. Our shooters are very experienced and very proficient. We always give a good showing for ourselves. Now, let me give you some historical background, Our club lost 20 shooters one year ago when a major manufacturing plant moved to China. We rebuilt the attendance with new CAS shooters from our club and surrounding CAS clubs. So today, we have 20 beginners with our 55 regular members. This is the beginner's first match."

I quickly added, "this is great, since we have a full membership of beginners." Randy then asked, "what do you hope to learn during your visit?" Sue said, "other than watching your club in action, we have some questions to cover before the match begins." "OK, go ahead."

1. "How do you select your target layout?" "We start with the written fantasy scenario, then match the gun with the target that reflects the scenario. This is all done the day before the match. The RO2, who wrote the stage, meets with paid workers and directs the target changes. It is a lot of work, but the match quality is the end result."

2. "What are your popular targets?" "The three popular ones are the shotgun slam fire knockdowns, the 5 target dueling tree and the rail sequential falling plates. I would like to add that over the past three years, our targets are getting smaller and farther."

3. "Would you explain the last two?" "The 5 target dueling tree has 5 red pistol targets on the left, and when hit, revert to the right side and show a black target. This is a quality tree that rotates the plates on bearings and does not allow a bounce back. After a full magazine of five shots, any red target left over is a miss. The falling plates on a rail is the most popular. Looking at the array, the shooter sees a large black plate with the #10 in white. As he hits plate #10, plate # 9 appears, and down the line. Let's say that he misses plate #3, he must continue shooting at it until his gun is empty or until the #3 falls. If he hits all the first nine plates, #1 is a small plate the size and color of an egg—a very difficult shot! All standing plates are misses."

4. "How many paid employees vs. voluntary shooters?" "We have two employees per stage, loading and unloading tables. Each stage has 3 volunteers" RO, RO assistant, and scorekeeper. The RO assistant is also an RO1 certified officer who will substitute for the main RO when needed. His main function is to pull the reset cables after the misses have been counted. Misses are clear with reactive targets, they are any upright targets leftover after a shooting string. Procedurals are called by the main RO, the assistant RO or the score- keeper. We do not have spotters or brass pickers."

5. "Who picks up the brass?" "Boy scouts." "Boy scouts! Does that mean you pay them for their service?" "No, at the awards ceremony, the troop scout master holds an auction. The 45 ACP are separated from the 45 Long Colt and the shotgun shells. I strongly suggest you stay for the auction– it is a sight to see."

6. What if you don't want range picked brass and want to keep your own?" "Simple, the boy scouts pick up your brass and shotgun hulls. They only keep it for the auction if you don't want to keep your own casings. If you keep your brass/hulls, it's customary to tip the boy scout with 1$." "So for 3$ you can end up with your own brass, and you

are supporting the boy scouts, heh." "Yes, and in some matches we use girl scouts."

7. "What is your house rule on moving with guns. The pistol, once unholstered, is caried to all shooting tables with the slide locked back and no magazines in the pistol–it will be shown clear at the last shooting table. The long guns are both carried with the action opened and a round in the receiver is allowed–not in the chamber. In short the RO expects to see a safe gun on the move or it is a safety violation. House rules must be checked by visiting shooters."

8. "Would you describe your loading protocol?" "As the shooter arrives at the table, he safely places all three guns on the table. The rifle and shotgun have their actions cycled and followed by slowly dropping the hammer on an empty chamber. The pistol, without a magazine, has the slide cycled and the hammer slowly dropped on an empty chamber. Then all three guns are loaded and the actions not cycled."

9. "Please describe your 'show clear and make safe' procedure?" "At the end of the shooting string, the shooter takes out his pistol magazine, cycles the slide, dry fires the gun and reholsters it. That gun is now been verified as safe by the RO. The shooter then goes to the unloading table to have his rifle and shotgun shown empty and safe."

10. "Is sharing guns a problem?" "We have beginners today and you will see a lot of gun sharing. We allow this since the cost of guns is always a deterrent to joining the sport. Since our posses and shooting orders are randomly selected, the gun sharers and disabled are exempt."

11. "How do you handle pistol jams?" "In our beginner meetings, we went over the common jams and the accepted methods for clearing them. We showed videos on many jams since seeing the clearing methods made them believers."

12. "How do you minimize gun jams?" "Once a 1911 is broken in, the gun should be field dismantled, cleaned and oiled after each practice. Before a match, completely dismantle the shooting mechanism and clean it well. Oil the suggested points, and my opinion is to use a synthetic slide grease made for these guns."

With the shooter's meeting terminated, everyone was heading to their starting stage. We watched the RO describe the fantasy scenario, and then the shooters started moving to the loading table. Randy pointed out that only two shooters were allowed at the loading table at a time. The first 3 shooters went through the bank stage without a problem.

The boy scouts were well informed and only approached the firing line once the shooter was at the unloading table. They politely offer the brass and hulls to the shooters. An occasional shooter kept his brass, and some only kept their finicky pistol brass–both with a tip.

By the time the fourth shooter came up, Randy said, "since we have 20 beginners, you are going to see some common violations. Being their first shoot, the violations are being waved–only applies to the beginners." Randy pointed out the beginners and we saw what he meant:

- We saw an accidental discharge within 5 feet of shooter. A Stage D/Q.
- Leaving a long gun with the action closed at the end of fire. A MSV(minor safety violation) of 10 seconds.
- Handing a broken gun to the RO. MSV 10 seconds.
- Some clearly unsafe gun handling. Stage D/Q.
- Broke the 170 degree rule with unloaded gun= Stage D/Q, and with a loaded gun= Match D/Q.
- Dry firing at the loading and unloading tables. Stage D/Q.
- Loading the pistol with a live magazine per protocol, but accidentally pulling the slide back. Stage D/Q.
- When drawing the pistol, cycling the slide before the pistol is 45 degrees downrange. MSV 10 seconds.
- The very common, moving with a finger in the trigger guard. 1st=warning, 2nd= MSV 10 seconds, 3rd= Stage D/Q
- Placing a loaded gun on the shooting table. Stage D/Q.

Lunch time arrived for each posse serially. We joined Randy for a BBQ chicken, macaroni salad and coffee. During lunch, Sue brought up the subject of violations. "Is it just me or do we have too many Stage or Match D/Q's?" I felt the same way and said, "don't you think that we should have more 10 second MSV and even add a 20 second SSV(severe safety violations). Otherwise we ruin people's chances of competing with a Stage D/Q or being thrown out of the match with a Match D/Q?"

Randy very carefully prepared his answer. "I agree with you and you can do this as a club house rule. If you affiliate with SASS you have to follow their rules. There are many clubs that prefer the former."

After lunch, we watched the shooters go through each stage. It was mid afternoon when Sue and I both felt very confident that we understood the operational methods. We thanked Randy for all his assistance. We both felt we would meet again.

With some time to spare before the boy scout auction, we decided to visit the vendor in the clubhouse. This was an older couple selling 230 grain 45 ACP bullets and 250 grain Long Colt bullets–the mainstay of WB shooting and also used in CAS and silhouette shooting.

We said hello and struck up a conversation. He was free since shooting was still going on. Sue looked at the bullets and said that they were perfect. I looked at the price and said, "Sir, you are selling these at 3/4 of the retail price and there is no shipping to pay. Why and how can you do this?"

"Well folks, I used to be a CAS and WB shooter before I got old and can't see well with cataracts. So today I practice my hobby with my helper, the Missus. We travel 5 days per month on a circuit of tire stores. We have very loyal store managers who charge the wheelweight salvage rate and I give the manager an extra management fee. When the 3/4 ton duel rear wheel with extra springs is full, we come home to unload with the use of the tractor and front end bucket. We then get back on the circuit through Missouri and Oklahoma for the remainder of the 5 day week."

"For the next 5 days, I melt the wheelweights in cast iron pots on high BTU propane cookers. Pour the hot lead into 10 lb. molds. The third week I spend 5 days making the 230 grain 45 ACP on my Magma Master Caster. I lube and size each bullet on my Magma Lube Master. The fourth week I convert my equipment and repeat the process to make the 250 grain 45 Long Colt."

"Why is the process a 5 day activity?" "Because on weekends we go to shoots and sell our products." "Sounds like a lot of work!" "Well we like the traveling week, and we like to keep busy. The machines do all the work and I enjoy supervising the machines, adding lead and converting from one caliber to another. Besides we do very well financially, and it is a hobby business that is the size I can enjoy. That is why I don't add the 38's used in CAS. The business would get too big for us." As we departed, we bought 8 boxes(#500) of each caliber.

Shortly thereafter, the awards ceremony started. The boy scout leader ran an auction. The brass was placed in bags of 200 rounds of either 45 ACP or 45 Long Colt and the shotgun hulls in bags of 200 hulls. He started by asking, "if anyone will pay $5 per bag, please come up and select what you want." Several shooters got up and made their choices. Then he said, "anyone willing to pay $3 per bag, please come up." Finally, "For 1$ take any bag." The remainder of the bags disappeared. Sue said, "I like this, we need to do the same. In addition, the boy scouts were very efficient when picking the brass, and this will speed up our lost time between shooters."

The awards ceremony was similar to the last one we had seen. There were 13 awards given out. Each category winner got a plaque that indicated the match date. The second and third place winners got a certificate with the date added. The match winner got the trophy.

I asked the RM where he gets these plaques, certificates and the trophy. He said, "We order the generic trophy and plaques from a supplier. We have the software to generate the certificates. The trophy and plaques already say WB, the club name, and match winner or first place. We have a stencil that allows us to engrave the date." He gave us the web site for ordering the trophy and plaques, and the name of the certificate printing software.

We then headed to our motel for the evening. We had another great dinner at the motel and went to see what was happening in the bar. They were planning a DJ controlled country dance. We reserved a table for two and went to our room to change.

The dance was a relaxed event with great dancing songs. We danced intermittently and reflected on our visits to well established WB clubs. We did not realize that the resident instructor and husband were enjoying the evening as dancing customers. Yet before the second intermission, with a full house, the instructor invited everyone to the dance floor and line up as couples. She then showed us a great waltz, called Just Another Waltz, to George Strait's You Look So Good in Love. This was a completely new technique for a waltz and something we would bring back home to the Country Roadhouse.

The next morning, we got up late but in time to enjoy the morning breakfast in the motel lounge. We then packed up and headed home. We arrived before lunch time and proceeded to start planning for our week's activities before our first competition match next weekend. RR had decided, with our approval, to eliminate the practice match and go straight to our first competition match–to be held on Saturday. A group e-mail was sent to notify all the expected shooters, and reminded everyone to arrive early for registration since the shooter's meeting would start promptly at 8AM.

CHAPTER 12

WB, Camp Therapy and First Match

Back home again, the next day began slowly. We got up late and had an extended coffee/news period. After coming alive, I said "Sue, we need to start thinking how to spend our week before the big WB day on Saturday." As we were talking, Sue said "other than our usual priming practice before a match, and your request to practice fast draw, I don't think there is much that needs our attention."

"Maybe we can get back to reading. You wanted to refer back to the reloading book, RELOADING, A Practical Hobby by Richard M Beloin MD, on issues related to loading 45 ACP and 45 Long Colt. I wanted to read his new book, COWBOY SHOOTING, On the Road. Allegedly, it's about a couple training for CAS and traveling out west—very similar to our lives last summer."

Amidst Sue's discussion, I was opening Saturday's mail. The last envelope was from a law firm, Cruzio,

Mann and Richardson. I opened the envelope and read the enclosed letter:

To Doctor Wil Summer,

I represent one of your old patients, Mrs. Elizabeth Morrow, who passed away 6 months ago. Mrs. Morrow was a rather rich widow who had only one heir. A large portion of her estate went to her heir, plus one medical school scholarship and one private donation. I am pleased to inform you that you are the fortunate recipient of her private donation. Mrs. Morrow told me that she always thought it sad that, as a widowed physician, you had no hobbies to add pleasure on your time off. She is leaving you a gift of $250,000 with conditions that we need to discuss. Please call our office and schedule an appointment with me ASAP.

Respectively,
Leonard Richardson, Esq.

I looked at Sue and said, "you need to read this." Sue read on and finally said, "this is quite an announcement. Has this ever happened to you before now?" "No, but I have heard that inheriting from well to do patients does happen. Guess we had better meet with Mr. Richardson."

That afternoon, I practiced my fast draw and by 4PM, I had shot 300 rounds. My times were hovering around 0.38–0.40 seconds. I knew that I was stuck on a plateau that would take a long time to move along. I said to Sue, "my last training session brought me to 0.38–0.40 seconds, and made me an experienced competitor. I am now starting my next training session, and my goal is to become a Master fast draw shootist, with shooting times in the 0.33–0.35 second range."

Sue had been reading her new novel, Cowboy Shooting–On the Road. The subject had her hooked. During the day, I had called the law firm and scheduled an appointment with attorney Richardson. To my surprise, we had been given a 9AM appointment with the attorney of record.

The evening was quiet since Sue could not get her nose out of that book–she kept saying, "been there and done that" or "this is a deja vu"

I spent the evening wondering what I would do with a $250K windfall. After an evening of day dreaming and wishful thinking, I came down with only one item that reverts back to my formative years in a small New England town.

The next day, while on the road, I asked Sue if there was anything she wanted. She said, I have the only four things that matter to me, health, family, guns/shooting and my husband. What about you?" "Those four are our fortunate given. But for materialistic things, do you wish anything?"

"No, what about you?" Yes there is one thing I would like, but will wait and see what the lawyer has to say."

Once the meeting started, after introductions, Mr. Richardson quickly got to the inheritance restriction. "Mrs. Morrow wanted you to purchase an item that would be pleasurable to you as a hobby. She did not want you to just get $250K to add to your checking account or investments." He continued, "according to the will, we would set up a trust that you and your wife could use to pay for expenses as long as they were related to the approved initial purchase."

There was a long pause and finally I said, "I would enjoy purchasing an isolated recreational home. A camp in the woods with 30 to 50 wooded acres." "For what purpose?" "As a winter haven away from the city. I would use the acreage for walking, snowshoeing, hunting, develop a hobby such as maple syrup production, set up our own shooting range, and possibly develop an ATV trail for riding."

The lawyer was thinking but quickly said, "Yes, that's a go. It would perfectly fit Mrs. Morrow's wishes. Meet with your real estate agent and start looking. When you find something, call me. The probate court is eager to close this estate since your inheritance is the only item that is pending. Just to remind you, if you buy something less than $250K, you can use the unused balance to pay for improvements, basic expenses and even taxes–as long as any expenditures are spent on site."

As we were heading to the real estate office, Sue asks, "where does this dream of yours come from?" "Well being raised in Vermont, I was exposed to my grandfather's hunting camp, and a maple orchard he had as his hobby. I always said that I would like to get back to that way of life. Plus the idea of a private range and a winter escape really appeals to me."

Sue paused and asked, "if you were raised in Vermont, why are you in Missouri?" "Well during my college years in Vermont, I decided late to major in pre-med courses. I had applied to many medical schools and had doubts in my future. After an interview, the first to accept me, with pre-med courses still pending, was our local Medical School. I guess they saw something in me that was a mystery to me. I did my residency here and falling into a local practice was the easiest transition." "This school gave me my once in a lifetime gift, medical school acceptance. In return, my loyalty to Missouri and this community has been everlasting."

———•●—•———

At the real estate office, we met with a young woman new in the office by the name of Rosemary. After introductions, we explained what we were looking for:

- Year round town maintained road access and withing 50 miles north of Springfield.
- 30 to 50 acres of isolated wooded land with camp– away from neighbors.

- The camp should be +- 500 sq. ft., with 1 bedroom–1 BR, water, septic system, propane heating stove and power.
- The woods must have the potential for a maple orchard.
- An open area of 150 yards to build a shooting range.

"Those are our minimal requirements, and all five must be met. Anything extra would be a benefit. When you have something that meets these requirements, call us." "Can you give me a dollar range that you consider in your budget?" "I will give you an absolute max of $230K"

Wednesday was a quiet day. We both did some reloading in the morning and Sue read all afternoon. I shot fast draw and actually started shooting 0.37 repeatedly. At 4PM, Rosemary called. I placed her on speaker phone, and her voice was clearly pressured and excited. She said, "you are not going to believe what came up for sale just a few minutes ago. This property meets your five minimum requirements plus the following:

- The maple orchard has 200 taps with installed tubing to all taps, as well as high tensile wires to hold up the main lines.
- The cabin is a cedar log cabin, fully furnished with new appliances and Ethan Allen furniture–plus phone service.

- It includes a three car garage. One unit is a sugar house, the second houses two included ATVs and a riding lawn mower, and the third is for one vehicle.
- It includes 50 acres of a mature forest, surrounded by 2000 acres of state land. Your nearest neighbors are one mile away–north and south. The acreage already has an ATV trail throughout the property. It includes a 2 acre clearing."

"Wow, I cant believe it is in our budget!" Rosemary said, "the executor of the estate wants a quick sale and he has it listed at $200K."

Sue said, "schedule a visit tomorrow morning." "I already did with the lawyer/executor and he put the listing on hold until our visit tomorrow."

Meet us at the office at 9AM and the lawyer/executor will drive us to the location."

En route with the lawyer and real estate agent, we bypassed the city and headed north. Before long we passed by our Desperado Club, and quickly found ourselves in forested areas. The executor said that there was one family member that had inherited all other assets, but the sale of this property was going to charity. He made it clear that the title was clear and ready for sale. The offered price of $200K was firm.

Arriving at the location some 45 miles from home, we saw a picture perfect home and grounds. The camp was a real log cabin with a front porch that looked at the open field and the high mountain in the background. The woods were all hardwoods on the right of the field and mixed type on the left side of the field. The cabin was surrounded by medium size maple trees for shade.

We parked next to the three car garage and went to the cabin. The porch had a hanging swing and two large rocking chairs. We entered the cabin and saw a magnificent arrangement. The kitchen was to the left with a dining table for four. The kitchen cabinets were a medium maple hardwood and the appliances appeared new stainless steel. There was even a washer/dryer behind closed doors. The furniture was high end Ethan Allen. There were two lazy boys rocker loungers, a flat TV on the wall and a full length couch. In the living room was a propane parlor heating stove. This cabin was an open concept except for the bedroom. It had a queen size bed, quality dressers, and plenty of closets. The bathroom had a large shower, a single vanity, toilet, and linen closets.

I looked at Sue's big smile and said, "this is more than acceptable." We then moved to the garage. Bay one was empty for a vehicle. Bay two had two modern ATVs an a 42" riding mower. There was a work bench fully stocked with carpentry, mechanical tools and a chainsaw. The third bay was a sugar house. It had a vacuum pump, large holding tank, a small reverse osmosis machine(called R-O), a press filter system, and a 2 X 6 foot propane fired arch with a stainless steel pan. The pan was also tig welded per modern standards free of lead solder. There were many accessories needed in the production of maple syrup. The lawyer looked at us and asked, "is this acceptable?" "Beyond belief."

We went outside and followed the sap gathering tubing and quickly walked into an amazing maple orchard. The trees were all 24–30 inches in diameter. Tubing went to each tree and most trees had two side branches for two taps. I said, "this looks like a well maintained old orchard. Simply beautiful."

The lawyer then took us to the ATV trail. As we walked through the two acre field, we walked by a large earthen berm backstop. We walked the trail for 10 minutes when Sue said, "we don't have to go farther, we will take it." So we came back to the porch and I said, "call Leonard Richardson and he will give you approval for the sale. The lawyer said, "Lenny is a good friend of mine," as he was dialing.

They talked for 15 minutes and all the lawyer said was, "really" "OK" "Yes" "Can do" "Certainly" "Free title" "Probate approved" and "tomorrow morning at 9AM will be fine." He hung up the phone, looked at us and said, "congratulations, such gifts rarely happen and I am happy for you. If you approve, we will have all the papers ready for a final sale in the morning. You are getting a great deal and the probate court will be satisfied since they set the price on this real estate. It is uncanny, but the owner of this place was a retired physician who loved his guns and his maple syrup hobby. I am glad to see their legacy being transferred to you."

That evening we loaded all the extra furniture, nick-knacks, and miscellaneous kitchen utensils that had been placed in storage, from Sue's apartment. We also loaded extra clothing, especially winter and work clothes. Our plans were to go to the camp after the closing and 'move in' so to speak. Plus we brought Wil's 44 Magnum pistol for the planned walk through the ATV trail.

The closing took one hour and we proudly departed with a deed and title. After the executor left, our attorney was clearly pleased with our purchase. He said, "sounds like you got just what you were after and more–this was Mrs. Morrow's wish. The real great thing is that you have $50K to spend in the future, as long as it is related to property–and yes a shooting range is part of the property."

"I have started a trust checking account in both your names to pay for your purchases. I will review your purchases every year just to confirm your sales are related–this is just a formality. As long as I don't see a $10K charge for a month in Europe, it will all be approved. It is perfectly OK to include minor purchases such as camp clothing, groceries, vehicle gas and the like. This $50K is to cover all expenses at the camp. Any questions?" "Do you wish to be consulted for a large purchase?" "No, If it's camp related it's automatically approved. The last item is this form. I am pleased to say that Mrs. Morrow's estate paid all Federal and State taxes on this inheritance. This form is signed by the Probate Judge and should be added to your tax report for this year. Have a good day folks."

When we arrived at the camp, we unloaded the truck, put everything away and headed to the woods. The trail was well groomed and well used. The woods were gorgeous. It was clear that the previous owner had another hobby. He had used his chainsaw and spent years removing brush and undesirable trees. There were many brush piles everywhere. These made a haven for rabbits. As we walked we saw clean sub trails for snowshoeing and even cross country skiing. The animals were plentiful: rabbits, partridge and deer—plus some bear tracks. The entire trail took one hour to walk and was thoroughly enjoyable.

On our way home, no one was speaking. Finally I said, "I wish Mrs. Morrow could have been alive to see what she gave us." Sue said, "I thank God for we are so fortunate. Let's use it for our pleasure and peace of mind. I respect the gift and will not flaunt it, but will be glad to share it with our family and even our friends." "Yes, sharing it is a marvelous idea. The first to share it will be RR and his wife. Sue then said, "and let's call it CAMP THERAPY. Ok?" "Yes, great name."

Saturday finally arrived. All the weeks of meetings, planning and training was coming to fruition–not just for us but for all the WB shooters. RR had e-mailed everyone to notify all of the 7AM early registration with free coffee and donuts, because of much to cover at the shooter's meeting.

The $10 registration was manned by three of the six employees. At the beginning, RR was called to settle an issue. He called me over to get my input. Couples were asking to be on the same posse. RR asked me what I thought. "I should recuse myself, but I believe that couples who practice and shoot in the same game should be kept together. We need to do whatever is possible to encourage shooting as a social event. Not to be corny but 'a happy wife is a happy life.' " I was expecting a wrap on the head, but Sue only said, "never were ever spoken wiser words!"

Another registration issue, two apparent gamers wearing Shady Brady hats and short sleeve shirts wanted to shoot on the same posse. RR made the call and they had to draw– getting a random posse color, and ended up on separate posses. They were not happy campers and RR made a note to watch them. I noticed the hats and shirts–to be discussed.

I watched the registration and identified illegal gear that needed mention at the shooter's meeting–holsters without hammer thongs, polymer/plastic holsters and pouches, and other illegal holsters. The other issue to discuss was rifle short stroke kits.

"Welcome to our first WB shooter's meeting and match. We began with the Pledge Allegiance to the Flag. Today we have 75 shooters and we will need to maintain a lively pace to be done at 4PM. We will shoot in three categories: Women's modern-13, Men's modern-46 and Men's traditional-16. No ladies registered in Traditional."

"I have several announcements. The first, tonight we have a free gala event with dinner two alcohol drinks and a dance, all paid for by Willard Stone. Events begin a 6 PM with a happy hour–so bring your spouse, significant other or date and join us in the main clubhouse."

"Second, we are not using shooters as brass pickers, We have an arrangement with the local boy scout troop. They will pick up the brass and offer it to you. If you don't want it, they will add it to their auction at the awards ceremony. If you want some of your brass, take it from them but it is customary to give the kids $1. Since there are only three stages, $3 to get your brass back is a good deal."

"Third, the mini clubhouse is open and will host our lunch. At lunch, pick up your keys to this building, the main clubhouse, and the gate. Your set should include all three locations."

"I have a long list of items to mention, so please hold your questions till the end. Sue and I will alternate discussing each issue:

- Holding up a pistol magazine, I said, this is a MAGAZINE(or mag), not a CLIP as non shooters like to call them. Mark your mags if you expect to get them all back.
- We have 6 violations: miss-5 seconds, procedurals 10 seconds, minor safety-10 seconds, Stage D/Q, Match D/Q and failure to engage-30 seconds. Today being our first match, we are not applying the penalties to your scores, but we will call them out-loud for all to appreciate.
- A broken gun is placed on the shooting table. Do not hand it to the RO.
- Tell your RO if you are sharing guns.
- There are many targets downrange–at least 40 per stage. Be careful not to shoot at the wrong array– that will get you a procedural of 10 seconds.
- You can slam fire your shotgun at any shotgun target, but the far targets may not fall down with a partial hit.
- Moving from one table to another. The rifle and shotgun rules are the same as SASS-CAS. However for the pistol, remove the magazine and lock the slide back before moving.

- Be careful moving with two guns in hands, You are likely to break the 170 degree rule.

- A dropped round or magazine on the table or ground can be picked up and used. This is our house rule.

- Holster issues. Polymer/plastic holsters and pouches left over from IPSC will not be allowed after today. Hammer thongs are required once off the firing line. The entire barrel must be covered by leather, including muzzle and ejection port. At lunch, we will have a local leather worker who makes a usable and legal 1911 holster for $50 and one for $80. His double leather pouches go for $12.

- Some of the CAS rifle short stroke kits will not qualify in this game. The lever must move 4 1/8 inch to be legal per hand-book measuring method. In the future, we will be measuring the lever travel of all rifles. Incidentally, this will also be a requirement for rifle silhouettes.

- At the end of the firing sequence, you will show the RO that your pistol is safe. You will remove the mag, rack the slide, dry fire and holster with a hammer thong.

- 1911 jams will occur. There are three common ones: failure to engage the magazine, a double feed and a stove-top jam. I demonstrated and described the methods for clearing a jam.

The best way to avoid jams is to clean your gun and oil all the suggested location. I also recommend a special lube for the slide. Otherwise, it depends on the gun.

- One shot per target–do not re-engage.
- Our fancy scenarios are short and to the point–such as a bank robbery, a jail escape and an attack on a outlaw camp.
- Loading guns. Rifles have 10 rounds, the pump shotgun has 5 rounds and the pistol magazines are all loaded with 5 rounds.
- Your most common violation will be to move with your finger in the trigger guard of all three guns, but more so with the pistol.
- More on the pistol. If ever you need to place your pistol on a shooting table, it must be safe(no mag and the slide locked back). Once the pistol is unholstered for use, it does not ever go back to the holster until it has shown "clear" at the end of the firing string.
- This is the last day for Shady Brady hats and short sleeve shirts–follow SASS protocol.
- A shooter's long guns is his/her responsibility. Do not pick up their guns and bring them to the unloading table.
- The RO assistant will pull the resetting cables and pick up the shooter's magazines. It's a lot to

accomplish, so feel free to assist him at both tasks. Remember to get the verbal OK from the main RO that missed targets have been counted before pulling at cables. The best way to avoid a premature reset is to follow the assistant RO.

- I saved the best for last. In the future, we will add the Texas Star to be shot with the 1911 pistol. We will also add the flying vertical clay bird–released by a shotgun hit at the base target. If any of you have other suggestions, please see me."

Since there were no questions, we proceeded to our posse's selected stage–gold posse on 1, red posse on 2 and blue posse on 3.

———————•━━●━━•———————

Sue and I were on the gold posse starting on stage 1– the bank, or more specifically, The Stone Bank. As the RO gathered the posse, he removed the disabled shooter's scorecard. He then shuffled the score- cards and when finished he checked the order to make sure the shooters sharing guns were not next to each other–giving them time to reload the guns. The disabled were offered first or last position. The RO then went through the order, requesting all shooters note who was shooting before themselves, so the shooters would step up to the loading table without being called up. That is when all hell broke loose.

Rowdy Bill, the gamer with the Shady Brady hat who had lost his bid to have his friend shoot on his posse, put up an objection. He said, "I don't want to be the first shooter." The RO came back and said, "the random pick is final, sorry." He requested a review by the RM. RR came over and listened to the RO's explanation of events. He even listened to the gamer's feeble demand. RR finally said, "sorry sir, it is what it is. Accept it or you are bordering on a Spirit of the Game violation–in short, sir, take it or leave it."

The RO then read the scenario, "this is a bank robbery. In the first window the security officer is fighting the robbers in the bank, he is shooting through the teller's window. He shoots 10 pistol rounds and 5 shotgun rounds by slam firing at the dumping targets. He then moves with his pistol to the outside window and fires his 10 pistol rounds and 5 rifle rounds at the robbers on the boardwalk. He then moves to the third window with his safe rifle and fires at the escaping robbers with his 5 rifle rounds and 5 pistol rounds. Total rounds, Pistol=25,Rifle=10, and Shotgun=5."

Sue then says, "so we have to move the rifle safely with 5 rounds remaining and the pistol is moved to all three windows with the slide locked back." "Yes, and we shoot a total of 40 rounds. Also, remember that the rifle targets require some careful aiming when you shoot the last 5 shots, since the targets alternate between large and small size–a perfect place for a miss."

Rowdy Bill reluctantly came up to shoot. He started at the first window by missing one dumping target. By the third window, he was going too fast and missed a small rifle target–as I had warned Sue. He then had a jam on the last 5 pistol targets. After making his pistol safe and holstering it, he said to the RO, "are those dumping targets properly set? I thought I had a good bead on it." "Sir, you had a total miss with the shot blast hitting the ground–off it's mark." As he arrived at the unloading table he was mumbling how some of those rifle targets were intentionally too small to make people miss them. I heard the unloading officer say, "or maybe they are small to make people slow down.!"

Fortunately, the next 5 shooters did very well and shot the stage without violations, and only a few misses. Their shooting times varied between 50–70 seconds. Sue was shooter #7 and up next. At the buzzer she took off like lightning. The 'bing' of lead bullets hitting steel and hearing the steel targets falling produced a smooth systematic cadence. Her deportment gave her a delightful stage performance. She finished the stage with every steel target down and the RO yelling, "clean and in 47 seconds." As she stepped to the unloading table, I heard many shooters saying, "nice run" "nice job" and "way to go." I could tell by the look on her face that she was proud of her performance. I said to her, "nice going, I guess practice makes all the difference, heh."

My turn came up. I worked hard all through the stage. My speed was good but I ended up with two misses. My time was 60 seconds. I said to Sue, "I am nearly moving as fast as you, but it's still a bit over my ability since I missed two targets." Sue added, "despite that, you are shooting as well as any other man in the modern category."

The next stage was the field course. The RO started, "a Pinkerton was invading an outlaw camp to arrest a murderer. On route, he encountered three ambushes before he got to the actual outlaw camp for a bold shootout."

Shooter #1(our gamer) did well with a clean shoot. Yet, his slow swagger walk between shooting tables cost him in time. At the end of his shooting string, he holstered his pistol and started to walk away. The RO stopped him and said, "sir, you cannot holster your pistol until you show me that it's clear and you dry fire it. Plus, this time slip the thong over the hammer. If you ever do this again, it will be a Stage D/Q."

At the field course, Sue was hustling between shooting tables. She had one miss and a total time of 64 seconds. I also had one miss but my time was 78 seconds. After the stage, I said, "Sue, you run like a 30 year old." She added, "I may be an old motor, but with the proper oil, I can hum like a new one." Trying to get her going, I said, "what brand of oil do you like?" *She just gave me that look, the one I might fare well with!*

This field course was a large 50 round course, 30 of which were pistol rounds. Several shooters had several jams and often had to sacrifice a magazine. Even if most shooters carried 8 magazines, with jams you can run out of ammo. One shooter who had several jams actually ran out and failed to engage 2 targets–a very costly event in time. The message was clear, if you have a problem 1911, you had better have more than 8 magazines.

After two stages, we broke for lunch. The main subject at our table was the coming Bar W Ranch Shootout. Several shooters had heard different stories. Apparently, a rain enclosure had been constructed at the WB range with it's own set of porta-potties. The three stages were all facades with a rain roof that would become permanent fixtures. They had a fourth range for a field course that had three shooting tables. The rumor was that they would have a stage solely for pistol shooting. The last news was that they had set up practicing ranges at the old CAS range for CFD and WB that would be open as early as Thursday morning.

On our way out, I stopped at the leather vendor and purchased 4 clip-on black double magazine pouches–to cover the need with pistol only stages. The clip-on feature was ideal for this type of stage.

The last stage of the day was the jailhouse. The RO read the scenario, "the sheriff is fighting off a bunch of outlaws trying to free their leader who was jailed for murder." The shooter started with a rifle as he tried to deter the outlaws as they were running their horses down main street. The last window was when he tried to stop them from breaking down the door to the jail. It was a straight forward shooting event. Yet we saw several violations. Shooters were getting cocky and not paying attention to their techniques.

We saw one shooter loading his pistol with the slide down before moving to the next window. One shooter had a squib load on his pistol and was stopped by the RO as he attempted to reload. Two shooters forgot to move the pistol per routine and accidentally holstered their gun. And finally, one shooter got an AD by slam firing his shotgun and hitting the floor just ahead of his feet. That poor RO turned green and had to stop the shooter–but gave him a reshoot.

One thing happened that no one had anticipated. A rifle shot took out two targets with one shot. The shooter kept on shooting and ended up with a spare round which he ejected. At the end of the string, he was awarded a failure to engage violation. The RO explained, "in this case a fragment of the bullet took out the nearby target. The shooter was suppose to shoot the next round at the spot where the free target had been. It is the same thing as any target that falls spontaneously. You get a freebie, but you must shoot in the vicinity of the free falling target. This is just like baseball's double play in the vicinity of 2nd base."

Sue shot this stage at her best. She got a clean shoot of 54 seconds with a 45 round stage. I also got a clean shoot but at 61 seconds. The real sad situation was seeing the gamer get more and more irritated. He showed up on the firing line again without the thong on his pistol hammer and was reprimanded by the RO. The last event that made him boil was when he shot a five string rifle array with his pistol that was meant for the rifle and did a vice versa with the rifle. At the end of his round the RO shouts out "clean" but with a 10 second procedural. The gamer went ballistic and was clearly rude to the RO. Finally, the RO explained what he did and at least the gamer left without embarrassing himself any further. This being the last stage, he went to his car and was obviously not staying for the awards ceremony.

———————•◗◖●◗◖●———————

At the end of the shooting event, our posse finished first. We all gathered in the clubhouse for liquid refreshments as we awaited the other posses. Sue started the conversation, "I was watching the boy scouts today. They were very proficient. They waited for the RO and shooter to clear the firing line before three boys moved in to pick up the brass and hulls," Sue and I had decided to buy back our pistol and rifle brass since we were shooting new Starline brass. That cost us all of $6 to get back +- 250 once fired brass.

Someone asked, "how many jams did you get today?" I said, "we got none." "How did you manage that?" "We have very clean, oiled, and greased Kimber guns. We also shoot new or twice fired brass that has been resized. After three firings, the brass is relegated to the practice pile. That way we avoid split cases that are notorious to jam a rifle or a 1911 pistol. We plan to follow this practice with Silhouette shooting in the future."

RR started the awards ceremony. First, the boy scout leader ran the auction. The shooters were willing participants. All brass and hulls were sold and the boy scouts left with $289–that averaged out to +- $4 per shooter.

For the awards, RR had found the source for the match winning trophy as well as the first place plaques. The dates were engraved in the generic awards and the 2nd and 3rd place certificates were printed using the club's computer software.

Sue was pleasantly shocked to make 2nd place in women's modern category. Her winning smile said it all. She had been beat by a well known CAS lady by the name of Kat Star. Sue said to me, "now I know who my nemesis is. I will eventually top her. Today she beat me by 60 seconds in overall time. I know she is at her maximum ability, while I am still learning and improving."

I was more than satisfied with my results. I had placed 14th out of 46 men in the modern category. Stan and Jack, who had been in the red and blue posses, had clearly beat me. Stan had placed 2nd and Jack had placed 3rd. Both got certificates. The match winner was a visitor from Vermont who had been visiting a relative in town–RR to everyone's surprise. At the photo shoot, I took a group photo of all 10 winners. I would make 8X10's and give them to Stan and Jack. I congratulated them as we shook hands.

At the end of the awards, RR remind everyone of the Bar W Ranch Shootout next weekend, He took a poll and found that 13 shooters were attending. Sue said, "and most of those also do CFD, heh!" He then said, "in two weeks we will hold the first rifle and pistol silhouette shoot. The range is built with permanent steel targets and the mini clubhouse is open for use. The pistol silhouettes are set at 25, 50, 75, and 100 yards, whereas the rifle silhouettes are set at 50, 100, 150, and 200 yards. Remember that silhouette shooting will be performed free style, except the 200 yard target will be off a railing."

"Last, we have a big evening planned. Free dinner, drinks and dancing–with one surprise. PS. This is a dress up gala event. See you at 6PM for happy hour."

While we were dressing for the event, Sue exclaimed, "I wonder, will this dress up event be a hit or a flop?" "We need to see if there is a social potential with this crowd. If there is, we can extend it to the other Cowboy Games.

I have been wondering for sometime. The way I see it, men will be attracted to free drinks and dinner, whereas women will be attracted to dressing up and dancing, heh! If Willard Stone is willing to fork up this bill, he must know something we don't know"

I wore a modern western attire of charcoal polyester pants with a black stripe, an open collar medium blue embroidered shirt and a western cut sports coat. Sue had a plain medium blue western princess type dress with shoulder straps and a combo turquoise/silver earrings and pendant. The jewelry and dress matched her blue eyes and golden hair–just like a Ladyslipper.

We arrived at the clubhouse at 5:30PM and people were already arriving. We had not planned a welcoming committee, but as we arrived, we saw Willard Stone in full western attire. He was already greeting the early arrivals. We went up to him and Sue planted a kiss and a big hug, almost mesmerizing him. Willard shook my hand and said to us, "other than my money, this evening is possible because of you two. My thanks to you is already in the works, and I am certain that it will be appreciated. Now I am looking forward to your next game, CRS and CPS. Enjoy your evening."

As we were heading to Stan and Miranda's table Sue asks, "what did Mr. Stone mean by his thanks to us was already in the works?" "Heck, he is related to Constance Whitehouse, so anything is possible."

Stan was still glowing from his second place win. Sue asked, who is joining us since we are at a table for six. Miranda said, "it is a surprise." "Stan added, "it will be more of a shocking surprise, believe me." RR came over and asked if we cared to move to the master table with Mr. Stone, himself and the missus. I said, "I believe that the three dedicated RO's need some recognition, so please add them with their wives."

As the food was ready, RR announced a random table call to the food line–of course after the head table served themselves. People had a choice of chicken parmigiana with linguini or lasagna with a side of fettuccine Alfredo– along with a creamy Italian salad, rolls and a dessert of Cannolis with coffee or tea.

After dinner RR managed to get Willard Stone to stand and accept the crowd's appreciation. Willard was quick with his words. "Thank you all for making this Cowboy Game possible. In reality, I just dumped money into this project, but the heart and soul came from Wil and Sue." The place erupted in applause and a total standing ovation followed. The clapping did not show any signs of stopping till Sue and I looked at each other and we knew we needed to simply stand and bow.

RR then requested that everyone gather outside while we clear the tables and set up a dance floor for the evening. Upon our reentry, tables were set for six and Stan and Miranda again joined us. I said, "where is this mystery couple that did not join us for dinner?" Stan answered, "I got a text while we were outside. They had a fender bender–actually they were rear ended at a stop sign by a local policeman." "Oh my, that must have been awkward." "Yes, especially when the lady was driving, and apparently read the officer the riot act–several times." "Well, I am certainly eager to meet this couple."

The dancing started and three line dances were introduced. Sue got up with several of the Country Roadhouse dancers. As the dance started, several of the other ladies joined in, and it lead to a full floor. The next dance was a two-step and at least eight couples from the Country Roadhouse joined us. We were surprised to see four other couples joining in. People were looking on and were smiling. The next dance was a waltz. It again created great interest from the onlookers.

On our way back to our table we saw we had new guests. As I sat down, I started laughing. Sue just about said "what the _ _ _ _," but stopped herself in time. Stan and Miranda were holding back an explosion of laughter. In front of us was Jack with his surprise date, Kat Star. Since Sue was speechless, I asked, "well Jack, how long has this been going on behind our backs?" Cynthia(Kat) said, "since your wedding, I was Jacks's date at the reception" and Jack added, "and we have been dating ever since. We thought it was time to stop hiding, since it is not just a passing thing" We finally congratulated them and had a decent conversation with Sue's nemesis.

The remainder of the evening was a continuation of these three dances, with the occasional slow dance that filled the dance floor to overflow status. At the peak of the evening, RR came over and said that many people were asking where they could learn to two-step and waltz. I answered, "I suspected that this is what W. Stone meant when he advertized a surprise this evening. I will make an announcement."

"I got to the microphone and said, "there seems to be a lot of talk about where you can learn to two-step and waltz. Well look no further, Sue and I will teach both dances starting the week after the Bar W Ranch Shootout. These lessons will occur at 6 and 8 PM Monday, Tuesday and Wednesday at the Country Roadhouse. These lessons are free. We are limiting each class size to 7 couples. If interested, come to our table to sign up with your names, e-mail and phone numbers. Just remember gentlemen, we can teach any of you to dance–no one will fail and the time to learn is when you are with other people that also do not know what they are doing. I promise that you will enjoy yourselves."

After a very successful evening, Willard Stone came up and said, "I knew you were dancers and was hoping this evening would go as it did. I think we are going to end up with a sixth Cowboy Game–Cowboy Dancing."

On the way home, Sue was looking at the sign up sheets. She said, "You were planning 6 classes of 7 students each." "Yes" "well you have a full house of 40 students.

Oh my, guess who is at our first class?" "No idea." "Jack and Cynthia of all people" "Well a confirmed bachelor is adjusting to a woman in his life."

Sue asked how I knew that the Country Roadhouse was available those evenings. "I had talked with the owner and he was very interested–adding dance lessons on those slow evenings would be very good for business. Some students would come for dinner and others would buy liquid refreshments. So it was a go."

So Sue, "we have three days before we leave for the Bar W Ranch. How do you want to spend them. "I want to practice WB during the day and possibly practice CFD at night." I said, "I just want to practice CFD since this is my last chance to fine tune my fast draw skills before I face that expert from Nevada and the natural talent on my heels, Stan."

After traveling several miles in silence, I said, "do you realize we have been together over a year and it has been a year of such extensive shooting, traveling and dancing?" "Yes, but more important, you still look at me with those undressing bedroom eyes. So take me home, we have had a wonderful day to celebrate privately!"

CHAPTER 13

WB/CFD, The Bar W Ranch Shootout

O ur three day preparation for the shootout started in the morning. Sunday was an expected slow day at the WB range after yesterday's competition. Sue went to the range and I stayed home to practice fast draw.

The shooters at the WB range were practicing for the next shoot at the Bar W Ranch. The four were, Stormin Sandra Jean, Tru Fak, Manor Queen and Lady Stitcher. By noon, Sue was home for lunch and would do some fast draw this afternoon. I had practiced fast draw all morning and was still on my 0.35 second plateau.

After lunch, we went man-on-man against each other. After a 5 round string, Sue said, "my goodness Wil, you are right there at 0.35 seconds consistently." I said, "a spectacular accomplishment is never preceded by less than a spectacular preparation–practice, practice and more practice." "Well, aren't you getting poetic?"

We practiced on and off all afternoon. In the evening we made a list of what we needed to pick up for our trip. Since all meals were furnished at the Bar W Ranch, the grocery list was short. Later, we went to the storage area and picked up our camper.

Monday was a repetition of the previous day. Sue went to the range and yesterday's four club members were still shooting. Smokemeat and Lucky Lady had joined the group. When Sue got back to the house, she said, "those club members were having a good time and were clearly becoming better competitors."

That afternoon, Sue went shopping. She said she needed a new swimsuit and other clothing items for the trip. She made arrangements with her daughter to meet for a late lunch and go shopping thereafter. I continued my quest—trying to get off that 0.35 second platearu. When she got back, I was still on my same lonely plateau, and she had several clothing bags and a few groceries. She opened her purchases and started modeling the items. When I saw the three swimsuits I was thankful that she had a well rounded display. One conservative two piece, one revealing mini bikini, and a standard one piece Miss America style.

That evening, we went through our ammo inventory. We prepared practice and match ammo for the three guns in WB. We also packed wax bullets for practice and competition. We did not know if the ranch was providing fast draw match ammo, which is commonly done to get uniform velocities.

Tuesday was our last practice day. Sue got back from the range early and said, "I am ready for the WB competition." After lunch, we loaded the camper with all our gear. Sue then started cleaning all our guns and I went back to doing more fast draw. Suddenly I said, "that's it, I am finally hitting 0.33 seconds at least 50% of the time and that is the practice game that I am taking to the shootout."

After dinner Gail and RR(Warren) called. They had a special event over the weekend and they wanted to learn to two-step. So I said, "come right over and we'll teach you." We barely had time to make room in our garage and they arrived. Without any delay, we started showing Warren the quick-quick-slow-slow and then showed Gail the matching steps in reverse.

They traveled in a counter clockwise fashion, and both were verbally repeating the quick-quick-slow-slow phrase. Sue and I were on the edge of laughing, but they were doing it correctly. Then we put Willie Nelson's All Of Me and they danced to the music. We showed them the most important maneuver–how to alternate positions and have the man go into reverse, and then resume driving forward. We emphasized that changing the lead and follower positions was needed to prevent fatigue. We then added how to make 90 degree corners. Finally, we varied the speed of the dance, from slow to medium and fast. They were quick learners and within one hour they were dancing with a respectable form and rhythm. Gail finally said, "Warren has never wanted to dance because he felt he had two left feet. Now I know better."

Warren added, "I never would have believed I could do this. So, many thanks. Now I know that your dance lessons at the Country Roadhouse will be a success." Our final tip was, "now go home and practice every day to smooth out your moves and you will be ready for the weekend."

That evening, we went to bed at 8PM and were up at 4AM for a cold cereal breakfast. With a large thermos of coffee, at 5AM we were on the road to the Bar W Ranch Shootout.

———————•▬●▬•———————

On the road, Miranda called to enquire where we were spending the night. Sue said, "we stop at the OK Campground which is 45 miles from the Bar W Ranch. This allows us to arrive early Thursday morning." "Why do you want to arrive early?" "Because all day Thursday, they have practice ranges set up for both WB and CFD."

We arrived at the OK Campground by noon. We set up the camper, had a light lunch and headed to the pool. Sue was modeling her conservative two piece swimsuit. At the pool, we met Stan and Miranda who had beat us to the site. We also saw some familiar faces, the WB guide, Randy Wooten and wife as well as Bo Duffer and wife from Colorado. There were several other Cowboys from last year's event that were returning for this year's shootout.

After swimming, we found ourselves floating on noodles and socializing with all of them. Stan pointed out that we were expecting a large contingency of our Desperado Club membership. Most were WB shooters but there was also a small group of very good fast draw shooters. Sue said to Miranda, "I did not know you had a camper." "We decided recently, to join the 'on the road' program. That way we can go to other clubs to shoot this summer. Also, most of the club members that are coming to the shootout also have campers–except for two couples who rented campers just for this event."

We managed to spend the entire afternoon at the pool. By 6PM everyone was heading to their camper for dinner. While we were changing, I said, "well, we haven't had a swimsuit disaster like we had last year. Sue said, "yes, that was funny and it lead to you know what." I came back, "you know, athletic directors tell their teams to not have sex the night before their big games–to preserve their energy reserves."

"Well excuse me but I am a free agent, and now is a good time to use up some of that reserve energy, heh." Yes Mam."

Thanks to a replenishing dinner of steak on the grill with many extras, our evening was complete with some reading time. I started reading that book Cowboy Shooting–On the Road by Richard M Beloin MD. We then went back to bed to sleep and replenish our energy reserves.

———•———•—•———•———

Wanting to take advantage of the entire day, we arrived at the Bar W Ranch access road gate by 9AM. The place looked the same as it did last year. The buildings on the left of main street included the Whitehouse family home, the large pool area, the meeting place, the corral for horse rides, the barn, a row of porta potties and the camping area. The camping area had four rows of 25 camp sites with power, water and sewage.

The right side of the main street had the permanent home of Charles and Tess Whitehouse, the owner's son and his wife. Next was the tack and saddle shop, the carpentry/plumbing/electrical building, the automotive center, the employee bunkhouse and the cook shack. The last building was the business office which substituted for the registration site. Beyond the registration site was a road to the WB range, and next to it was a private home for Jim and Eleanor Beecher(ranch foreman and business manager). The Beecher's home was directly across from the camping area.

We stopped in front of the office and was greeted by Eleanor, who stepped from her counter to give us a welcome hug. After much discussion of what was happening at our club, we got down to business. We paid for three nights camping, all meals, fees for WB and CFD competitions, Friday evening high stakes bingo for Sue, open pistol shooting for me, and Saturday dinner/dance.

Today we have attendants who will run the WB stages and the CFD electronic targets. Feel free to spend the day practicing if you wish. Sue said, "we will do WB this morning and CFD this afternoon."

Eleanor then says, "you have a very large contingency of people from your Desperado Club. Here is a printout of your members and their camping locations:"

1. Doc Derby and Lady slipper–Site # 6
2. Tru–Fak and Stormin Sandra Gene–Site # 5
3. Trak–Man and Manor Queen–Site # 4
4. Guest and Kat Star–Site # 3
5. Jay–Dee and Miss Productive–Site # 2
6. Butcher–Blok and Lady Stitcher–Site # 7
7. Gerry Rigger and Blondie Quickstep–Site # 8
8. Stan Winslow and Miranda Currier–Site # 9
9. Smoke-Meat and Lucky Lady–Site # 10
10. Special guest and wife–Site # 11

Sue asked, "who is the guest with Kat Star?" "I won't know till they arrive since I did not get the name." I asked, who are the special people on Site # 11?" "Emma Whitehouse told me that if this one got out before they arrived, that I would end up picking turnips in Iowa!" "Ok, so we have to be surprised, heh." "Actually, it's more like Mrs. Whitehouse's private payback–so she said."

We opened the camper and headed to the WB range for practice. All 4 stages had a ranch attendant and being early, we had complete freedom in using all the stages repeatedly. The stage we performed most often was the pistol only stage. The targets were challenging since they were set up at different distances and were of different sizes. The upright poppers were the most intriguing since they fell with a bouncing clamor. The new feature at this new range was the roofed structures for the four permanent stages as well as a large roof enclosure for spectators. By lunch we were satisfied that we were ready for the WB competition.

Through out the practice, it became obvious that one of the practicing shooters was a seditious character with faults. Sue asked what I meant by seditious. "A trouble maker." Sue said, "well his faults are more like chasms, to me." "Unfortunately, he will likely cause trouble at tomorrow's match."

Heading to the cook shack for lunch, as we were looking at the menu, Sue said, "this is the same menu they had last year plus a few new entries." "Yes, but why would you change excellent choices." The menu included:

BREAKFAST. Biscuits and gravy, steak and eggs, oatmeal and corn bread, skillet Texas hash, beans and salt pork. All orders include homemade toast, peanut butter, jelly and coffee.

LUNCH. Beef stew with vegetables, hot roast beef sandwich, beef burger and steak fries, cattle drive casserole with chipped beef in a white auce, refried beans and tacos. Any of the above with sweet biscuits, a mixed bean salad and coffee or drink. Dessert includes Cowboy honey dipped cookies or sugared Bearpaws.

DINNER. Steak and more steak. Standard 10 oz. sirloin steak. 10 oz. BBQ strip steak, dutch-oven Swiss steak, Cowboy beef brisket, and a 10 oz. fried steak. Choice of side dishes: beans with green chile, baked or mashed potatoes, choice of hot vegetables and garden salad. Dessert includes: traditional canned peaches, Cowboy double layerd chocolate cake or old fashion bread pudding.

We had the beef stew and cookies. We went to get our wax shooting guns and gear and headed to the automotive carport parking garage–the CFD enclosure. The four double lanes were managed by ranch employees. They functioned as RM, side and extra judges, electronic target operators and announcers. Shooters were the customers and did not have to perform any functions other that shoot their best practice game.

With four double lanes, the employees were processing 8 shooters every 5 shot string. This gave the heavy shooter attendance the opportunity to shoot as much as they wanted to. Some of our club members were already at the practice to include: Stan, Butcher–Blok, Gerry Rigger, and Trak–Man. They were all shooting at least 0.45 seconds, but we all knew that this was a conservative time. They were all saving their best times for Saturday– so was I.

The attendants informed us that the morning elimination would be done with ranch prepared Dead Eye wax bullets–for uniform velocity.

In addition, the Magnificent 12 shoot-off would also have three grains of Triple Seven black powder substitute added for effect and show. Since many of us had never shot with black powder, we were not accustomed to shooting through a white smokescreen. We were allowed to practice with 50 powder loaded wax bullets. Despite fans to dissipate the smoke, it was still difficult to properly see an early starter light–but everyone was in the same boat.

After a long afternoon of practicing fast draw, we cleaned our guns and went to the camper for R&R. Suddenly Amos and Emma Whitehouse showed up to visit. The first subject was what we were accomplishing at the Desperado Club to make Willard Stone's dream come about. Emma added, "and all that work without remuneration as I expected. Well remember that my cousin is like an elephant, he never forgets activities done on his behalf. I suspect he is already planning something in that regard."

The subject changed to, "why did you change your shootout from CAS to WB/CFD?" Amos said, "well after last year's shootout, most of the comments and popular opinions centered on WB as a progression of CAS into more modern times with new guns. Of course, everyone wanted a piece of fast draw after seeing the demo last year."

"With this background, a retiring CFD expert moved from Fallon, NV to an inherited family homestead in our nearby town. The long and short of it, he quickly established a local CFD club with plenty of enthusiastic beginners. Then, the president of a nearby large WB club approached us to add WB at the shootout. He would provide all the targets and set them up. I had to provide permanent stages. Then the CFD club got into the fracas, they would provide the electronic targets and train my ranch hands how to operate the electronic equipment. They would use the carport for the shooting enclosure."

"The long term effect of this arrangement was that if the shooters want more of this type of shootout, I would provide the WB targets and electronic targets, and promise to continue the new trend for the next two years." Emma added, "Amos is still wondering who got the better deal out of this agreement, heh?"

The subject changed to the ranch. "How are things working out this year?" "We have had a banner year. Plenty of rain, coyotes under control, large increase in calves and beef prices are up. The best news is that Charles and Tess are ready and planning to take over the ranch. We spent all of last winter in Alamo, Texas in a mobile home park and enjoyed it. We are traveling more and working less. We have agreed to a generous retirement income from the transfer of ranch ownership." Emma even added, "and since the CFD electronic targets got here, Amos has been practicing every day and is enjoying it. It was that DVD by Quick Cal that convinced him to try out this sport." "I won't be competing this year, but I'm planning to next year."

As the Whitehouses were leaving, we saw several of our club members arrive at the registration and the camping area. Sue was watching site # 3 and I was watching the surprise at site # 11. Finally a pickup was pulling a popup camper and parked at # 3. I recognized the bright blue new truck but said nothing. Out of the truck appeared Kat Star as expected, and the driver finally showed his face, P–Shooter. Yes, "my good friend, neighbor and CAS teacher, Jack!"

Sue was standing with her arms akimbo and her dropped jaw. She says, "this is obviously more than just dating." Cynthia said, "yes, and both of us have enjoyed our commitment since the WB dinner/dance." Jack simply shrugged his shoulders and said, "I thought I would be a life long bachelor, until I got mauled by this cat!" The shock continued as we saw an obvious RV rental pull up to site # 11.

The RV got parked, and out comes Warren and Gail– the one and only president of our Desperado Club. Sue and I went over and a said, "what are you doing here?" "Well it is a short story. Willard Stone showed up at the house with two round trip tickets to Amarillo, Texas for Thursday and return Sunday evening. In addition, he paid for this RV rental, my two days off taken without pay, my fees at this ranch and all other miscellaneous expenses. All he said to us was." "This is a token of my sincere appreciation for everything you have done for this club. Have a nice holiday and see you at the Bar W Ranch."

By 4PM, all our club members arrived. In a short time, we all gathered at RR's site and had a party going. That is when Willard Stone arrived with a van full of appetizers, beer and wine. He also mentioned that the cook shack would hold a late dinner at 6:30PM for our crowd of 18 attendees. After the late dinner and the partying, we decided to put off the pool till tomorrow evening.

<hr>

The WB competition started promptly at 8AM with the usual Pledge Allegiance to the Flag, and the shooter's meeting. The three posses had been randomly chosen at registration. It was nice to see that couples were allowed on the same posse. Our club members were well distributed throughout all three posses. Fortunately Jack and Kat were not on our posse because of the fierce competition between the ladies.

The shooters were all experienced shootists over a long standing period of time. Because of our extensive practices, we were able to keep up with their pace. Sue was better than me. She moved faster and was more accurate. It was clear that her performance was appreciated by the three different RO's. When Sue finished a string of fire, the smiling RO would yell out, "clean and fast time of…"

The RO's were all ROl from other well established clubs. The RM was Bull Slinger, from last year's CAS match. The match was moving along well with the goal of establishing the Magnificent 18 by lunch time. The only trouble was caused by that seditious looking individual. He managed to complain at all three stages. The bank windows were too short for his tall stature, the jail window bars were too close, the targets were too far or two small, and the field course had too much running.

Of the three, each RO made light of his negative comments. However the RM(Bull Slinger) did not. He approached him after his last stage and said, "I hate to see someone so unhappy at a friendly charitable competition, so if you wish, we would refund your other registration fees." "No thanks, I came here especially for the fast draw competition, and I plan to show everyone how we do it in Arkansas."

Just before we broke for lunch the Magnificent 18 were announced. Six in Modern Men, six in Modern Ladies, and six in Traditional Men–there were not enough shooters for Traditional Ladies. The shoot-off would be 35 rounds of the 1911 auto pistol. There would be three award winners in each category. Sue made it to the Magnificent Six Modern Ladies category–as well as Kat Star, Stormin Sandra Gene, Blondie Quickstep, Eleanor Beecher and Tess Whitehouse. I made it in Modern Men category as well as Stan, P–Shooter, Smoke-Meat, Charles Whitehouse and Tru–Fak. The Traditional Men finalists were all unknowns from other clubs. This last group must have been from one club since they all had different military uniforms dating back to WWI.

The talk at lunch was about the expected hot competition this afternoon. Everyone knew that the line up included the best of the best. As we gathered at the range, the RM gave us the rules of engagement. "Every shooter gets to have two non sequential runs at the pistol array. The higher of the times will be eliminated. In order to have an awards ceremony, we are not announcing the positions of the top three shooters. Their times will be certified by the RO, the RM, Amos Whitehouse, and be revealed at the awards ceremony on Sunday morning. Today we will name and eliminate the bottom three shooters–keeping the suspense of the top three shooter positions alive, heh."

Sue's time on her first run, according to my stopwatch, was 49 seconds because of one miss. I said, "you need to pick up speed with 100% accuracy." Her second time was 42 seconds with all hits. I said, "that's a good time and will likely 'slip' you in the top three. Nice job, Ladyslipper." The bottom three shooters were announced, sixth place–

Stormin Sandra Gene, fifth place–Tess Whitehouse, fourth place–

Blondie Quickstep. Sue was satisfied with any position in the top three.

The men's shootout was also hot and agressive. The shooters were running and hitting the targets. Sue was timing me on our stopwatch. I was consistent, 47 seconds on each run. I said, "that is the best I can do." The bottom three shooters were announced, sixth place–Tru-Fak, fifth place–Charles Whitehouse, and fourth place–Smoke-Meat. I was shocked, I had made it in the top three. Sue was wrapped around my neck saying, "hell, what a result for a newbie in the sport. I am so proud of you, heh!"

After the tense WB competition we were relaxing at the camper when Jim Beecher showed up. He sat down and started, "So I hear you are very active in adding shooting disciplines at you Cowboy club. The one that interests me is CFD. I joined that club in town started by the fella from Nevada–Winston Burns. I have been practicing a lot in my back yard on a steel target and I go to the club twice a week to shoot at the electronic targets. I heard that you won your last match with a show stopping time of 0.36 seconds. Is that right?" "Yes that was a lucky Hail Mary shot." Sue said, "it was not. Trust me, you better be on your best game to beat Wil tomorrow."

After dinner our crowd was heading to the pool for an evening of relaxation. We arrived as the adult evening schedule started. Everyone got two free drinks from the pool bar–located this year in the shallow end of the pool.

All our friends and club member, especially the men, were staring at Sue's mini bikini. Some were trying not to stare, but some were not bashful–whatsoever. When Sue walked the diving board to dive, it was like a slow motion video of following eyeballs and smiles. *My thoughts were, "I hope her top stays in place–well at least the bottom half stayed up."* Everyone wanted an encore but Sue had learned her lesson–as she stayed in the deep end while she moved things back in place. My response was to have a third pina colada. It was RR who saved the day when he said, "well Sue, that was certainly one for the team, heh!"

The remainder of the evening was very pleasant surrounded by our friends and club members. That is when I said to Sue, "not to sound poetic or the result of the third pina colada, but as I sit here with our surroundings, this thought comes to mind. At a certain age, people get comfortable with what they have, what they know, what they do and who they share it with. I guess it's called contentment where there is no anguish, boredom or want. The shooting sports has made it possible." "Yes, and I call it a touch of happiness."

As we were all floating on our noodles, Jim Beecher started thinking back at last year's shootout event. He said, "many of you may remember the famous resuscitation conducted by Doc Derby. Many remember that famous 'precordial thump' that drove many a shooter to the sidelines where they turned green. But the climax was when that 6 inch cardiac needle was plunged into the chest. A dozen good men dropped in place to their knees and lost their lunch."

The Beechers and the entire group of bobbers were laughing out of control. That is when Charles Whitehouse turned green and said, "I have spent the entire year trying to get that needle sight out of my head, and the deja vu has brought it all back. Fortunately, Charles wife, Tess, was laughing so loud that even Charles started laughing. As the tone quieted down, it was clear that no disrespect was intended.

Shooters were at the range for an early start. There was a delay because one of the side judges was ill. Amos Whitehouse, the RM, came to ask me if I would volunteer. I said, "Warren Whitaker(RR) was the RM at our CFD tournament. I explained that he knew the rules better than anyone I knew, including me. Plus he is not a shooter today, he is a guest of Willard Stone." Amos turned around and saw Willard who was listening. Willard said, "without a doubt, you are lucky to have him." RR was pulled out of the crowd, and he was obviously proud to participate.

After the usual Pledge Allegiance to the Flag, Amos explained that the first stage of elimination, to process 100 contestants, would be a 2X elimination to get to the Magnificent 12 by lunch time.

The competition started, I was shooter #74. I had plenty of time to watch the shooters. I saw some fantastic fast draw talents. I was proud to see our three club members, Trak–Man, Gerry Rigger, and Butcher Blok give a great showing for themselves. I was not surprised when they made the Magnificent 12.

Sue was shooting her usual 0.45 seconds, but her vicious poker game was devastating for unaware competitors. She had perfected her false tactics: groaning, bluffing, slowing down, missing and suddenly picking up speed. As soon as the competitors realized what she was doing, she then gave them her best practice game–a consistent 0.45 seconds.

She made it to the Magnificent 12 with pride, even if she knew she would be eliminated at that level.

The only problem encountered was a call by a side judge who claimed that the trouble maker from Arkansas had started his draw before the starter light came on. Amos came over to hear both sides of the argument. Then Amos looked at RR who was standing next to the side judge. He said, "Warren, did you witness the event?" "Yes I did, the side judge is correct, the competitor had his gun lifted at least a full inch before the starter light came on." Amos issued a failed round and awarded the competitor an X. Mr. Arkansas left the firing line in an obvious foul mood.

By lunch time we had found our Magnificent 12. My usual lunch in this situation was a sweet dessert with regular coffee–quick energy and caffeine to keep my neuro reflexes at peak response. The competition was kept at 2X until the bottom six were eliminated. The next stage were the final six: Stan, Trak-Man, Winston Burns(the instructor from Nevada), Gerry Rigger, Jim Beecher and me.

Amos then announced the rules for the final six–sudden death. Yes, if you get a single X, you were eliminated. When we get to the final two, the best two times out of three is the match winner. As the competition started, I eliminated Trak-Man and Stan. Winston eliminated Gerry Rigger and Jim Beecher. So here we were, I was going against a fast draw expert from the CFD capital of the USA.

Moving ahead, Winston had seen my best time as 0.35 seconds, and Winston's best time was also 0.35 seconds. It was clear that we had to find some energy or willpower to push the envelope. With 175 spectators holding their breath, I went into the zone and the starter light came on. The overhead display yielded soft groans–we both shot 0.35 seconds. Amos cut the ice and said, "if this keeps up we may be here past dinner." I could see Sue's lips, "you can do it."

The next round was ready, it was delayed because I asked Amos for a pause. We got ready, I heard SET, and I swear I saw the starter light flicker to come on. My time was 0.33 seconds to Winston's 0.34 seconds. There was applause. The final round came around, while getting ready I paused again but this time I heard a familiar voice in my head, then heard SET and the final light came on, again in slow motion. I remember hearing the two shots and expected another tie. The overhead display showed Winston's time as 0.33 seconds and mine at **0.32 seconds.** All I remember after that is Sue breaking my neck and crying like a crazy woman.

The applause, hoots, and hollers were overwhelming. Amos and RR came over to give their congratulations. Winston was next in line and stated, "nice job, and the competition was as good as I ever had." The next to congratulate me were all our club members. The last straggler to give me a hand was Willard Stone, who had tears in his eyes, nodded, and never said a word.

On our way back to the camper, Sue said, "I saw you request a pause before your last two shots. What was that all about?" "On the first instance, I said a short prayer and actually asked for divine assistance. On the second instance, I felt I had exhausted my reserve of divine assistance. So, I asked my departed 1st wife for a sign that she approved of my lifestyle and my new wife." "Wasn't that a bit of a risk?" "No, I suspected for the past year that she approved. Just as the SET command was sounded, I heard her voice saying, 'yes, and you're good to go.'"

———————•———◼━●━◼———•———————

Saturday evening was the shootout's social event. A true gala with dinner, dance and some promised surprises. When preparing our wardrobe, I chose a well embroidered Western Tux. A high bowler Cowboy hat, striped pants and dancing boots. Sue wore a strapless dark blue floor length gown with a high slit on one leg. With her diamond earrings and pendant, she looked like a queen. Sue asked how she looked? "Like a real shocker, but fortunately not the same type as the pool escapade. I got that look, a new one, a mildly threatening type with a smile."

Amos and Emma were greeting all attendees. Mrs. Whitehouse gave us a prolonged hug and said, "it has been a pleasure receiving your Desperado Club members, and we are pleased with your showing." Amos said, "we are seating you at the head of your club's table. As we sat down, we noticed that we had a long table of 20 places–plus the round tables had all been replaced by long tables. Winston Burn's club also had their own two tables. By looking at each table's name tag, they were seating people by clubs, local shooters, and other miscellaneous groups of shooters. They had a large table of non shooters who were invited Whitehouse guests–politicians, friends and business associates.

The dinner was a choice of steaks–T-bone, delmonico, tenderloin, plus a small side of beef brisket. You had a choice of mashed, baked potatoes, potato salad and three hot vegetables. Dessert was tapioca pudding, custard pie or blackberry squares/ice cream.

There were very well planned seating arrangements. We were seated across from RR and W. Stone was sitting next to Sue. Stan and Miranda were next to RR. After all guests were seated, Jim Beecher came to the microphone. He said, "dinner is ready. We have 150 steaks being placed on the fire pit and will cook them 5 minutes on each side. Sorry, we cannot risk any beef less than medium. I will call tables randomly and when 150 guests have picked up their steaks, the second team of 150 guests will have to wait +- 15 minutes for the second round.

Our table did not make the first round, but we were the first table on the second round. I took the T-bone and Sue took the delmonico. During dinner, RR said, "I hear this is this ranch's beef. This has to be the most tender and tastiest steak I have ever had." Sue and I looked at each other and said, "the product of their cross breeds—more later."

After dinner Jim Beecher came back to the microphone. "It's time to vote. How many of you shooters, by a show of hands, would like another two years of combined WB and CFD instead of CAS. There was a sea of hands that covered the hall. Well Amos, looks like some of your ranch profits will go towards electronic CFD targets and WB steel knockdown targets for the next two years.

Jim's second point of interest was, "I saw in the past two days some amazing specialty shooting. The match winners need special recognition" Doc Derby in CFD and Kat Star in WB. These are natural talents and the pride of their organizations. Ladies and gentlemen, bring your hands together in their honor. Applause and a standing ovation followed.

During the interim, the long tables were exchanged with round tables to make room for a dance floor. The dancing started on the band's first production. A two-step. RR and Gail got up and danced the two-step. We stayed sitting down so we could watch our club members. We were not surprised to see a good attendance on the floor, since most were regulars at the Country Roadhouse.

Sue added, "after the dance lessons starting Monday, we are going to end up with our own dance group and public dances at the clubhouse. I joined in, "look at Warren and Gail, they look like old hands despite being green beginners, heh!"

The evening was a classic but a modern Western dancing event. Halfway through the evening, Jim made an announcement, "In the past year, we have had an instructor that has been teaching the two-step and the waltz. Tonight we are having a two-step dance-off."

Jim welcomed everyone on the dance floor for two-stepping. "We have three judges circulating among you. If you get tapped on the shoulder, you have been eliminated." The dancing started and after three different songs, we were down to six finalist couples. Sue and I, Stan and Miranda, Gerry Rigger and Blondie Quickstep, Tru-Fak and Storming Sandra Gene, Trak Man and Manor Queen and an unknown that turned out to be the local dance instructor.

During the final dance, the three judges were conferring and systematically one judge would wander and eliminate one couple. They would meet again and another was eliminated. It finally came down to Sue and I against the lady instructor/husband couple. A full song was played and the four of us danced and gave a demo of all the moves and turns we knew. At the end of the dance the Whitehouses joined the judges and Amos announced the winners, "The winners of our first dance-off are, with a unanimous vote, Doc Derby and Ladyslipper."

After an exhausting day and pleasant evening, we went to our camper. With all competitions completed, there was no reason to preserve our energy reserves for tomorrow—so we decided to completely drain our batteries. . . . .!

Sunday morning we had a replenishing breakfast at the awards ceremony. After our third serving at the buffet style display, some of our friends were looking at us in amazement. Sue said, "If they only knew why we are so famished?" "I can spill the beans if you like" All I got from Sue was that look, the one I don't fare well with. Fortunately, Amos started the awards ceremony. "I would like to thank Winston Burns for the use of his electronic targets, and several WB clubs for their steel targets."

The WB status was based on total time to complete the course.

WOMEN'S MODERN CATEGORY:

1st place—Kat Star—40 seconds. Awarded the match trophy.
2nd place—Ladyslipper—42 seconds. Awarded a plaque.
3rd place—Eleanor Beecher—45 seconds. Awarded a plaque.
4th place—Blondie Quickstep—51 seconds. Awarded a certificate.

5th place–Tess Whitehouse–53 seconds. Awarded a certificate.
6th place–Storming Sandra Gene–54 seconds. Awarded a certificate.

MEN'S MODERN CATEGORY:

1st place–Stan Winslow–38 seconds–Awarded the match trophy.
2nd place–Sheriff Jack Cummings–40 seconds. Awarded a plaque.
3rd place–Wil Summer–47 seconds. Awarded a plaque.
4th place–Smoke-Meat–50 seconds. Awarded a certificate.
5th place–Charles Whitehouse–54 seconds. Awarded a certificate.
6th place–Tru-Fak–61 seconds. Awarded a certificate.

MEN'S TRADITIONAL CATEGORY.

Awards given for similar six categories.
A photo shoot followed, We took many shots to enlarge in the future.

COWBOY FAST DRAW

1st place–Wil Summer–0.32 seconds. Awarded the match trophhy.
2nd place–Winston Burns–0.33 seconds. Awarded a plaque.

3rd place–Stan Winslow–0.35 seconds. Awarded a plaque.

4th place–Jim Beecher–0.36 seconds. Awarded a certificate.

5th place–Trak-Man–0.38 seconds. Awarded a certificate.

6th place–Gerry Rigger–0.41 seconds. Awarded a certificate.

A photo shoot followed, and congratulations were extended.

With a great holiday coming to an end, we headed back to the camper. Sue mentioned, "well, I guess Mr. Arkansas did not show you hicks how to do fast draw, heh" I answered, "it never ceases to amaze me how some people's mouths just brings out their character faults."

We then hooked up the camper, said our thanks and goodbyes to our club members, the Beechers, the Whitehouses and Willard Stone. On route home, I said, "well Sue we are finally heading down hill. We need to research the next game, Cowboy Silhouettes, prepare a shooters meeting and or a club meeting." Sue adds, "and practice, me with the rifles and you with the pistols."

BOOK THREE

CHAPTER 14

SILHOUETTES, Training & Meeting

We got home late Sunday evening after traveling some 500 miles from the Bar W Ranch. Consequently, we got up late, made coffee, and just sat around listening to the news broadcast. We didn't have the energy to make breakfast, and I said, "guess we are getting old. Traveling 500 miles after spending three days at competition, is carrying its toll. Despite our worn out state, by noon we made a full brunch and started communicating."

I started, "well here we go, Cowboy Silhouettes will be the last game we will develop and train for. We will develop CLR but not participate or train for that game. Sue, you will naturally do well with free standing rifle shooting. You are fast and accurate, and will need most of your training for the long range targets at 150 and 200 yards. I won't even consider rifle silhouettes. I look forward to pistol silhouettes using my two Ruger Super Blackhawks." Sue adds, "I would never try Pistol

Silhouettes, the guns are too heavy with too much recoil for me."

"So let's divide the work. You do the research on the rifle portion and include a presentation for the club meeting as well as the shooter's meeting for the competition match. I will do the same for the pistol division. We can even farm out some portions of rules and other areas to RR, who has shown interest in this sport, because Gail will be training and performing in this game."

Sue asks, "as I am doing my research, what points should I cover at the club's meeting versus what I need to discuss at the shooter's meeting." "During the club meeting, you need to cover the guns, ammo, reloading and other gear, before the shooters go to Ed's Mercantile with their orders. RR will gladly cover targets and the sighting in process."

"At the shooter's meeting, you need to cover the operational methods for this competition–everything the shooters need to know once they get on the firing line. This involves which target for each rifle, how to address each array, and how to deal with misses. This also involves the house rules and specifics of this range."

We both did several hours of extensive research. We read many articles and watched every video available. Hour by hour, we were adding to our club presentation and shooter's meeting. We made copies or all our outlines for distribution. After two long days, we were ready.

———————●━━●━━●———————

RR welcomed the shooters. "Welcome to our first club meeting on this new game, Cowboy Silhouettes–Rifle or Pistol. This is a great sport that only requires two rifles or one pistol. Fortunately, many of the guns are already in use from other Cowboy games. Today we have 55 people in attendance and how they choose their category depends on this evening's presentations by Wil and Sue. So let's begin with Sue."

"This category requires two rifles. A lever action rifle in pistol caliber and a high velocity hunting rifle. The rifle characteristics for both rifles are":

1. Rear sights–open, tang, or receiver sights are OK.
2. Can use smokeless, black powder or black powder substitutes.
3. Lead cast bullets only. Coated lead bullets are OK.
4. No coaching, spotting scopes or binoculars during competition.
5. Shooting jackets, vests or shooting gloves are not allowed.

RR will now present some info on the targets. "All our targets are knockdown targets set to fall with a 200 grain bullet at 800 fps. Each array has 5 targets. The targets are

AR-500 steel and will ring like a church bell. The sizes are as follows:

RIFLE SHORT RANGE: PISTOL CALIBER
50 yards, Chickens, Black, 13X11"
100 yards, Pigs, Red, 22X14"
RIFLE LONG RANGE: HIGH VELOCITY CALIBER
150 yards, Turkeys, White, 19X23"
200 yards, Rams, Orange, 32X27"

"The reset of these knockdowns are powered and automated. By pressing the four buttons, the arrays will all reset without pulling cables or going downrange."

Sue took over, "now specifics of each rifle. For the short range targets, the rifle pistol calibers are usually 44 Mag or 45 Long Colt, but any caliber greater than 25 caliber can be used. If you use the 357 Magnum, use the 180 grain gas checked bullets at 1300 fps or greater, but do not use the Model 1873–the mechanism may not be strong enough to withstand this load, so use a Marlin 1894 CB. For those of you who reload the large bore calibers, keep your velocities under 1200 fps. to avoid barrel leading. There is no reason to have velocities over 1200 fps. for short range targets. Ed's Mercantile is carrying an inventory of Marlin 1894 CB for $1000–and a more economical Marlin version 1894C for $800."

For long range shooting, most shooters use one of their hunting rifles. The classic caliber is the popular

30-30, 32 Winchester Special or 35 Remington in lever action models. However and caliber greater than 6 mm is OK. This is a list of other characteristics for this gun at this range–house rules:

1. Maximum gun weight of 10 lbs.
2. Release triggers are not allowed.
3. Maximum barrel length is 30".
4. Belted magnums are not allowed.
5. Trigger pull must be 2 lbs. or greater.
6. Bolt actions are allowed with a magazine limited to 5 rounds.
7. If you reload, the maximum allowed velocity is 1600 fps. That means you need to use gas checks over 1200 fps. Fortunately, there are many bullet makers that provide these lead bullets with gas checks.
8. With short stroke kits, the lever must travel a minimum of 4 1/8"."

"RR will now present his ideas on sighting-in your rifle." "Competition day is not the time to sight in your rifle. With both range categories and the two different yardage of each, you need to know the POA and the POI of your rifle. The time to know these facts is now. That way, you can start practicing after the initial sighting, which is done on a fixed rifle rest and with a spotter on the spotting scope. For example, using the short range

45 Long Colt. The average 250 gr. bullet has a ballistic coefficient of +- 0.13. Using the short range trajectory tables in your reloading manual at 1000 fps., with a zero POI at 100 yards, the POI at 50 yards is 4 inches high. To summarize, if you are shooting at the 100 yard target, aim dead center. If you are shooting at the 50 yard, you better aim 4 inches low. This is the way to sight in your rifle— do not plan on changing the sight's elevation between yardage. It is not allowed according to our house rules."

"For another example let's take the 30-30. A 170 grain flat point bullet has a ballistic coefficient of +- .22. If loaded to 1500 fps. for long range shooting, with a POI of zero at 200 yards, the POI at 150 yards is 5 inches high. To again summarize, if you are shooting at 200 yards aim dead center, if you are shooting at 150 yards, you better aim 5 inches low."

"By sighting both rifles in this manner, you have to aim low at the near target and dead center at the far target. It is no more difficult or complicated than that." The shooters were very attentive and certainly appreciated RR's simple and basic method of sighting a rifle.

So come with a spotter, use the fixed targets at all 4 yardage. These targets are the same size as the official knockdowns. Once your rifle is sighted in, move over to the automated knockdowns and practice. Remember, if you show up at a match with unprepared rifles, you will not be allowed to participate."

Sue added, "I am certain you realize that a free standing shot at 200 yards is difficult to do. Maybe we will entertain this feat in the future, but for this coming first match, the 150 yard target will be free style, but the 200 yard shot will be off a standing railing." Loud applause ensued. Sue then hands me the microphone. "Before I begin my pistol silhouette presentation, are there any questions?" "Yes, The last two games, CFD and WB, have the potential of being competition sports between other clubs. With this current game, are there any plans for competing against other clubs or is this a local club sport?"

"First of all, Cowboy Silhouettes is a free standing game that will have its own shooting day. It is usually a club event, but we have three clubs within reach. One is in Kansas City, MO at 160 miles, and the others are in Fort Smith, AR and Wright City, MO both at 200 miles. If we have a yearly inter club event, we can send an invitation to all three clubs. If they attend, it would mean overnight housing. It also means that we, as a club can also attend their matches. For now, it is a local club game for us to enjoy."

"Moving on, pistol silhouettes is actually the fourth game we are starting. Although, it will be shot in the afternoon and the rifle silhouette will be shot in the morning.–same day. Like the rifle division, we will have a short range and a long range. The targets are:

25 yards–10X8–black–short range triangles

50 yards–15X10–red–short range clover leafs
75 yards–15X12–white–long range round targets
100 yards–22X14–orange–long range squares."

"Other points of interest include:

- We have our own range, #4 adjacent to to the rifle range
- Our firing line, like the rifles, is under a roof
- Our targets are colored to avoid shooting at the wrong array
- The typical calibers are 44 Magnum or 45 Long Colt
- If you are using one pistol for short and long range, an estimate when sighting your gun is to zero your pistol at 75 yards yards. A guide is to aim, the 25 yard target at the base, the 50 yard 1/3 up from the base, the 75 yard dead on, and the 100 yard target at the top. If you use two guns, sight your short range pistol dead on at 50 yards and adjust for the 25. The long range pistol is sighted dead on at 75 yards, and aim at the top of the target for the 100 yard. The advantage of two pistols is that a longer barrel is more accurate than a short barrel for the 100 yard shot.
- In pistol silhouettes, caffeine is your enemy.
- The typical calibers used are 44 Magnum or 45 Long Colt

- Since I use two pistols, I load the short range 240–250 grain bullets at 900 fps and the long range at just under 1200 fps–thereby avoiding gas checks. If you load one pistol, 1000 fps is a good compromise for 240–250 grain bullets
- You can use a 357 Magnum in this game, but I recommend you use a 180 grain gas checked bullet loaded to 1300–1400 fps. Just make sure your pistol can handle these pressures.
- Note that we have fixed targets on the side for sighting in
- Like the rifle range, the knockdown targets are automated
- The knockdown targets are set to fall with a 200 grain bullet at 800 fps with a center hit.

"You have ten days to practice. Willard Stone is providing a digital chronograph with an operator for the next 10 days between 8–11AM and 6–9PM. This is a great opportunity to set your loads to your desired velocity for all guns. This feature is available to all club members.

"Before we close the meeting, are there any questions?" "Yes, what is a usable operational method to shoot the knockdowns when there is a large group of shooters wanting to practice?" "We suggest that two shooters address two arrays for 10 shots each–one at the short range and the other at the long range, and then they move off the firing line. The next two shooters do the same thing. Also, don't forget that if there is no one on the fixed sighting-in targets, you can use this range for practicing, since all targets are the corresponding size at different yardage. During practice days, you have to pick up your brass."

"Next question." "Are the match operational methods the same as these three other clubs?" "No, I have contacted all three club range masters, and found out that only one club follows national standards. The other two have set up their own house rules, targets and operational methods. At their recommendation, we decided to use a combination of these two club's methods for our range."

With no other questions, see you on the range for the next 10 practice days. Our first match is next week on Saturday. Registration starts at 7 AM at the new clubhouse.

That evening we loaded ammo for several practice days.

Rifle short range, 45 Long Colt–250 grain bullet at 900 fps.
Rifle long range, 30-30–170 grain gas checked bullet at 1400 fps.
Pistol short range, 44 Mag short barrel–240 grain bullet at 900 fps.

Pistol long range, 44 Mag long barrel–240 grain bullet at 1150 fps.

The next morning, we were first at the chronograph station. We were happy to verify that our reloads were all in the chosen velocity ranges. We then moved to the sighting range for rifles. Sue was the shooter and I was the spotter on the spotting scope. She sighted her 45 Long Colt dead on at 100 yards and had to shoot 4 inches low at 50 yards. The 30-30 rifle was zeroed at 200 yards, and had to aim 5 inches low for the 150 yard target, since the POI was 5 inches high.

I then sighted my pistols with Sue on the spotting scope. The rear sights had been changed to a one hole Warren Custom peep sight. The 9/32 peep was placed on the short barrel Ruger and the 7/32 peep placed on the long barrel Ruger. The front sights were painted with Sight Brite–a florescent orange. The short barrel Ruger was zeroed at 50 yards, and had to shoot below center at 25 yards. The 7 ½ inch Ruger was zeroed at 75 yards and a high aim at 100 yards was a center hit.

After one hour, our guns were sighted-in on solid rifle and pistol rests. It was time to get off the bench to start shooting free style.

We went to our respective ranges and joined the lines. We shot for one hour and then took a break. Muscle fatigue was a real problem from extended shooting times. The routine of shooting 10 rounds and then stepping off the firing line to rejoin the waiting line, should have prevented muscle fatigue, but it did not. All the shooters quickly realized that breaks were needed, and gathering at the clubhouse became a welcomed routine.

The next morning, we saw RR and Gail at one sighting bench and Stan and Miranda at the other sighting bench. The boys were spotting for the ladies and within an hour the girls were heading to the knock-down range. As they were leaving, a single red headed lady showed up to sight in her rifles. Sue recognized her from CAS as Karut-Hed. I said, "now I have seen many redheads, but a carrot color is real striking isn't it?" Since she did not have a spotter, I volunteered. Her sighting in process was quick and she moved to the knockdowns.

Sue watched Karut-Hed shoot the rifle at both the short and long range. She looked at me and said, "Oh great, looks like I have my work cut out like I did with Kat Star in WB! That gal can shoot fast and accurately." We then joined the shooters and practiced on and off all morning—Sue on the rifle range, and me on the pistol range.

At lunch time, Sue was pensive and eventually said, "If I don't win this competition, I will likely get the nickname 'Miss 2nd Place.'" That is when I said, "In competition, any shooter vies for placing." "What do you mean by placing?" "To take, 1st, 2nd, or 3rd place. It's not a dishonor to place second or third. Remember that life as a 1st place winner means that there is always someone ready to replace you, and that is usually the second place winner. No one can keep a throne in competitive sports, since there is always someone able and ready to throw you off your pedestal." "I agree with you, but I saw you take first place at our CFD match and at the Bar W Ranch, and I want to experience that feeling someday." "Trust me, you will eventually."

After lunch, Jack arrived and we went to the pistol range. We teamed up. Jack did the long range and I did the short range on the first round. The next round we alternated. Jack also had two pistol like I did. It was clear that Jack had been practicing–he was fast and accurate. I said, "we are about equal in marksmanship and speed. It is going to be close match, heh." Jack then surprises me by saying, "I have been practicing in the evenings with Stan. Let me say, we have problems.

Stan is way ahead of me, and if he continues practicing, he's going to take this match." I said, "he's been a frequent 2nd place winner and it is simply a matter of time before he takes over."

During the next break, I walked over to the rifle range to see how Sue was doing. The first shooters I saw was the team–Gail and Miranda. I was amazed at the progress these two beginners had achieved. While the boys were at work, these gals were at the range, practicing all day. Sue was also doing very well, I saw her shoot the short range arrays with no misses and the long range arrays with two misses at the 200 yard shot on a railing.

Standing there I got cornered by several shooters. They wanted to know my technique for loading the 30-30. I answered, "I use the two stage system outlined in 'Reloading–A Practical Hobby, by Richard M Beloin MD.' I lube the cases with Hot Shot and then size and decap each case on a single stage Rock Chucker press. Then I remove the sizing die off my Dillon XL–650 progressive press and finish the loading to include adding powder, case belling, seating and crimping. This is a personal approach that works for us, since the difficult sizing step is best done by us on a strong single stage press. Some reloaders perform all functions on their progressive press. Try it each way, and you will quickly decide what works for you."

We finished the day with 100 % accuracy at our respective short ranges, but we both were having trouble with our long range targets, We were both hitting 2-3 out of 5–and that was still unacceptable. Just as we were preparing to leave, the evening working group of shooters were arriving. Sue alerted me to a problem. One shooter pulled out a 300 Win Mag rifle with factory loads of 180 grain jacketed bullets.

I said, "sir, you cannot shoot that rifle with jacketed bullets at our targets. This is a low velocity lead bullet range only." "Oh come on, why is that?" "Because that bullet will place a ding in the steel." "So what?" "Because a ding in the steel will cause lead bullets to bounce back intact at the shooters instead of splattering on impact." "I don't care." "Well you had better care, because one ding and it will cost you $100 per shot per target." "Well I still don't care and I am not paying."

"Very well, go ahead and fire away, and when you place a loaded magazine in the rifle, I will call 911. I will request the sheriff's assistance. You will likely get arrested, fined and then will be banned from this range for life." As the shooter started to give me the aggressive and evil eye, several of the shooters came to my support. One big and burly man, the type that looks like he sprinkles nails over his Cheerios, came to my side. He added, "when our leader calls 911, we will put you down and tie you up into a neat package for the sheriff."

The arrogant smart ass picked up his gear and left the firing line. Sue followed him to his car and came back with his auto tag number. I said, "we need to inform RR of Mr. X's behavior and give him the auto tag number."

Just before leaving for the day, a shooter came off the line and we heard him say, "that is it for me." I asked him what he meant and he said, "I just got laid off and supporting the family with a wife and two kids on unemployment makes it difficult to buy ammo and pay for competition fees." I asked him to follow me to the clubhouse. "Your name is?" "Roger Cramer." I filled out two papers and said, "give this voucher to Ed at his mercantile and he will give you 700 45 Long Colt and 300 30-30 ammo. Then present this second voucher at registration, It is valid for the next 5 registration fees and

5 free lunches. In addition, I will speak to RR and you will be offered a range job, to help compensate your income beyond unemployment benefits." The man looked at me and could not speak. I quickly said, "you're welcome and enjoy your sport."

That evening, Friday, we made plans for the weekend. I said, "the weekend will have a flood of shooters at the range. What do you say we go to our new camp, set up some targets and practice our long range pistol and rifle silhouettes?" "That sounds great, what do we use for targets?" "Fear not, already provided for." "Then lets pick up food for the two days, our four guns and ammo, and let's go tonight!"

Within an hour, we were on the road. A 50 mile trip was a short jaunt to another world. As we arrived and I pulled into the driveway, Sue punches me in the shoulder. "I figured, 'fear not, already provided for,' how did you achieve this?" "I called the target company and had eight correct size targets delivered to RR'S home. I then hired three of the range workers to arrange for a sand berm at 125 and 225 yards. Afterwards, the workers took the size specific targets/steel posts and laid them out according to the map I provided them. I can tell you that the targets are regulation size and are at the proper yardage. l also had them build a roofed area, with a table and sitting bench–including a standing shooting railing." "Well, I guess you deserve a special thank you, heh?" "Later, now I want that rack of ribs on the grill"

After dinner, we walked the range to inspect the installation. Afterwards, we practiced for an hour before dusk. The remainder of the evening was peaceful while reading and sitting by our fireplace. Sue interrupted the silence and said, "time for us to initiate this cabin, and check off the special thank you I owe you - - - - - - -."

The next morning, after a replenishing breakfast, Sue comes out with a wrapped item. I unwrapped it and found a sand blasted painting of the camp, including the mountain behind our camp. The title of this painting was, Camp Therapy. I looked at Sue and did not speak, words were not necessary. Sue said, "Happy Birthday, my loving 62 years old husband."

We went to the range and banged away all morning. The roofed firing line was certainly appreciated because of a soft rain for an hour before the sun came out. With many breaks, we shot to our hearts content. By 4PM we quit, showered and headed to the Country Roadhouse for dancing. Ironically, the club was 5 miles away from our home on the same road to the camp. So we had a +- 45 mile trip to the dance club from our camp.

The evening was another great dancing event. During intermissions, we visited with friends and club shooters. All the shooters were pleased with the club developments and changes. It was Miranda who said, "and we know what you did for Roger Cramer. That was a nice touch, but more importantly, a sign of commitment above and beyond!"

As the evening progressed, the DJ announced that phase one of the two-step lessons starts Monday evening at 6 and 8PM as scheduled.

The next day, we again spent at shooting on and off till noon. We had finally improved our long range accuracy. We could usually hit the target some 80% of the time. The short range targets were usually 100% hits. We finally closed up camp and headed home.

On our way home, Sue commented, "We have three evenings of dance lessons plus a general dance the fourth night. We have five days off before our competition. How would you like to plan our day's activities?" "I think we still should shoot in the mornings. Monday afternoon we do our shopping, run errands and do house work to clear the slate for the remainder of the week. Tuesday, Wednesday and Thursday afternoons, we should spend with dancers who were having trouble the previous evening–like when we needed to offer special training to some CFD shooters. Plus we will have to find some time to reload. If we do all this, we will have Friday as a free day before the competition on Saturday." "Sounds fine with me–let's move on."

CHAPTER 15

SILHOUETTES, Dancing Lessons and Competition Match

Monday morning we were late getting to the range. During my first break, several shooters wanted to know how to correct a pistol shooting to the left when using fixed sights. We had several Cowboy shooters using their Cowboy pistols with fixed sights for pistol silhouettes. It was not a problem at the short range but at 75 and 100 yards it was an issue. Most shooters had to shoot to the right side of the target to get a center to left side hit on the target. I answered, "if you are not comfortable with 'Kentucky windage adjustment,' you need to bring your gun to a gunsmith."

"He will place the pistol frame in a vice and be able to tighten or loosen the barrel in the frame. A pistol that hits to the left can have its barrel tightened, forcing the sight to lean to the left. This will result with the POI moving to the right. Once the barrel is turned, the POI will hold true only for that load. You need to decide if this pistol is used in other games before you take this step, or use this same load in other games."

"Both my silhouette pistols have adjustable rear sights for elevation and windage. So I don't experience this dilemma. I have adjusted the rear sight so that my POA matches my POI for both guns."

We practiced all morning and by afternoon, we went home to catch up on household duties and errands. This cleared our slate and allowed us to be available for shooting and dancing lessons.

We arrived at the Country Roadhouse at 4:30PM for dinner. That gave us plenty of time before the 6PM class. We started the lesson on time. "Welcome to all eight couples. We are going to make you two-step dancers by 8PM. We are going to show you how to dance in a counterclockwise direction along the dance floor perimeter. We will teach the man to dance forward(drive) as the lady dances backwards(passenger). Then we will reverse the process and have the man dance backwards and the lady dance forward. This will include the technique for changing direction and resuming direction. We will also show you how to make a 90 degree corner turn and we will show you the basic inside/outside lady's turn. Incidentally, it is customary for the man to drive forward 60% of the time–and that is beginner two-step."

Sue adds, "at the end of the lesson, we will be offering a private lesson tomorrow afternoon, at our home, for anyone we feel needs extra help. I you feel you are in this category, please tell us. Remember, it's not a shame to need extra help, we all learn differently. We hope that these extra lessons will keep undecided dancers from dropping out."

The lesson started, the eight men were shown the four basic steps–quick, quick, slow, slow, in forward motion. The ladies were shown the same steps but in reverse. Each individual was going around the dance floor, humming the QQSS phrase. Then the couples united in proper form and all eight couples were going around the dance floor humming that QQSS phrase. Sue almost lost it, she had to turn around to hide her smile and silent laughter.

We then showed them how to reverse direction and how to resume. I would call out the order and the teams followed–reverse, resume, reverse, resume etc. When the students had to reverse/resume on their own, is when we saw a problem–some men just couldn't pull the trigger to reverse or to resume. Despite this we put the music on and we could see the light bulbs go on in at least six of the eight couples.

During a short break, I said, "it's up to the man to decide to reverse or resume. Learn to pull the trigger, don't wait for your partner to say, 'well dear, are you going to drive all night, my hips are killing me.'"

After the break, we showed them how to perform a gradual turn at the end of the dance floor, or to perform a 90 degree turn. The last thing we showed them was the lady's inside/outside turn. We then played the music and watched them perform. Again we had two problem couples.

We took another break and decided to talk to these two couples. The first was really having trouble pulling the trigger, and the other was just unsure of themselves. They were both happy to meet tomorrow for the extra help. We then finished the lesson by varying the speed of three dances, medium, lively and fast. All eight couples could handle the first two, but the problem two couples could not handle the fast dance.

At the end of the lesson I encouraged them to practice every day till our Thursday dance. Sue whispered to me, "six couples are ready for Thursday night and we will salvage the other two tomorrow."

The next class had arrived for the 8PM slot. The 1st class wanted to stay and watch the 2nd class. I said, "NO, all beginners have the right to be instructed without the stress of observers. We are all too self conscious to tolerate this. So go home, practice and see you Thursday evening at the beginner's dance."

The second class stepped up. Jack was in this group. He came to me and said, "I have never really danced, but this is important to Kat and so I will do my best." The lesson began with the same format. This group had six natural dancers and two scarecrows–Jack and another elderly couple. The latter two were offered a private lesson tomorrow afternoon and both gladly accepted. Otherwise as the lesson finished, we again knew we gained another six couples, and two more would likely join after their private lesson.

As they were leaving, one lady asked a question. "Who is the lead person and who does the work?" I answered, "the man is the lead and that is why he drives 60% of the time. The man decides when to reverse and when to resume the line of dance. He also decides when it is time to trigger the lady to do an inside turn or an outside turn. With the next lesson, you will learn many new turns, all of which are instigated by the man, But the lady does the turns and she is the one that gets all the credit with advanced moves. So yes, the man leads, but you ladies do all the work and only you ladies look good on the dance floor, no one appreciates what the man does." *Applause followed with smiles.*

Tuesday morning was another practice at the range. We were home by noon for a quick lunch. Our first students arrived just before 1PM. It was the unsure couple. They performed for us and we said, "you have been practicing, yes." "Yes we did last night and this morning."

Well you look great, so dance to a few songs and we will add pointers if necessary. That couple left, proud as a peacock.

The next couple had the man who could not pull the trigger. We trained his wife to tap his shoulder at the end of a QQSS which is when one performs an event—that is on the quick, quick. It worked. We then had her do the same shoulder tap to resume line of dance. They were very capable dancers with nice rhythm otherwise. Sue explained, "eventually your husband will no longer need the shoulder tap and will become the true lead." They also went home very satisfied.

The third lesson was for the couple that danced like scarecrows. Both man and woman danced standing straight without, joint flexibility, body rhythmic gyrations or facial expressions–they were doing the steps without musicality. I said to Sue, "dance with the man and I'll dance with the lady. With a song heavy on rhythm, we danced. I was adding directions, "bend your knees slightly to add a bit of bounce to your steps, show me some body gyrations, follow the song's beat and add a smile. This is not a punishment, dancing is a pleasure and an accompaniment to the song at hand. After several songs, they were finally showing signs of understanding the art of dancing with musicality. We told them that they needed to practice and would be ready for Thursday.

The last lesson was Jack and Kat. When they arrived we had them dance to a medium two-step as we watched. Halfway through the dance, we knew what the problem was. At the end of the dance, I said, "it is very clear to us. Kat you are leading, and Jack you are following. That will not work and we need to reverse the roles." I started dancing with Kat. She tried to drag me into reversing and

I resisted. "We will reverse when I am ready. The same thing happened when trying to resume the line of dance. Kat took off on her own and resumed the line of dance. The next time she did this, I held her in place and her face showed an element of surprise. I said, "you resume when you feel me push my hand on your back." Kat was doing the inside/outside turn whenever she felt like it. I stopped her again. After two full dances, Kat had gotten the picture.

I asked Sue how things were going with Jack. "Come to find out, Jack knows all the steps and moves. When I danced in a passive role, Jack was free to instigate all the moves. He was actually a rhythmic and smooth dancer. If Kat is ready to follow, the problem is resolved." We resumed the dancing, and Jack and Kat looked great as a dancing couple.

When they finished their lesson, Kat came to us with an apology. She said, "since my divorce I have become a dominatrix out of necessity. Being in a relationship is changing all that, and today's experience is a perfect example of proper role playing–thank you for your guidance."

The remainder of the week was smooth sailing. We practiced in the morning and taught dancing in the evening. One evening we had a couple that went out of step whenever the man tried to reverse. I asked the lady to dance with me. As I went to reverse the line of dance, I saw the problem. Her right foot was in the way, so I kicked it out of the way to go into reverse. We then stopped and the lady said, "why did you kick my foot?" "Because it was in the way and would likely trip me. You have to get your right foot out of the way when the man starts reversing." The problem got resolved without a private lesson.

One lesson exposed us to two uncontrollable situations. One man simply appeared unable to perform the QQSS basic step. I took the man aside and said, "sir, you are faking, anyone who is not comatose, can perform this simple task. If you don't want to do this, don't humiliate your wife any further, and walk out or get with the program." As the next dance started, we saw this couple walk out.

The second insurmountable and rare situation was when a dance partner could not hear or pick up the beat of a song—he was no better than deaf. Sue and I watched him demonstrate the beat of a song by hand motion and his beat did not belong on this planet. I said, "this is a difficult situation. We can show you the beat for this first song and you may be able to follow. However the next song will have a different beat and you will be lost, get out of step and confuse the other dancers. Sorry, but it is not going to work out."

That evening we generated no private lessons. Seeing a free Wednesday and Thursday afternoon, we e-mailed all 46 registered students, and informed them that we were opening both afternoons to all dancers. Anyone with minor problems, questions or just simply wanted to dance in our presence, were invited to come at any time.

Wednesday afternoon turned out to be a dancing party. At all times we had at least four couples on the floor. Even with the Wednesday evening last dance lessons, no one needed private time. Yet on Thursday afternoon the garage was packed with beginner dancers. We knew the enthusiasm was real when even the working class took the afternoon off to come and practice in our garge. It was so packed that afternoon that we had to use both garages and push equipment outside for the afternoon.

The Thursday Beginners Dance started at 7PM. Most of our students arrived early for a light dinner, They had all been warned, "you cannot dance on a heavy meal or too much alcohol." All our students arrived in western attire with a minimum of Cowboy hat, boots and jeans. The DJ started the event and invited Sue and I to the dance floor for the evening's first dance. We started dancing and performed the same moves we had taught—nothing fancy for now. Halfway through the song, the DJ invited all beginners to the floor. The floor flooded with bodies, and there wasn't room to spare, even with the massive Country Roadhouse dance floor.

The evening was certainly a success. All our students looked great on the floor. Halfway through the evening, the DJ invited Sue and I to the floor to demonstrate the set of turns we would teach starting next Monday evening. We danced and demonstrated, the sweetheart turn, the promenade, the pull through, around the man with a whip and under the arch. *The dance finished with a resounding applause.*

Three songs later, the DJ again invited Sue and I to the floor. He said, "you will also be taught the second most popular country dance in this club–the country waltz. The music started to Kenny Roger's "Someone must feel like a Fool". We demonstrated the basic waltz and even enhanced it with a few basic turns. When the demonstration was done, there was total silence in the club. The DJ finally said, "well folks, what do you think?" *The place exploded with shouts, whistles and applause.* The DJ added, "looks like it will be a keeper, heh."

As the evening was coming to an end, we reminded everyone that the phase two lessons would follow the same schedule as phase one. Departing greetings were extended and we received a special thanks from Jack and Kat. That meant a lot to Sue who was finally warming up to her.

Friday was our day of rest. We got up late, but by 11AM we started to put up our gear for Saturday's competition. By lunch, we prepared a cold lunch and headed to the clubhouse. We were there for the comradery and the gun talk discussions–our hobby.

The subject for discussion today was started by a shooter. "It is clear that with these five shooting games, we are all needing more ammo. Unfortunately, it is expensive to buy a progressive reloader with all the accessories needed. The old method of buying loaded ammo is getting too expensive to sustain these shooting games."

Another shooter said, "what is the solution?" "One suggestion is to provide a reloading press, like you all did with loading wax bullets for CFD." I joined the discussion, "that means we would need three Dillon XL-650 progressive presses to reload for 45 ACP, 45 Long Colt, and 44 Mag. The 30-30 and 45-70 for CRS and CLR could be loaded on a Hornady single stage press with bushings. That way each caliber would have a preset loader. This can be expensive for the club, if the insurance carrier even allows it. This may be possible but I need to bring this to RR first, and later to Willard Stone at our next meeting."

That evening Sue started to give me "signs and hints" before bedtime. I said, "remember our discussion on preserving our energy the night before a competition." Sue gave me that look–the one I don't fare well with, and said, "I am not a football player, I am an aging woman. My motor needs regular oiling before it seizes permanently. So we had better do well at the games tomorrow, or the guns go on the back burner for a while, heh!"

Saturday finally arrived. Registration started at 7AM. Each shooter paid $10 and took a random number—Sue got #10 out of 30 for Rifle and I was assigned #4 out of 20 for Pistol. By 8:30AM the shooters meeting started with the Pledge Allegiance to the Flag. RR announced, "a free dinner/dance this evening at the clubhouse. Rifle Silhouettes will be this morning, Pistol Silhouettes will be this afternoon, and the awards ceremony at 4PM." Then he said, "Silhouette shooting is not a volume shooting sport. It involves precision shooting at a healthy pace. It is a timed event and misses are added to your time. All targets are engaged once only—a miss is not reengaged. We are planning to send each shooter to the firing line twice for a total of 40 rounds. He then handed the microphone to Sue.

"I will now present the operational method for Rifle Silhouettes:"

1. "On the buzzer, you shoot, free style, your pistol caliber rifle a total of ten rounds. Five at the 50 yard and five at the 100 yard targets. The scorekeeper records your time, misses and procedurals."

2. "While still on the firing line, on the buzzer you shoot, free style, five rounds with your hunting rifle at the 150 yard target. Your total time is again recorded."

3. "After reloading five rounds, on the buzzer, you shoot five rounds off the railing at the 200 yard targets. Your total time is again recorded.

Note: your times will be added to your second round at the firing line, and are recorded without a public announcement–to be revealed at the awards ceremony. Each shooter may look at his/her own scorecard."

Sue hands me the microphone. "The operational method for Pistol Silhouettes is similar to Rifle. Every 5 shot rounds start on the buzzer, is free style and ends on the 5th shot. Each five shot round is assigned a time and given to the scorekeeper. Each shooter may look at his/her own scorecard. Just remember that pistol shooting is a challenge, is difficult to attain speed, misses are common, and it's impossible to make up for a 5 second miss by speeding up–speed promotes more misses."

The competition started and was moving along rather smoothly. We were done with the first round for all 30 rifle shooters by 10:30AM. The results by my stop watch and quick math gave me a estimated score for the top 5 shooters in seconds.

Karut-Hed 41, Sue 45, Kat 49, Gail 62, Miranda 68.

My observation during this match was that everyone seemed to enjoy the organized shooting, and everyone seemed interested in watching the performance of their competitors. There were several very interested spectators–most were the shooter's friends or family. The second and final round was similar to the first round. I did not attempt to keep score. I was enjoying just watching the event, and noted that the top shooters times again appeared to be close.

The Pistol Silhouettes started after lunch. I was shooter #4 and so would not get to watch the other shooters. I knew I had to watch out for Jack and Stan. The problem was that I had not seen too many hotshot competitors during the day practices. I assumed that the hotshots were practicing in the evening as Jack had suggested.

When my turn came up, I arrived at the firing line with both my guns loaded with 5 rounds. On the buzzer, I made quick work of the five 25 yard targets. Got a clean quick time, reloaded and on the buzzer I again shot clean at the 50 yard targets–just a bit slower. Changing guns, on the buzzer, I took aim at 75 yard targets, slowed down and knocked all five down. The scorekeeper recorded my time. After reloading, on the buzzer, I took very careful aim at the 100 yard targets, and started knocking them down. I missed one and I knew my time was slow as expected. I never looked at my score card, I was happy with my performance. Sue showed me her estimated times in seconds.

Me 80, Stan 85, Jack 90, #1 Hotshot 95, #2 Hotshot 99.

The second and final round quickly followed and we were done by 4PM. Sue had watched the second round without using her stopwatch. On our way to the awards ceremony, I admitted, "I never worked so hard at a competition as I did today." "I agree, plus I had to witness that lightning Karut–Hed blow past me–how discouraging." "No Sue, she's just another challenge that you will eventually overcome."

RR conducted the award's ceremony. He started the event by saying, "several observers saw much enthusiasm among spectators, many of which are CAS members. I suspect we will have a higher attendance on our next shoot. I seems that every one liked the painted targets and the choice of guns. If that is the case, Silhouettes would become a two day event–one for rifle and one for pistol. Time will tell."

"It was a great match today and I am proud to hand out the awards.
Rifle Silhouettes–total times of both rounds:

5th place, Miranda 121 seconds–a certificate. *applause*
4th place, Gail 115 seconds–a certificate. *applause*
3rd place, Kat 98 seconds–a certificate. *applause*
2nd place, Sue 94 seconds–a plaque. *applause*
1st place and match winner, Karut-Hed, 83 seconds–a trophy." *applause*

Pistol Silhouettes–total times of both rounds. Keep in mind that this game is much slower because of the longer times to attain a sight picture.

5th place, Roger S.(#2 Hotshot) 201 seconds–a certificate. *applause*

4th place, Noah B.(#1 Hotshot) 192 seconds–a certificate. *applause*

3rd place, Jack 180 seconds–a certificate. *applause*

2nd place, Stan 168 seconds–a plaque. *applause*

1st place and match winner, Wil 160 seconds–a trophy. *applause*

Sue steps up and congratulates Karut-Hed. Gail and Miranda were boiling over with their placing. RR was proud of his "non-gun" wife. RR closes the event with a reminder–"tonight we are having a free dance and dinner with liquid refreshments. This is a great opportunity for the two-step beginners to join our new hobby–Country Dancing!" Mr Stone, our benefactor, will be here to greet all of you. The dress code is jeans, western shirt, Cowboy hat and boots."

The shooters, dancers and their guests were arriving by 6PM. Willard Stone was wearing a high end western attire with Cowboy hat and boots. He greeted everyone. The 200 guests filled all the tables. The hall was set up with new round tables. The match winners were seated at the head table with Mr. Stone, RR and Gail. As we were seated, Sue said with a smile, "here I go again, Miss 2nd place sitting with Mr. 1st place again, heh!" *For the first*

time, I gave her that look—the one that would not fare well with me—with a smile.

'The dinner was country style and catered. Pork roast, baked potato and carrots. The tables were served by random drawing of table numbers. Dessert was custard pudding. After dinner, Mr. Stone gave a small speech. He said, "look around, the place is packed. I have decided that we will extend this clubhouse by 50% and we will start next week. It is clear that we need more room. People are taking dance lessons and we will be hosting shooting events that will attract other clubs. *The attendees were shaking their heads in disbelief and applauding to express their thanks and support.*

The dance began and all the students were up enjoying the dancing festivities. They filled the dance floor and it was clear, we needed a bigger hall. It was a pleasant evening.

During an intermission, RR brought up the subject of club sponsored reloading equipment. Willard held up his hands, "my spies have already informed me of that discussion. I have checked with our insurance carrier. Their engineer and risk management personnel have ruled that it is a low liability addition, and they have approved it. When we build the clubhouse addition we will also include an end-enclosed room, with a double wall separating it from the clubhouse—all per the insurance carrier's specs. I am told that you would need three Dillon XL-650 presses, one Hornady single stage press with bushings, and the miscellaneous accessories–tools of the trade.

Would a budget of $4,500 cover the equipment?" RR sheepishly said, "of course. You told us weeks ago that we could have whatever else we needed to make these games a reality. I hope we are not overextending our privilege." Willard said, "not at all, all your requests have been right on the mark." RR came back with, "and by the way, I am now on the hunt, I will find out who your spies are, with a smile." Mr. Stone also acknowledged with laughter.

On our way home Sue says, "you were correct in preserving our energy for this Silhouette competition plus an entire evening of dancing. I guess our guns won't have to go to the back burner, heh." When we got home, Sue started undressing in the living room, through the kitchen and finally standing naked with hands akimbo in the bedroom door. "Well, my motor needs servicing." I responded, "synthetic or natural oil. . . . .!"

CHAPTER 16

CLR, INTRODUCTION/MEETING

The next morning, after a replenishing breakfast, I said, "what are we going to do about long range shooting(CLR)–the last new game on Mr. Stone's wish list?" Sue says, "We promised RR and Mr. Stone that we would do the research, prepare a club and shooter's meeting and organize the game till match day." "Yes, but you and I agreed that we would not train or participate in this shooting game."

"That doesn't change the fact that we have to be the range masters for the first competition. Thereafter, the new RM will take over this shooting game. We'll be left the other four games to manage for the remainder of this season, and likely all next season as well!" "Ok, let's begin our research."

After two days of reading several articles, watching videos and visiting different club's web sites, we started organizing our materials into handouts–for the club meeting and the shooter's meeting.

"Welcome to the first CLR meeting, we have 44 shooters in attendance and we hope to convince all of you to join this game. CLR is not a standardized shooting sport. It varies from club to club and is usually organized to match the available distance for the furthest shot. This is general information regarding the sport:

- Your matches will occur on their own scheduled date.
- Scoring is based on the number of hits in an allotted time.
- All our targets are shot off a railing while sitting on a bench.
- Expected requirements include a decent modern rifle, the best sight you can afford, consistent ammo, shooting skills and patience–this is not a moving and active sport."

"We have set up fixed white targets at five different locations:

100 yards for sighting in and free style shooting–26X32" (W X H)
200 yards–26X32" for Marlin 1895 lever action(same as 100 yards)
300 yards–34X50" for H&R 1871, 1885 single shot or Marlin 1895 lever
400 yards–38X60" for 1885 Highwall single shot
500 yards–48X72" for 1874 Sharps or Rolling Block"

"Since this sport is based on the tools of the trade, let's begin with the guns. I had a long meeting with Ed at his mercantile regarding the needs of long range shooters. The guns I will present are from Taylors, Cimarron, and Marlin which is where Ed gets his best discounts. Before you purchase a gun, let's agree on the caliber to maintain a level playing field–this is a 45-70 caliber as the game's standard. Of course, other caliber will be accepted but smaller calibers may be a problem as we will discuss later. In addition we are a smokeless powder club, but if you wish to use black powder, it's OK.

Marlin 1895 in 45-70.

- "Ideal for 300 gr. GC bullet at 1300–1500 fps. (200 or 300 yds).
- 26 inch octagon barrel with a weight of 7 pounds.
- The stock has a straight grip.
- Priced at +- $800.
- Tang sights with elevation and windage by Marbles are good to 350 yards and sell for $125. An alternative is the Smith Ladder Sight which I will discuss later. Just keep this one in mind."

H & R 1871 Buffalo Classic in 45-70.

- "This is a break-open single shot that is a great gun to 300 yards with simple open sights. It is now out of production but easily available on Gunbroker.com.

It usually sells for +- $500. By adding a Smith Ladder Sight, it is good to 400 yards. Remember, you are buying a used gun, as much as they are known to be accurate, you are purchasing a pig in a poke."

1885 Highwall in 45-70 by Uberti(Taylors).

- "This is a fast reloading and very accurate rifle for 400 yards.
- It comes with a 30 inch round barrel and a straight grip.
- It generally weighs +- 9 pounds. with a case hardened receiver.
- Needs a vernier sight (see below).
- Priced at +- $1100."

1874 Sharps in 45-70 by Pedersoli(Taylors).

- "This is the classic buffalo rifle used during the harvest.
- It has double set triggers, weighs +- 10 pounds and has a 30 inch barrel.
- It comes with a quality vernier sight.
- Priced at =- $1500."

Rolling Block in 45-70 by Pedersoli(Taylors) or Cimarron.

- "Choice of 30–36 inch octagon barrel.
- Case hardened frame.
- Weighs +- 11 pounds.

- Checkered pistol grip.
- Double set triggers with silver fore-end tip.
- Priced at +- $1800. Plus also needs a vernier sight."

Note–shooting beyond 350 yards really requires a vernier sight."

Regarding vernier sights, this is Ed's recommendation. You don't need a long range vernier sight to 600–1000 yards at this range. What you need is a mid range sight to 600 yards. He suggests:

A–Pedersoli Soule type. Mid range with 3 inch of height for elevation changes to 600 yards for +- $300.
B–For a more economical mid range sight, he suggests the Pedersoli Creedmore sight also up to 600 yards for $200.
C–For those with poor vision, add a Hadley cup with varying size eyepieces to accommodate different lighting conditions.

From the audience a question was asked, "can you explain how a vernier sight works?" "Yes, after the meeting I will gladly explain the mathematical and practical applications of the vernier sight, and I will also include the Smith Ladder Sight."

"Now let's talk about consistent ammo–the key to accuracy in long range shooting. I am convinced that you cannot effectively compete with varying brands of factory ammo. Store availability may force you to change brands. Each manufacturer's brand has different powders and other variables to affect your POI. Therefore, reloads is the only way to maintain consistency."

"Assuming that you are using the same cases and primers, the only real variable is the powder. With this sport, the 45-70 405 grain bullet is loaded to 1300 fps. and the popular powders used are either H-4198 or A-5744. The 405 grain bullet is usually not gas checked, but the 300 grain is fired at 1300–1600 fps and needs a gas check to prevent barrel leading. Of note, 1300 fps. is the old black powder 45-70 load of 70 grains of powder by volume(not weight). So if you have a powder load that is accurate at 100 yards with two inch groups, then use it to work up to 200 yards and beyond."

"With no questions let's move on to sighting. Like silhouettes, it is up to you to know the sight settings to move from one target to another. During my discussion on sights I will give you estimated changes to help you get a hit at different yardage. The key to this sighting method is a good spotter who can shorten the sighting process. Remember, don't come to the match with unsighted firearms."

"Now let's discuss some rules of the game:

- Guns are period correct between 1860 and 1899.
- Rear sights can be open, ladder, peep/tang sights or verniers. Tang/peep sights must be mounted on the rifle's metal tang, not mounted on wood.
- Front sights can be blade or hooded inserts with or without a spirit level.
- Fiberoptic or painted sights are not allowed.
- Wind gauges. The club with maintain a wind gauge and sock. You may use these findings for estimating wind velocity and direction.
- During competition, the club will maintain three RO's on spotting scopes.
- Hits are confirmed by the audible ding of the bullet on AR-500 steel. If no ding is heard, a hit can be confirmed visually by at least two of the three spotters. This is the major reason for using the 45-70 bullets. The lighter bullets don't produce a loud enough ding, and you may end up with more misses because of lacking confirmation. A miss location will be given to the shooter if seen, but a hit location will not be given to the shooter. It is what it is."

That does it for the information portion. Sue and I have agreed to manage CFD, WB and Silhouettes next season. However, we need a manager, for this long range game, for next season. Although we are not accepting pay, all new managers will be paid $20/hour in the future. The number of working hours spent weekly will be set by the managers but approved by RR. For those interested in the CLR manager position, give us a note with your plans for the future of this game.

This ends our meeting, for those who wish to hear my talk on vernier and ladder sights, feel free to stay.

VERNIER SIGHT–ELEVATION.

Sue says, "you might as well just continue, no one is leaving." "Well, I know that many of you have used vernier sights in the past." "Yes, many of us have, but most of us don't know how it works, heh"

"In that case, let me say that I have researched and studied this sight and I feel comfortable with my presentation."

"At this range, you can determine your vernier setting for every target on the range–and from one target to the next one. This only leaves operator skills and weather conditions as variables to affect your POI."

"Looking at the chart, each major line on the left side is equal to 5 points. So 4 major lines equals 20 points. Plus the distance between each major line is divided into 5 minor lines on the right side micrometer, and each minor line equals one point. So 27 points would be 5 major lines equals 25 points plus two minor lines will now equal 27 points. Now keep this knowledge on the back burner for a bit and we will return to this."

"Now lets sight your rifle at 100 yards, Set the rear aperture at the approximate elevation of you front sight. This will put you on paper. Then remember that at 100 yards, one point equals one inch. So move your scale by points to get to the bull's-eye. Hint, one minor line is one point–right?"

"Once you are zeroed in at 100 yards, you have to use the ballistic and trajectory table of your manual, to get to the next target at 200 yards. Don't panic. I have computed this for you. To move from the 100 yard zero to 200 yards, add 40 points on your scale(8 major lines). Now look at this 'master chart' of points from 100 yard zero(estimated):

200 yards–add 40 points(8 major lines)
300 yards–add 55 points(11 major lines)
400 yards–add 65 points(13 major lines)
500 yards–add 85 points(17 major lines)"

"Of course if you are moving from 200 to 300 yards you add only the difference between the two or add 15 points to your 200 yard zero and so on."

"Now the last thing to remember. Let's say you added the 15 points to the 200 yard setting and your spotter says that you shot 6 inch below the target at 300 yards.

How many points do you have to add to hit center. Well remember this chart. A point at 200 yards equals 2 inches. A point at 300 yards equals 3 inches. A point at 400 yards is 4 inches and of course, a point at 500 yards is 5 inches. Makes sense, yes?" A loud clamor erupted with a loud, Yes. So with the example above, wanting to change the POI lets say 15 inches at 300 yards you would add 5 points, or 15 inches divided by 3. Did I loose you? A pause. If there are no questions, let's discuss other vernier sight tips.

- The weather will affect your settings on match day. You will get two shots at the 100 yard target to make changes for the day's weather. On a cold day you need more elevation and on a hot day you need less. The sock and wind gauge will make you use Kentucky Windage to compensate the winds drifting effect on a bullet. Experience will guide you.
- Use the largest lollipop front sight insert you have. Unlike posts and beads, lollipops don't cover targets.
- Use the rear sight's aperture eye cup hole that gives you the clearest focus. The rotating Hadley cup has eight different hole sizes that gives you the choice needed, given the daylight's actual brightness."

VERNIER SIGHT–WINDAGE.

"When you are sighting you rifle at 100 yards is when you set your windage to zero. This is a hit or miss process. For example, if you are shooting four inches to the left, remember that each micro line is a point or one inch. So try to move your sight 4 points to the right and take another shot. It is a trial and error method."

"Remember, after this initial windage adjustment you will likely be using Kentucky Windage to compensate for wind. A tip–if you have to shoot 3 inches to the right to compensate for wind at 200 yards, you will have to increase your compensation at 300, 400 and 500 yards. The longer the distance to the target, the greater the wind drifts your bullet."

LADDER SIGHT.

"This is the commonly used fixed sight used for the lever and single shot Buffalo Classic. I am referring to the Smith sight that Ed has on the shelf. This sight fits in the dovetail groove of both gun's barrels. *A large paper schematic displays the Smith sight.*"

"First, remove the front sight and replace it with the gold bead provided by Ed. With the ladder down, the base of the sight has a V-notch that is your 100 yard setting, which matches the new front sight. Take a shot, I am told that most guns will place a shot within six inches of elevation–either too high or too low. Remember this finding, for if you are shooting 6 inches low, you have to compensate your POA for a 100 yard shot. Windage is now set by sliding the sight in the dovetail groove."

"Now flip the ladder up. More than likely, you may be on center of the 200 yard target. Or you may have to elevate the v-notch slide up a few clicks. When you move the slide up you should hear and feel the clicks as the notching system in under a spring/ball tension system. Once you find the correct setting, count the lines the slide moved up and write it down. Then mark your ladder with paint or an engraving mark for quick access. The engraving is durable but can be repaired with bluing, the other may magically disappear during a match—not good."

"The next is the 300 yard target. It is a hit or miss system. Once someone has found the settings, I will remember the number of lines the v-notch slide moved. That will make it easier for other shooters sighting their guns. Finally, if you are shooting an 1871 H&R Buffalo Classic, you have to repeat the process you just performed on your Marlin 1895 lever."

TANG/PEEP SIGHT.

"I am certain that many shooters with CAS experience, using a tang sight, will rely on this sight for both 200 and 300 yards. It is not as handy as a ladder sight, but it can be done. Most tang/peep sights are good up to 350 yards, and so are ideal for the lever. 'They will not fit on the. Buffalo Classic."

"Start at 100 yards. Turn the rifle sideways and set the peep at the approximate elevation of the front sight. That will put you on paper at 100 yards. Next set your windage and then walk the sight over to get a center hit. This is your zero."

"Move up to 200 yards by a number of full turns of the peep knob. Once we know the approximate number of turns, we will pass it on to you. Then you refine the turns to hit center. This process is repeated for the 300 yard target. For example, if it takes 7 full turns of the peep knob to get to the 200 yard target—remember this. Then if it takes 9 more turns to get to the 300 yard target—remember this as well. Basically, you will need to remember only the two numbers above, and the fact that you need 16 turns to get back to the 100 yard setting. It's that simple, heh."

"That brings our meeting to an end. Are there any questions?"

"Yes, long range historically is shot off shooting sticks. We will be shooting off a rail which is a modern version of shooting sticks. So why did you hint that free style may be a future shooting method?" "Ok, at the first match, you will shoot free style at the 100 yard target. Each hit will add a hit to your total number of hits. Since the target used for this free style shot is the same size as the 200 yard target, everyone should be able to get some positive results."

"In the future, we may extend these free style shots to 150 yards or possibly 200 yards. This free style shooting is being tried as a potential user friendly demonstration for spectators. If it is a failure for shooters and spectators, we will eliminate this short range free style shot."

"Why are each shots timed–meaning that they must be shot in a certain time frame or loose the shot within 5 seconds of the bell?" "We have contacted several clubs that host long range shoots. They all agreed that many long range shooters can take a long time to set up, aim and finally take the shot. If we don't limit the time to take your shot, we are going to turn off other shooters and most spectators. If spectators leave because of a slow boring event, they will never come back!"

"You have ten days to sight in your guns and practice. Since Sue and I will not be training and shooting this sport, we will be available with our spotting scopes to help shooters sight in their rifles. We will be available from 8AM–4PM and 6–9PM daily until all shooters have sighted their rifles. Don't hesitate to bring your own spotter since it may be crowded during the first three days. Once you return for practicing, it is best to come with your own spotter who can locate your hits and misses. Sue and I may even help practicing shooters when we are done sighting rifles."

"The last bit of news. As you know, Willard Stone has expanded the clubhouse. At the end of the expansion is a room for a reloading center. It now includes, three Dillon XL-650 presses set for 45 ACP, 45 Long Colt and 44 Magnum. It also includes a RCBS Rock Chucker and powder measure, and a Hornady ambidextrous Lock-N-Load single stage press, that utilizes bushings for your own 45-70 and 30-30 dies. Once you set your dies into your own bushings, then your settings will maintain their zero—three bushings sell for +-$15. It also includes a priming upgrade and a powder measure. All reloading accessories will also be included. You have already spent enough for your guns, we hope the reloading center is a benefit to you."

On our way home, I asked Sue, "what did you think of the meeting?" "Well I watched the audience and this is what I found.

First, this is the most attentive group of shooters I have ever seen. Either you were some incredible charismatic speaker or we have a group of serious shooters!" "I think it is the latter because when I closed the meeting and moved onto vernier sights, no one left. To me, this was a sign of serious shooters who like precision shooting."

The next morning we were at the range at 7AM. After an extended coffee/donut hour, we set up the club spotting scopes. These were high quality scopes–Leupold 16–48X with a good 60mm field of view, high lens clarity, and a 6 foot solid tripod base. By 8AM we had one shooter ready for sighting. We decided to work with this shooter who had experience with vernier and ladder sights. This would give us standard sight settings to pass on our next shooters.

Starting with the lever rifle, using the ladder sight, and 300 grain bullets at 1500 fps., the unflipped ladder base was 6 inches high at 100 yards–more than acceptable with a low POA compensation. The shooter then flipped the ladder and lifted the V-notch slide approximately 1/4". He hit a foot below the 200 yard target. He made another blind adjustment and hit dead center at 200 yards. He then added the total lines on the ladder that the slide had moved to–a total of 8 lines(noted for the future). We repeated the process and found that he had moved the slide up another 12 lines for a center hit at 300 yards(again noted for future use). These ladder slide changes by the line would make it easier to sight ladder sights in the future.

The next gun to sight was the single shot 1885 Highwall. Using a 405 grain bullet at 1300 fps., we sighted the elevation and windage by hit or miss till we had a center hit at the 100 yard target, and marked the vernier and windage zero settings. According to the 'master chart(on page 328 of the club meeting handout), we then added 40 points and were surprised with a low target hit at 200 yards. He then wanted to go up 8 inches and so he went up 4 more points(a point is 2 inches at 200 yards). We then documented the 44 point setting for future use. We then sighted at the 300 yard target by moving the aperture 15 points up.

This shooter wanted to sight his Rolling Block rifle at the 400 and 500 yard targets. We simply continued the process. After getting his zero set and documented at 100 yards, we moved his rear aperture a total of 65 points and walked the hit to a center location. We then added another 20 points per the 'master chart' and sighted him with a center hit at 500 yards. Sue added, "that is simply amazing, to think you can hit that buffalo at 500 yards without a scope–heck, I can barely see that 48X72" buffalo!" Total sighting time was one hour for three guns.

Meanwhile, several shooters had arrived and were attentively watching the sighting process. Sue and I each took a shooter and both guns were sighted in 45 minutes. We continued straight till noon. Several spotters were watching us through the process, and we gave them the tentative settings on both the ladder and vernier sights. By 10AM, we had 2 spotters who agreed to join us for the day. By 4PM we had processed 17 shooters.

We went to the local diner for dinner and came back at 6PM for the evening session. The method used for sighting was very effective. At 6PM we were shocked to see RR arrive with Gail. "What made you decide to join this game?" "Long story, I will tell you later." I sighted Warren within a half hour. Gail wrote down all the settings. Gail then said that she would be Warren's practice spotter for the next 9 days.

We continued spotting for the next two days and evenings. By 9PM on day three, every club meeting registrant was sighted in. All shooters were now in the practice mode, and anticipating the first match in seven days.

CHAPTER 17

CLR, Competition Match

D ay four was the beginning of a week long practice period for all long range shooters. We came to the range with the intentions of spotting for anyone who came to practice without a spotter. Since the shooting rail could hold 5 active shooters, guns were blazing away. It was impossible to hear your bullet dinging the target. A spotter was needed to inform the shooter of his bullet placement.

Throughout the day, it was amazing to see so many shooters coming to the range. It was clear that, this was a competitive sport which required confidence in hitting a long range target repeatedly. Sue added, "and that is why the shooters are swarming the range–practicing is not just a pleasure but it is the only way to guarantee one's ability to call the shot placement at excessive yardage, as we have in this game."

The week passed quickly and then Sunday arrived. After a quick registration and random shooter selection, the Pledge Allegiance to the Flag was performed and the Shooter's meeting began.

"This shooter's meeting is centered on the operational methods for shooting long range at this club. They are as follows:"

1. "Five shooters are called to the firing line and five shooters are called to the on deck circle. Those on the on deck circle place their unloaded guns in the gun rack with their ammo. On the command, those on the firing line load their lever rifle with 3 rounds and place them on the shooter's table. Then shooter #1 stands, on the command he racks his lever and has 30 seconds to fire free style at the #1 100 yard target. If he does not fire before the 30 second bell, the shooter will hear a five second count down as follows: one thousand 1, one thousand 2, one thousand 3, one thousand 4 and one thousand 5–LOST SHOT. This is repeated two more times and then shooter #2 follows the same routine. The round finishes with shooter #5. Yes, it is a lost shot after one thousand 5."

2. "The second string is two shots at the 200 yard target–off the railing. On the command all five shooters load 2 rounds in their lever rifles. Then shooter #1, on the buzzer, has sixty seconds to fire at the 200 yard target before the timing bell. Then he repeats everything for his second shot.

Afterwards the other four shooters perform the same two shots."

3. "The third string is the 300 yard target using either the lever rifle, the single shot Buffalo Classic rifle or the 1885 Highwall. Same two shots within 60 seconds for all five shooters."

4. "The fourth string is the 400 yard shot with either the 1885 Highwall, the Rolling Block or the Sharps rifle off the railing. Same two shots and 60 seconds for all five shooters."

5. "The fifth and last string is THREE shots off the railing with the Highwall, Rolling Block or the Sharps. Same three shots and 60 seconds for all five shooters."

"Now some shooting tips:

- How do we determine when a shot is a hit? This is a clanging or gong sport. An audible 'ding' is a hit. Our three spotters have had a hearing test and all have perfect hearing. If a ding is not heard, but two of the spotters saw the bullet hit through their scope, it is a hit. So each shot is either a hit or a miss and is reported to the scorekeeper.
- Scoring is based on the total number of hits—out of a 12 hit max.
- If you have a miss, it's hoped that at least one spotter can tell you where you hit, so you can make

adjustments. If you have a hit, they will not tell you where you hit on the target.

- We have computed the time for each string and have come up with an estimated 45 minutes per string. Starting competition at 8AM, and taking one hour for lunch, should finish the match by 4PM.

- The awards ceremony will be held at the firing line after the last shooter. We will award 1st, 2nd and 3rd place winners. Any ties will be eliminated with a sudden death shoot-off.

- This operational method is for this first match only. Procedures can be changed, in the future, as recommended by shooters or your new range master."

"Any questions?" "Yes, spectators can be noisy. This game requires careful aiming and concentration. How do we damper a noisy crowd of spectators?"

Sue answered, "This is a friendly club shoot and we want the spectators to socialize and have a good time. If we loose the spectators, we will eventually loose the game. We expect that when the shooting starts, the spectators will quiet down. Unfortunately, it is what it is, and we have to accept it. Time will tell if changes are needed."

"Next question?" "How are you going to handle safety violations."

I answered, "house rules–loss of hits as follows: Each minor safety violation will result in the loss of one hit. Each Spirit of the Game violation will result in the loss of two hits. Each major safety violation will result in the loss of three hits or a D/Q depending on it's severity. Again, this is an experiment and we are trying to follow other club's protocols until final decisions are made." "With no other questions, let's go shooting."

I was the RM and Sue was an observatory judge. I called five shooters to the firing line, the ones holding #1–5, and 5 shooters to the on deck circle, the ones holding #6–10. The entire first string was smooth sailing. Everyone got misses, especially the 400 and 500 yard shots. We started seeing problems and violations by the third string.

The first was a shooter seen adjusting his stool's height after the buzzer sounded. I let him take the shot and then said, "once the buzzer sounds, it is time to shoot. You adjust your stool's height before the buzzer, during the load and make ready command. To complicate matters, you also had the hammer pulled back as you were fiddling with the stool. This is a MSV and you have lost a shot.?" *I noticed that all the shooters got the point.*

The second event was unacceptable behavior. A shooter had done poorly and as he left the firing line, he was swearing and threw his rifles in the gun rack. I immediately got in his face and said for all to hear, "your behavior will not be tolerated, this is a family event. I am charging you with a Spirit of the Game with a two hit loss. I also suggest you go home and don't come back without an attitude change.

The third event was an accidental discharge. A shooter set his rear trigger and the gun fired. Fortunately the bullet hit far downrange. He was given a MSV with a one hit loss for faulty equipment—then was handed a screwdriver and asked to tighten the set screw.

The fourth violation was a cheating charge. Sue had noticed something and had given me the alert sign—coughing and pulling on her earring. I watched the shooter and immediately saw the problem. I went to the shooter and said, "Sir, I am charging you with cheating and giving you a Spirit of the Game violation of two lost hits. If you accept my charge and the violation, nothing more will happen. If you challenge my charge and I can prove you cheated, you will earn an official D/Q which will stay on your record. The shooter said. "I am sorry, I will never do it again and I accept the double lost shots. Out of curiosity, how did you know?" "You did not change your sight to go from 300 to 400 yards, the angle of your gun stayed the same, and we all heard the ding but the spotters never saw your hit at 400 yards—because you shot the 300 yard target four times. I know I was born at night, but it wasn't last night!"

By lunch time, we had processed 5 strings for a total of 25 shooters. At lunch, we sat with RR and Gail. Sue says, "we are surprised that you are participating in this game and your turn is coming up this afternoon. What is the story?" "Well, after the silhouette shoot, I was so proud of Gail that I started thinking about long range for me. Then Willard Stone wondered why I did not consider joining CLR and enjoy one of these new games instead of always working at no pay. So we went home and Gail convinced me that I should reconsider." Gail added, "Warren has always been interested in the era of the buffalo harvest and the guns used. He has read many books on the subject and was fascinated how these people could shoot a rifle with vernier sights at incredible distances of 600 yards or more."

So one day we went to Ed's Mercantile. He had everything I wanted. A Marlin 1895, a 1885 Highwall, a Rolling Block, a Smith ladder for the Marlin, two quality vernier sights, 1000 rounds of GC 300 gr. bullets, 1000 rounds of 405 grain bullets and all the reloading components I needed."

"My bill came to $5400. As I wrote a check, Ed was smiling. I handed him the check and he proceeded to tear it up into pieces. He then said, "Willard Stone will take care of this. Enjoy your hobby, Warren.""

After you helped me sighting in the rifles, Gail and I went to the range every night from 6–9PM, two complete weekend days and two full afternoons. I shot till I became proficient at all yardage. I got so good that I could call my shot placement. Now I am a very comfortable long range shooter and looking forward to the competition." "Ok, so what number did you draw?" "Would you believe it, #40–the last shooter!"

The match resumed by 1PM. A shooter on the first string, known to be a better than average marksman was getting many misses and was all over his targets. I stopped him and said, "Ralph, you are getting a different audible report on your shots. Something is wrong. I took three rounds and gave them to Sue. "Would you dismantle these and weigh the powder." Once the string was finished shooting, Sue came and said, "the powder weight varies 5 grains either way." "Well Ralph, your powder measure is broken and I'm afraid you will have to dismantle this last batch of reloads, and fix your powder measure, I'm sorry."

The remainder of the afternoon was uneventful. We finally got to the last string. Of course shooter #40 was last to shoot. He was amazing. All his shots were before the warning bell. The crowd picked up his tempo and was cheering with every ding. He nailed the three 500 yard targets like they were standing at his feet. When he finished he had 12 hits–but we had a tie, someone else had 12 hits. The 2nd and 3rd spots were clearly won without ties.

As the two contestants came to the firing line I noticed RR's opponent. His name was Gabby and he looked the persona of the actor Gabby Hayes. But he had a real Sharps–top quality for +- $12,000. A real challenge for RR's $1800 Rolling Block rifle.

The rules of engagement for the 1st place sudden death shoot-off were announced. "You have five 500 yard targets to fire at with a 3 minute time frame. When the bell rings, you will have a firm 10 second audible count followed by 'lost shot.'" Everyone knew this was a real difficult feat to accomplish and the spectator crowd went silent.

The shoot off began, "are you ready, stand by, the buzzer goes off. The first round is loaded and the guns start blasting. All the first four shots were hits for both shooters. As RR loaded his fifth round, the bell rang. Gabby was just ejecting his 4th round and so was behind RR by a few seconds. RR fired on the sound of "one thousand 4" with a fifth hit and Gabby fired on the sound of "one thousand 9" but missed. The crowd erupted in cheers, whistles and applause. Gabby stepped to RR and proudly shook his hand and congratulated him. *I thought, what a competition and what sportsmanship.* I asked Sue to get me something.

The award's ceremony was held in place on the firing line as Sue arrived with a package. I then announced the third place winner with ten hits–a plaque for Jim B, *applause.* The second place winner with 11 hits–a small trophy for Vince T, *applause.* A first place shoot-off–a small trophy, for honorable mention to Gabby H. *applause, hoots and cheers.* And first place/match winner– our RR, Warren Whitaker. *applause, cheers and hollers.*

As the room was clearing out, RR came up to me and asked if I found a manager for the long range game. I said, "not yet." "Well stop looking. I guess I am hooked on this game for a multitude of reasons, and would be honored to become it's range master and organizer." "Thought you would never ask." Willard Stone came over and congratulated RR for stepping up to the plate. He said, "it's about time that you participate and enjoy one of the games you helped to organize."

"Now that the season is coming to an end, could the five of us have a private meeting. We moved over to the main clubhouse, set a pot of coffee, and Willard spoke up. "It has been a great season of five new games, and you have made my dream come through. So how do I repay you for all the hours you have spent on this project?"

RR exclaimed, "well that $5400 bill at Ed's Mercantile was certainly above and beyond my pay grade. Gail and I thank you so much. Willard came back, Warren you have been working for over 10 years as president of this club and now the intense past year—did anyone ask you to learn all the rules of these games etc etc etc."

As Willard hands Warren and envelope, he says, "this is my thanks to you for all these years. RR opens the envelope and pulls out a certificate of deposit. He hands it to Gail who says, "Mr. Stone, we cannot accept this." "Too late, the funds are already in the bank. Enjoy it, and let it make your employment work load easier." Gail shows us the CD initial deposit of $100,000.

With RR speechless, Willard looks at Sue and I. That's when I put my hands up and said, STOP. "I checked with my patient list at my old office. I found out that Elizabeth Morrow had only one living family member. This family member was the heir who did not contest the estate's distribution of $250K. That was you, Mr. Stone."

Willard smiled and said, "I knew you would find out, and that is ok. So are we all square now?" Sue said, "above and beyond." "Now shall we get back to the business meeting? I have two proposals."

"First, for the next year, I will finance the four of you, to travel anywhere in this USA, to shoot at the game you choose. I will pay for all your expenses, through the club credit cards you carry. I offer this in hopes of attracting other shooters and clubs to join us. While on the shooting trail, you will be this club's representation. My goal is to make this club a haven for all six Cowboy games. Yes, I include the original game, Cowboy Action Shooting. You also have two couples that are your next leaders–Stan/Miranda and Jack/Kat. I would also include them as club representatives and ask them to travel on our behalf–either on their own or with you guys as a team. Look at it as paid vacations."

The second proposal may be a shock. I am prepared to finance a cowboy shooting extravaganza to include, CFD, WB, CRS, CPS and CLR. This would be a free event, to include registration, lunches, dinner and dance for all club members and their guests. We would also invite the clubs you visited and offer their club leaders/officers the same free benefits, as long as they pay for their own lodging."

The four of us looked at each other–totally mesmerized. Sue finally broke the silence and said, "fall is a nice time to host something, just before winter." Gail added, "foliage season is the best weekend." RR looked at Willard and said, "it's a lot of work, but if you include all the employees we need, well maybe it's doable." I added, "we could get our backups involved, Stan and Miranda–Jack and Kat."

RR looked at Willard and said, "this could mean an attendance of 200 club members/guests and may include 100 outlying clubs/guests.'

Willard countered, "that is why we extended the clubhouse by 50%, heh. I am certain it will hold 300 people, and if not, we can add a circus tent."

There was an extended period of silence as everyone was thinking of all the ramifications for such festivities. Well Willard, are you willing to give us total control of the reins, and stay out of the planning completely?" "Of course."

There was another long period of silence, when we started looking at each other and started nodding to RR in approval. Suddenly RR spoke up. "OK guys, let's do it, we know we can do it. We'll call it the Willard Stone Cowboy Games Extravaganza."

CHAPTER 18

Stone's Cowboy Games Shootout

T he next morning, Sue and I were digesting the proposed season's closing activities. Eventually, I piped up, "This multi game shooting extravaganza is going to be a lot of work, and we cannot do it alone. This is what I propose:"

1. "We ask RR to permanently take over the CLR event before next season. To organize, manage and be the match's range master."

2. "Similarly, we ask our backups to temporarily step up, and take over the different games as organizers and range masters. Kat for WB, Stan for CFD, Gail for CRS, Jack for CPS, and Miranda to take over registration and the club's computer for score's entries."

3. "Sue, you become the public relations officer. You would need to take over announcements, advertising, and invitations. You then become

the festivities organizer and my partner for other duties."

4. "We will share organizing the breakfast and lunch wagon menus, the dance's band, and work with dinner caterers to set up a dining menu."

5. I will meet with our range masters as a group to assist them in leading their specific Cowboy game. I will also train every employee, since we expect them to understand their job description, work as a team, and independently when needed."

6. "I will also undertake the task of finding vendors that can support all five games. This is an opportunity to provide the tools of the trade, and the support needed with necessary accessories, at a fair price."

7. "You and I will not shoot in any game. We will be the match directors who will settle issues beyond our range master's abilities, we will be their substitute RM when their turn comes up to compete. Our job is to make sure that all games are moving along smoothly, and maintaining the total ambience of the shootout."

"What do you think, Sue?" "I like your plan. I especially like the idea of not shooting. First, with so much prep work, we don't have the time to practice and train. Secondly, I like the idea of giving our better shooters a chance to excel, by removing ourselves from the shooting equation, heh. I am certain that many other issues will come up, but for now we need to start by notifying our club members and outside clubs of the event. So, we might as well get started. We have three weeks to set up the event, and allow our shooters some preparatory practice time."

"What should my e-mail to club members include?"
"It should cover these headings:"

1. "Announcement. To reserve the date for a 5 game two day shooting extravaganza–Oct 20–21."
2. "Provide a schedule of the times and days for each game, when available. Make it clear, they can shoot in as many games they wish."
3. "Shock them with the 'great news,' this is a totally free event for club members and their guests. To include, registration, breakfasts, lunches, dinner and dance. Just bring your guns and ammo."
4. "Send them a list of proposed vendors, when available."
5. "Ask them to fill out a preregistration form. We need to know which game they plan to shoot, and who is coming so we can start planning our meals."

"I can do that, afterwards I will send an invitation by e-mail and regular mail to the clubs we visited or contacted during our research days. As W. Stone said, we are also offering a totally free event to the club officers or leaders. Their only expense is their travel and housing."

"Finally, I will send a personal invitation to Mr. & Mrs. Amos and Emma Whitehouse, Charles and Tess Whitehouse, and Jim and Eleanor Beecher at the Bar W Ranch in Texas."

"Closer to the shootout weekend, I will advertise in the local papers and invite spectators to the shooting events. Thereafter, I will help you out and start working on the extra duties that develop as the weeks progress."

I started working on a vendor list. After two days on the phone, I came down with a nice list of vendors, who agreed to be present for both days, and provide products appropriate for one of the five games. It was the set up that got me a nice group of vendors. There was no registration fee, all vendors would be under a separate circus tent, armed security would be provided Saturday night to allow vendor set ups to stay in place overnight, and an estimated attendance of over 300 people. I then presented the list to Sue:

- "Guns–Ed's Mercantile will have a display of the guns used in the five games. Any Saturday purchase would be delivered Sunday.
- Cowboy Cart–Ed's carpenter would display his three models and have units for sale as well.
- Gunsmith–Ed's regular gunsmith would be available on site for simple firearm repairs, and take orders for complicated problems.
- Clothing–Eve from Ed's Mercantile would provide all CAS apparel for men and women. She would even provide a portable changing room.
- Bullets–we contacted an elderly couple that we had met on our travels. They provided 45 ACP and 45 Long Colt lead bullets at very good prices.
- Components–we contacted a mail order house from Kansas City. They were regular providers of primers and powder. They would also include 38 Special, 44 Mag, and 45-70 bullets to complete the needs of the different games.
- Holsters–we contacted a private holster manufacturer that had demonstrated his product during the CFD meeting. His holsters were top quality at affordable prices, with or without belts. He also made ammo and shotgun slides, and nice leather pouches for holding spent ammo. Plus

he liked black leather products since they stayed cleaner with gunpowder.

- Steel targets–our MO manufacturer would bring samples of targets for personal use in private ranges. He would also have a truckload of ready to shoot targets for sale.

- Reloading presses–fortunately MO has a store that specializes in reloading equipment. They would display and demonstrate their presses to include: Hornady single stage press with bushings, a RCBS or Lyman turret press, Dillon Square Deal B and a Dillon XL-650. Plus would display vibratory cleaners, scales and other accessories. Some items will be ready for sale.

- Eye protection–a manufacturer of poly-carbonate OSHA approved impact lenses with side shields will display his glasses. Choice of clear or tinted lenses. These are high-end lightweight titanium frames at reasonable prices, ready for sale.

- Ear protection. This is the free product for all registered shooters. An individually poured silicone/foam ear insert molded in your ear canal. This is courtesy of your Desperado Club membership. For non members, a $10 charge. Also available are high tech electronic ear muffs and other inserts.

For spectators, an economical set of ear muffs for under $13.

- Others. Once things get rolling with newspaper adds and word of mouth, we expect other retailers and manufacturers will call and request a vendor site–especially since it is a free vendor site"

Sue adds, "lets try to keep vendors appropriate for the games."

--------●━━●━━●--------

The next thing on my agenda was meeting with the range masters. As people were arriving, Jack said to me, "you floored Kat when you called and asked her to take over the WB. She always looked at herself as the hostile outsider. Now you are including her. She is still wrestling with the notion that she is not only being included, but asked to lead one of the games. This is a real positive personality game changer for her–and I appreciate it."

"Welcome and thanks for stepping up to the administrative level of the shooting sports. I have several points to cover:"

1. "When you are preparing your shooter's meeting, use the handouts I gave you during our general meeting and shooter's meeting. Choose the items that are appropriate for this shoot, but always include the operational shooting method for each

game. This sort of repetition is very useful before each match–because we all forget, heh!"

2. "We hope that each of you will compete in your own game and in others if you wish. Sue and I will relieve you as RM when you shoot."

3. "Sue and I will be the match directors, and we will not compete those days. We will be everywhere and be available to you if you need our assistance to settle issues."

4. "I need the number of employees you will want to operate your game.

Let's go over each game.

<u>CFD</u>. You need 4 employees. An officer to fill the on-deck circle and bring scorecards to the scorekeeper, a scorekeeper, an announcer, and an unloading table officer. You will also need an assistant RO and RR has volunteered for this spot. He is also our resident rules expert.

<u>WB</u>. You also need 4 employees. Two cable resetters who also function as brass pickers. One loading table and one unloading table officer. This game has a lot of brass on the ground, and you should encourage shooters to help in the picking. You also need an assistant RO from the shooters, which you have to choose and announce to the shooters.

CRS. You need 2 employees. A power operator, and a brass picker. You also need an assistant RO to be chosen amongst the shooters.

CPS. Two employees, just like CRS.

CLR. You need 3 employees–3 spotters on club spotting scopes. You also need your own assistant RO. Brass pickers are not needed, if shooters elect to dump their spent ammo on the ground, it is their choice and they can pick up their own brass.

MIRANDA. Kat and Gail will help you with registration. Then you will spend your day on the computer, entering scores and doing the match computations and standings. Plus you have to visit the scorekeeper to get their completed scores in stages–so you don't get flooded at the end of a match."

"Please note, the assistant RO is there to relieve you when you need them, but they are also your best safety officer. Their job is to look around and maintain a sight in every direction. Establish a working relationship with them. We will also relieve them when they shoot."

"So you need a total of 15 employees. Plus we need one for parking, one as grounds keeper/target painter, two for cleaning the clubhouse, and one for backup in case of illness. I will arrange for 20 employees and it's my job to train all the employees. In addition, Sue will teach you, Miranda, on the use of the club's computer software."

By the time I finished with the RM meeting, Sue had sent several additional e-mails–it was easy since she had all the club members in the same group. She sent one giving the schedule, CFD Sat. AM, CRS and CPS Sat PM. WB Sunday AM, and CLR Sunday PM. Sue asked why the silhouettes were scheduled for Sat. PM. I said, "those two games will likely extend beyond 4PM. Since there is nothing on the agenda for Sat. night, it's no big deal if the event extends beyond 5PM."

Sue sent another e-mail once we had firm confirmations from the vendors. With the schedule of shooting events and the list of vendors, preregistration forms started coming in droves. By Oct 10, 93 club members had responded and most chose two games to participate. Most shooters chose one event each day, but there was a mixture of choices. The point being, there was a positive acceptance of Willard Stone's proposal.

The real shocker was the invitations to outlying clubs. Many clubs were sending 4 representatives with their guests. It did not take long to get to 100 invitee, which went along with our predictions. That is when Sue asked, "do you think the clubhouse can hold 300 people. According to Willard, there are now presently 300 chairs, set up 8 per table–as the addition was designed. Besides, we will have the circus tent still up for Sunday evening and we can set up tables in there if necessary."

Sue said, "great, since 300 or more is our working attendance. I'm done with the preregistration and I'm now ready to help you. What is next on the list?" "Breakfast and lunch menus." Sue took that over and met with the lunch wagon cooks and agreed on this menu:

Saturday AM. Coffee, with egg/ham on a muffin or triple flapjacks with molasses.

Saturday lunch. Grilled chicken leg or breast with macaroni salad, roll and a drink. Lemon cake for dessert.

Sunday AM. Coffee with scrambled eggs/sausage or French toast with Vermont maple syrup.

Sunday lunch. Meatballs/sauce on a bulky roll or classic cheese burger. Either one with egg/potato salad. Dessert of apple squares/ice cream.

I was amazed how these food wagons could serve these crowds in a timely manner. Sue explained, "all cold items are prepared the night before and refrigerated. Many of the meats are cooked the day before, refrigerated and reheated the day served. Some items are cooked from scratch on the many grills under the control of several cooks. In any event, they guaranteed me that the breakfast crowd would be served between 6:30–8AM and the lunch crowd between 11AM–1PM."

The dinner menu was a bit more complicated. They had to serve 300 guests within an hour. They would use a modified serving method used in Western Chuckwagon dinners. The main meat was pork via several pig roasts. Each roasted pig would have a carver cutting up the meat and holding the prepared meat in a warming dish. It would also include several hot vegetables and cold salads.

Randomly selected tables would guide the guests to serve themselves along the buffet table.

The last item was finding a country band that would play line dances, two-steps, waltzes, and slow dances. That turned out to be an easy one. Sue scheduled the band frequently used at the Country Roadhouse–a band that would be a hit with our dancers.

Once we got our planning and scheduling out of the way, we started training the employees. We met with small groups with similar goals. It was an easier process than anticipated because all our regular employees were shooters chosen by RR–this was a group that needed to supplement their income because of hard times or low retirement income. We also took the easy route and placed people into the same games they had supported in the past.

We each took three individual groups, for 1 hour each. I took the grounds, CFD, and CLR crews. Sue took the WB, CRS and CPS crews. After three hours, it was apparent that everyone was confident they could perform their duties, and we were reassured that a smooth sailing organization would follow.

With all our ducks in a row, we had five days left over, and we decided to visit the range to see how practices were progressing. The mornings at the clubhouse were a social gathering. With coffee and donuts provided, we had anywhere between 25–40 retired or day-off shooters every AM. As the shooters moved to the different ranges, we followed as eager observers.

The first thing we saw was employees at every range provided by W. Stone. CFD had an electronic target operator, WB had cable pullers and brass pickers, Silhouette range had brass pickers and power target operators, and the CLR had at least two spotters. The range was in a dynamic and lively state.

We also went to the evening practices. Every range was again supported by employees. The crowd of shooters was now the working class. As we walked through the different ranges, we saw our newly chosen "shootout" range masters in operation. Stan was showing a fast draw time of 0.34 seconds. Kat was streaking through the auto pistol targets like they were attached to her pistol. Jack was hitting his long range pistol targets with 100% accuracy. Gail was working that lever as if it was a hot knife through butter. RR was hitting the 400 and 500 yard targets repeatedly without even using the spotters.

After seeing this advanced marksmanship, Sue said, "Wow, it don't take long to get behind when you don't practice." I added, "yes, especially when you're over 60 years old, heh." Sue didn't like my answer and came back with, "I know every cowboy eventually takes off his gun, gets on his horse, and rides off into the sunset—well I'm not ready for that. Next year is another season and I will be ready for it."

———•—━━•——•——•———

The shootout weekend finally arrived. Friday was our dress rehearsal day. With the range closed for preparations, the activities included:

- The clubhouse was cleaned and tables were organized for breakfast/lunch meals.
- Breakfast/lunch wagons arrived, and set up their different serving tables and cooking equipment.
- Every steel target was painted.
- Stages were cleared of debris, and the RM's were checking out their ranges and their assigned workers.
- The massive circus tent was set up for the vendors—now up to a count of 17. Tables were set out for the vendors to use. Some vendors arrived to set up their displays and shelves for their wares—many needing electrical support. Nothing was left of value since there was no security till Saturday night.
- We did full testing of audio, electronic and power resets.
- Sue gave some fake scorecards to Miranda to process in the computer, and set up master sheets for each game.

- The five range masters reviewed their shooter's meeting notes with me.
- The parking lot size was mapped out. It was clear that it easily held 100 vehicles. Sunday dinner/ dance may need extra parking. We could use the access road to the range for some extra parking, but we decided to pass the word around by e-mail, that car pooling would be the best way to avoid parking lot congestion and overflow to the access road.

Willard Stone spent the entire Friday rehearsal at the range. At the end of the day, he came up to Sue and I and said, "you are nicely set up and how many are we expecting for the games and the dinner dance?" Sue said, "our current predictions include: 200 preregistered shooters, or more, in the five games. Most shooters are participating in two games. By Sunday evening we will have 300 guests for the dinner/dance. " Willard just smiled and said, "you have made it happen, as I knew you would."

The next morning we arrived at the clubhouse at 5:30AM. The club attendant had already prepared coffee/ donuts for the vendors and staff—the vendors wanted to be set up as early as 7AM. The three registrars, Miranda, Kat and Gail, were setting up by 6AM and went to work by 6:30AM. The real surprise of the day was when Sue's grand-daughter came to register for CFD. Miranda was surprised and looked at Sue for guidance. Sue simply nodded and Bailey signed up. Sue went to Bailey's mom and dad. She asked, "is Bailey really ready? Sam said, "we think so, she can shoot 0.37 repeatedly and the occasional 0.35 seconds. Plus she is very sure of herself after extensive practicing."

By 8AM, we had a tentative total registrants as follows: CFD 43, CRS 47, CPS 35, WB 64, CLR 52– for a total of 241 contestants to process over the next two days. This broke down to 93 club members and an amazing 52 shooters from outlying clubs, for a total of 145 competitors. That confirmed the fact that several shooters joined more than one game, and we were up to 300 guests for dinner.

Starting the general meeting, after the Pledge Allegiance to the Flag, I welcomed everyone to our first yearly multi-game shootout. I started, "we had engineered the matches to all run 3 hours but with the heavy attendance, we are likely looking at closer to 4 hours per match. We are providing many workers for each game, but extra brass pickers would be greatly appreciated. Stay alert, and keep up a good pace to help us stay on schedule"

"We invite shooters to write anonymous suggestions for possible changes in next year's event, and place them in the clubhouse suggestion box,. Other than that, remember that SASS safety rules always apply. From here on, the RM for each game will take over for their own shooter's meeting." Shoot safe and enjoy your chosen game–starting with CFD this AM and Rifle/Pistol Silhouettes this PM.

—————•——•——•—————

Sue and I planned to watch every event since only one game was competing at any one time. We would watch at a reasonable distance since we did not want our RM to feel like his/her performance was being observed and graded. As far as CFD, it was a smooth and an organized competition. We did not have to get involved for the resolution of an issue. We relieved Stan when he went to shoot.

Stan had a great stage presence. He shot with a range of 0.33 to 0.35 seconds and he made it look so easy. You could tell that his competitors were uneasy with his times. Sue commented, "it looks like the winner could be winning by hundred's of seconds."

Next string brought Bailey up to the firing line. As she was getting ready, all eyes were on this child–our protegee. The overhead display showed her times, 0.35, 0.35, 0.36, 0.37, 0.38–a five shot average of 0.362 seconds. The spectators erupted in cheers and applause. Bailey came off the firing line with a face showing a major achievement. Once off the unloading table, Bailey's mom came up to hug her, and was crying like a proud mother should be. Sue was also in the tearing huddle and said, "well Bailey, you made us proud today–you done good. We may have trained you, but you are the one who brought your training to competition level. You are a natural talent and you have the potential of going to the national level–if you choose to." *I thought, this was one of those events that will stay imprinted in our minds forever.*

The competition came to an end. Everyone enjoyed the menu's double choices for lunch. By 1PM the Silhouettes competition started. The rifle division ran over their predicted time and so the Pistol division started at 4PM. The spectators stayed right to the 7PM finish.

During the Rifle Silhouettes, Sue added, "Karut Hed is still hot and has not missed a target. Yet, Gail is tight on her tail. Although we did not know the contestants scores, we knew the top three would be at a photo finish.

The Pistol Silhouettes were just as dynamic and fast moving as the Rifle division had been. Jack was shooting like a pro. He shot at all the targets with an amazing 100% accuracy. He was a bit slower than other shooters who had one or more misses. It was clear that the awards ceremony would likely have a second battle for first place.

The next morning, registration started at 7AM. There were only a few that had not registered Saturday. With breakfast done by 8AM, the main meeting started with the usual Pledge Allegiance to the Flag. There was only one announcement, "the Awards Ceremony will be right after the CLR match and spectators are welcome."

The WB was a fast and dynamic match. To our surprise, there were 3 firearm malfunctions. Since we had brought our guns as spares, the three shooters took our guns and were given a reshoot at the end of their posse.

Kat did well. She was amazingly accurate with only a rare miss. What was so dramatic was the way she moved between shooting tables on the field course. She looked like a wild cat on the kill. She saved precious seconds by running at full speed. Yet the shooters were top quality, and it was obvious that we were heading for another finish with hair splitting stage times.

After another great lunch, the CLR started at 1PM sharp. RR kept the shooters moving at a good clip. The spectators got involved with every clear ding, by cheering the shooter. The shooters who got at least 10 out of 12 targets got a rousing line, "another 10 from Len" as a spoof from DWTS.

Sue was the RM when RR came up to shoot. He got 12 hits and all taken before the limiting bell rang. It was clear that RR owned this game. Because a tie was settled by the times taken to achieve this tie, it was clear that taking the maximum allowed time was not in the shooter's interest if he was going for a high placement. It was apparent that there were several good shooters, with high-end firearms, from our outlying clubs. Everyone could feel the tension amongst shooters.

The Awards Ceremony started promptly at 4PM. I started the event, "We have chosen the top five shooters of each game. We will give engraved plaques for the 4th and 5th places, a small engraved trophy for 3rd and 2nd place, and a 1st place/match winner engraved super trophy.

<u>CFD,</u> we have 2 club members and 3 visiting club members. The club members took 1st and 3rd place and three visiting club members took the other three places. Each winner was called to the stage but when we got to the 3rd place, RR got up and said, "I am proud to intervene and give this 3rd place trophy to the future of our sport, Wil and Sue's protegee and granddaughter, Bailey with an average time of 0.362 seconds. After the 2nd place award, the 1st place winner was announced, Stan Winslow our RM, with an average time of 0.345 seconds. *Applause*

<u>WB,</u> we have 3 club members and 2 visiting club members. The first place winner is Kat Star, our RM. The visiting club members got 2nd and 3rd places with our club members at 4th and 5th place. *Applause*

<u>CRS,</u> we have 4 club members and 1 visiting club member. The visiting club member won 3rd place and the others were club members. The 2nd place winner was Karut Hed and the first place winner was Gail, our RM. However, I may add that there was only 5 seconds separating 1st and 2nd place. *Applause*

CPS, we have 3 club member and 2 visiting club members. Our 1ˢᵗ place winner is our RM, Jack. *Applause*

CLR, we have 1 club member and 4 visiting club members. After all the other awards, the 1ˢᵗ place winner is RR, our club president and RM. *Applause and cheers*

In my closing words, I said, "we are grateful for the competition from our visiting clubs. We are all aware that the 1ˢᵗ place of each game was won by club members. That is because, our entire club has had a busy summer practicing for the new games. In addition, we have had a marathon three weeks to refine our techniques. You, visiting shooters, came here with your experience and gave us a good showing, without the extensive practice we had. It will take us years to match your skills." "Next summer, we hope to do some traveling to your clubs and we hope we can give you a good showing for ourselves. So thank you for coming to our shootout. One visiting shooter got up and yelled, "Who do we appreciate? Desperado, Desperado, Desperado!"

Last item, "try to car pool for the dinner/dance. We are expecting 300 guests and parking will be tight, or will extend to the access road. See you at 6PM. This is a Western black tie type event, so dress in your best duds if you have them. If not, wear your CAS costume–but come."

6PM arrived and guests were arriving. The ladies were wearing Western evening gowns, and the men wore a Western coat, tie and Cowboy hat. Everyone was greeted by a team consisting of Willard Stone, RR, Sue and I. The master table included, Willard Stone, RR and Gail, Sue and I, Stan and Miranda and Jack and Kat.

Sue went to check on the meal and came back saying, "we have three medium size pigs that are now being carved by three carvers. We have coleslaw or choice of two salads, three hot vegetables, baked or potatoes in white sauce and pre cut pork in several warming dishes. Plus the usual rolls, butter, cold pickle dishes and choice of three desserts."

After the master table, the remaining tables were called by random order. By using a double line at the serving table, everyone was served within one hour, and all the hot foods were hot. During dinner RR mentioned to Willard, "can you believe the attendance at dinner and the shootout. This must have cost you a fortune. How do we thank you?" "Not necessary, what is important is that this is a dream come through."

After dinner, I knew that RR had a presentation to make. RR goes to the microphone and gets the crowd's attention. "At the end of our shooting season, the Desperado Council, made up of three original CAS leaders and myself, met and made these two rulings. The first was a thanks to Willard Stone for his generosity in developing our club. The council voted unanimously to permanently change our club's name to STONE'S DESPERADO COWBOY GAMES." Sue got up, gave Willard a hug and planted a corsage on his lapel. A standing ovation followed, and I saw tears on Willard's face. *Applause*

After breaking Willard up, RR was on a roll. He added, "the second council ruling involved its own membership. The council felt that it was time to include the Cowboy Games in the council. So the council unanimously voted to include two new council members, Wil and Sue Sumner." Another standing ovation followed. We graciously accepted, and we were glad to sit down out of the limelight.

After dinner and the ceremonies, everyone moved to the circus tent. The clubhouse was picked up, and the tables moved around to form a dance floor. The band was setting up and then everyone was called back to the clubhouse. The band started with Willie Nelson's "All of Me" and the floor filled with two-step dancers.

Willard came over to Sue and asked her to dance. Sue's mouth just about dropped. She graciously got up and Willard easily guided her, and danced with amazing grace. During the dance he pointed at the Whitehouses and the Beechers and said, "more on that later, heh!"

After the dance, Willard explained what had happened. "After the dance at the Bar W Ranch Shootout, Amos hired a dance instructor. I was invited to their home to join in the lessons. For 4 days we danced and the instructor gave us three, two hour lessons. We not only learned the two-step and waltz, but we learned a half dozen turns as well."

During the first intermission, we went to visit with the Beecher's and Whitehouse's table. Amos said, "can you believe that we learned to dance the two-step and the waltz, and we love it." Emma added, "there is so much interest by the locals, that we are planning to start dance lessons at our meeting room, for the purpose of building a dance group. We will eventually host dances at the ranch."

After the intermission, Sue and I were invited to the dance floor, as the local dance instructors, to perform a country waltz. The request came from the visiting clubs that only performed the two-step. The band played "The Last Cheaters Waltz" by Boz Scaggs. We danced with as much elegance as we could. We performed several turns but mainly concentrated on weaving left to right in a skating pattern. One of the visiting club leaders came to our table and wanted to hire Sue and I as dance instructors. *I thought, better add that function to next year's list of possible activities–dance instructors!*

Emma and Tess Whitehouse came over after the dance. Emma said, "my goodness, you looked like you were lovers floating on a cloud.

Amos interjected, "remember dear, we are too old to perform like that, so just keep on dreaming you are on that cloud, heh!"

The dance came to an end. The last dance was "Goodnight Sweetheart." As we were dancing, we saw Willard Stone dancing with Karut Hed. Sue softly says, "unbelievable, that old man is still full of surprises, heh?" *I was thinking of adding the old saying, just because there is snow on the roof doesn't mean there is no fire in the stove, but I decided against it. I would only get that look, the one I don't fare well with.*

Epilogue

Afew days later, Sue and I were reliving our past shooting season and looking to the future. Sue said, "with the season's end, we now look forward to Thanksgiving, Christmas, multiple get together with friends and family, and Stan and Miranda's wedding. We always have our weekend dances at the Country Roadhouse, and hopefully we can go south this winter to either southern Texas or Florida, with our camper."

"I agree, but even going south for the winter still brings us back to next shooting season. By early March we have to prepare for either shooting our many Cowboy Games in our own club, or consider traveling to outlying clubs as club representatives. We have a third choice, maybe it's time to start teaching country dancing to outlying clubs, when we go shoot at their clubs or just hire out as instructors."

Sue was pondering the three choices and asked, "do we have enough energy to perform all three activities?" I answered, "well we have all winter to think about it, but sometimes natural events have a way of dictating the future!"

As I got that look, the one I knew I would fare well with, no matter what path we took.

Abbreviations

AD	Accidental discharge
ACP	Automatic Colt Pistol
CAS	Cowboy Action Shooting
CFD	Cowboy Fast Draw
CFDA	Cowboy Fast Draw Association
CRS	Cowboy Rifle Silhouettes
CPS	Cowboy Pistol Silhouettes
dia.	Diameter
D/Q	Disqualified
fps	Feet per second
FYI	For your information
ga.	Guage
GC	Gas checked
gr.	Grain
JFF	Just for fun
IMHO	In my honest opinion
LC	Long Colt
lr	Large rifle
lp	Large pistol
mag	Magazine
PF	Power factor

POA	Point of aim
POI	Point of impact
RO	Range officer
ROI	RO with training–can run a stage
RO2	RO with training–can design a stage
RNV	Ruger New Vaquero
RSBH-H	Ruger Superblackhawk-Hunter
RN	Round nose
RNFP	Round nose flat point
RM	Range Master
RR	Ranger Rooster
SASS	Single Action Shooting Society
SA	Single action
SIL	Silhouette
SR	Small Rifle
SS	Stainless steel
WB	Wild Bunch
209 PRIMER	Shotgun primer

Printed in the United States
By Bookmasters